I'VE GOT NEWS
FOR YOU

I'VE GOT NEWS FOR YOU

by John Wheeler

E. P. Dutton & Co., Inc.
New York   1961

Library of Congress Catalog Card Number: 61–6015

This book is dedicated lovingly to my late daughter,

ELIZABETH WHEELER ELLISON

CONTENTS

7

LIST OF ILLUSTRATIONS

(Cartoons)

Sports and characters at the Willard-Moran championship fight, by Clare Briggs, page 18.

Irvin Cobb at the Illustrators' Ball, by Wallace Morgan, page 92.

Brisbane's Park Row Pups, by Tad, page 116.

First *Mutt and Jeff* strip drawn by Bud Fisher in 1907, page 212.

(Photographs, between pages 96 and 97)

Baseball writers covering the New York Giants, 1908.

Richard Harding Davis in the trenches at Salonika.

Mexican troops, including Raul Madero, with Bud Fisher and the author.

General Villa's private railroad car.

Ring Lardner acting as a lion tamer.

President Harding, Grantland Rice, Ring Lardner, and Henry Fletcher before a golf game.

Three lousy golfers: Deac Aylesworth, Roy Howard, and the author.

Captain Eddie Rickenbacker and John Wheeler arriving in Mexico City after first flight of Eastern Air Lines.

Helen Reid, General Leon Johnson, Hugh Baillie, John Wheeler, and Jimmy Doolittle at a state dinner at the Lotus Club, 1954.

John Wheeler.

I. GHOST-WRITING—HOW IT STARTED

When I was an undergraduate at Columbia University, I served as the *New York Herald* correspondent there. One day I decided to investigate a mysterious old guy with a beard whom I noticed hanging around campus and going to classes regularly. He looked to be about 65. I found out his name was Kemp, and I began talking to him one day.

"How come you are still in college?" I asked him.

"Well, you see," he explained, "when my uncle died, he left me a handsome allowance as long as I went to school. If I quit, it was cut off, so I've been here ever since. The only trouble is I am running out of courses to take."

My story got a big play, and the other New York papers tin-canned after me. Probably that's why I am in the newspaper business today. When I graduated from Columbia in 1908, I took a job with the *Herald*.

This first newspaper job wasn't too exciting until I got to be a baseball reporter and then became a ghost writer, possibly the first in newspaper history.

I was traveling with the New York Giants in 1911 when I got a wire from my boss, the sports editor, which read about as follows: "Sign up Christy Mathewson to cover the World's Series exclusively. Offer up to $500 but try to get him for less."

This referred to the outstanding pitcher of that day, also known as Matty and Big Six. I looked him up and promptly offered him the $500, telling him it was my limit. He took it since this was a new source of income and ballplayers did not get such big money in those times. I was assigned to confer with Matty after every game and then turn out the expert's masterpieces. The Giants' opponents were the Philadelphia

11

Athletics. A cane-carrying *Herald* staff star named Fitzgerald (not Scott Fitzgerald) was to write the color stuff on the games.

Everything went along well until a gentleman named Frank Baker, who played third base for the Athletics, got hold of one and knocked it over the fence, thus busting up the ball game. A famous left-hander, Rube Marquard, was pitching for the Giants. That night Big Six and I turned out a very informative piece pointing out that the southpaw had served the wrong kind of a ball, and, if he had aimed at Baker's weakness, all would have been jake. As I recall it, Rube should have pitched one on the outside instead of the inside.

This erudite contribution to literature was widely published and stood up very well until the next afternoon when Matty himself, the old master, was in the box. Up came Home-Run Baker with two on. The last seen of the ball was when it disappeared over the center-field bleachers into the street outside. There was considerable razzing from the stands, evidently by some of the fans who had read the article on how to pitch to Baker by Christy Mathewson. We had a tough time working out a story that night, and finally Big Six decided to admit he had thrown a wrong one to Baker, too, and Baker was a great hitter anyway. This was characteristic of Matty's sportsmanship.

In those days, as I recall it, it was the best five out of nine, and about midway of the Series, we got a long rainy spell. I hung around with the ballplayers, and Mathewson and I turned out a dope story every night which made money for my employer, since the *Herald* syndicate was selling the service to other papers at so much a word. The prima donna with the cane came to Philadelphia only in clear weather when there was a game. Much to my surprise, after the Series a notice appeared on the *Herald* bulletin board awarding Fitzgerald a bonus of $25 for his good work in covering the event, while I didn't even get the time of day.

The next winter Christy Mathewson and I wrote a series of weekly articles for the McClure Newspaper Syndicate on "Inside Baseball." This sold very well. Subsequently, the collection was published in book form by Putnam. The title was *Pitching in a Pinch*. Matty and I each had a half interest. It kept on selling even after he died, and I then turned my share of the royalties over to Mrs. Mathewson. It was a damn good book.

When it was published I was still working on the *New York Herald* as a baseball writer, and there was a nice old fellow named James Ford who did the book reviews. I watched closely to see if *Pitching in a Pinch* was mentioned, but no soap. One day I met Mr. Ford in the hall and stopped him. I am not sure he even knew I worked on the paper, because he operated from a kind of ivory tower out front.

"Have you read the Christy Mathewson book *Pitching in a Pinch?*" I asked him.

He seemed slightly puzzled.

"No, I haven't," he answered.

"I thought maybe you would like to review it," I suggested.

"Have you read it?" he came back. "Could you review it for me?"

Had I read it? I could practically recite it and so could my whole family. I let myself go, and I very much doubt whether any book ever got a more favorable review.

In 1913, after the *Herald* turned down my request for a raise, I left and started an organization modestly called the Wheeler Syndicate. I hired Matty and a lot of other ballplayers for winter articles and covering important games. I was the most active spook practicing. Besides the book for Christy Mathewson, I wrote a later one for Ty Cobb entitled

Busting 'Em. In one World Series I was turning out expert copy for about eight stars.

The idea spread, and the old *Tribune* signed up Wild Bill Donovan, the American League pitching star, to expert for it. Bill MacBeth was his ghost.

Bill didn't believe in handicapping himself by getting the ideas of his star, so he wrote a story for publication on the opening day predicting the Boston Braves would beat the Athletics in four straight. Philadelphia was a heavy favorite, for it had a team made up of great players with big reputations who were supposed to scare their opponents as soon as they walked on the field. Donovan, being an American Leaguer, was searching for MacBeth with murder on his mind. He insisted MacBeth's prediction was ridiculous and made him look bad.

Boston won the first game, and Donovan began to cool off a little. After the Braves came through in the second, Donovan stuck his chest out and praised himself as a prophet. When they won four straight, he claimed MacBeth had had nothing to do with the prediction—that it was all his.

Eddie Collins, who was playing second base for the Athletics, and I went to college together, and I made him an offer before the Series, but he got a better one and took it, which was all right with me and part of the racket. We did sign up Johnny Evers, the fiery little second sacker for the Braves.

"Is Collins writing for you?" he asked me.

"No," I replied, "he got a better proposition than we made him."

After the Series, Evers was telling me how they rode the Athletics.

"We had that Collins so up in the air he couldn't spit and hit the ground," boasted Evers. He meant when a fellow gets nervous, his mouth dries up.

"What did you ride him about?" I asked him.

"We kept yelling, 'So you would throw down an old pal for fifty bucks, you cheapskate.'"

"Who was the pal?" I asked innocently.

"Why you were," explained Johnny with a laugh.

One of my saddest experiences was with Big Jess Willard, the prizefighter. We had signed him before his bout in Toledo with Jack Dempsey for the heavyweight championship, and I was to be the boy behind the typewriter as usual. We knocked out some good preliminary stories together which didn't give the challenger a chance—Dempsey was too small and all that. Willard foolishly let Jack Kearns talk him into bandaging their hands outside the ring. The Champion was trying to save money and doing his own managing.

The night before the battle Willard visited Tex Rickard, the promoter, to talk about his future plans. According to reliable reports, during the discussion he consumed a bottle of gin. Even an old-timer like Tex was surprised.

"Ain't that pretty strong medicine you're training on?" he asked.

"Don't worry," replied Big Jess, "I'll only be in there for exercise tomorrow. Jack's too little to hurt me."

The day was scorching hot—July 4, 1919. I was to meet Willard right after the fight in his dressing room to get his ideas. The first round was a bloody one. Dempsey, in perfect condition, laid his opponent's face open with nearly every blow he hit him. He cut him to ribbons. This led to the false report he had something besides fists inside his gloves, like Plaster of Paris or tire tape. Jess looked as if he had passed through a meat grinder.

There was also a rumor Dempsey and his manager, Jack Kearns, had bet $10,000 against $100,000 the battle would not last more than one round. It was close. With Willard on the deck, the referee counted him out, and the challenger rushed from the ring to his dressing room, thinking he had won. The timekeeper in the excitement had either forgotten to pull the string or Ollie Pecord, the referee, had not heard the bell. If Willard had had a smart man in his corner who could have claimed the decision on the grounds Dempsey had departed from the premises, it might have been different. The fight finally ended as the bell rang for the fourth round with our man a battered hulk and bleeding from practically every pore. His seconds threw in the towel.

After taking one or two looks at him, I realized he wouldn't have any ideas for a week or ten days, unless it would be to cut out some paper dolls. I didn't even go to his dressing room, but wrote the best story I could on my own. There wasn't much to say except about the devastating power of Jack Dempsey's punches. At the end I had Willard express the hope he would live.

Another worn-out fighter, Battling Nelson, had been assigned by the *Chicago Daily News* to cover the championship fight. By this time the poor fellow was punch drunk.

For some reason, Nelson set up housekeeping in a tent out by the arena where the contest was to take place, although this location was miles from the scene of the preliminary activities. Maybe he thought the promoters might try to hold the contest secretly some night, and he would be on hand. Even though it was during Prohibition, some of the other boys used to celebrate pretty good with the help of Jack Kearns, Dempsey's manager. Along about 2 o'clock in the morning somebody would suggest—usually Tad, the cartoonist—that they go out and visit Nelson. This consisted of approaching his tent stealthily and pulling out the pegs which naturally made it collapse. The culprits would escape before he could untangle himself.

The old battler, being a cleanly fellow, used to walk down to near-by Lake Erie armed with a towel and a cake of soap and take his morning bath. The weather the day of the fight was frightfully hot. The concessionaire had moved several barrels of lemonade out near the arena the night before, anticipating a rushing business. Nelson arose as usual the morning of the battle and headed for the lake.

However, on the way, he saw a hogshead filled with what he thought was nice clean water, so being in a hurry and having a busy day ahead, he hopped into it, soaped himself off, and finished his bath. He told several friends of his good fortune, and the word spread through the crowd that Battling Nelson had doused himself in the lemonade. Of course, there was no way of telling which barrel had entertained him. The result was nearly everyone steered clear of the drink, and the concessionaire was practically ruined.

Ring Lardner got a release from his *Chicago Tribune* contract in time to cover the Dempsey-Willard brawl for us. Also out in Toledo was Ring Lardner's shadow and a faint carbon copy of his literary output, a fellow named H. C. Witwer. Tad got to addressing Ring as "Witwer" and vice versa. Witwer is dead now and so is Lardner, but it is my bet if they arrived at the same destination, he is still following Ring around and eavesdropping.

Irvin Cobb, the humorist, was discussing Witwer's talents with Charles Hanson Towne, then the editor of *McClure's Magazine* which was publishing some of the author's stories.

"Don't you think Witwer is a good writer?" asked Towne.

"I am not sure about him being a good writer," replied Cobb, "but I do know he is a damned close reader."

Cartoon by Clare Briggs showing some of the sports and characters attending the fight for the world championship between Jess Willard and Frank Moran. (Clare Briggs)

II. SPORTS AND SPORTS WRITERS

SPORTS writers were a tough and colorful lot back in the days when I first started in the business. But probably the screwiest of them all was Bill Phelon.

Phelon had a strong aversion to water, either bathing or drinking, and for this reason George Ade once said he should have been called Hydrophobia Phelon. When I first knew him, he was writing baseball for the *Cincinnati Times Star* as his regular vocation.

While he was working on a Chicago newspaper, he rented a house in a respectable neighborhood and began to give late and noisy parties. These kept the honest residents awake long after their bedtimes. Finally the landlord notified Phelon he would have to move since he was a nuisance and had broken the lease. Of course, Phelon protested that his conduct had been beyond reproach.

This made no impression on the landlord, so Phelon went to the stockyards and bought the carcass of a pig which had recently been butchered. He smuggled it into his residence at night, tore up some floorboards, and buried the pig in the cellar. After allowing three or four days for it to ripen, he telephoned the police from a pay station and informed the desk sergeant there had been a murder in the house.

When the gendarmes broke in, the strong smell made it evident there was something rotten in Denmark, and they began to search for the corpse. Since it was hard to detect the source of the fragrance, the police began to rip the house apart to find the body. Of course, Phelon was in no way identified with this project, but he got reports of its success from spies.

19

Eventually, the police located the pig and went looking for the perpetrator of the hoax, but the sports writer had left town.

Working on the old *New York Herald* was a nervous, oldish hypochondriac named Bill Hanna. He was one of the best baseball writers in the business. One evening after he had finished his work, Hanna was strolling up Broadway when he met Bill Phelon walking down.

"Hello, Bill," said Phelon with a wave.

"Hello," answered Bill, sullenly.

Then Phelon continued for another block and boarded a trolley car going uptown. After four or five blocks, he dismounted, and started back again. Of course, he met Hanna.

"Hello, Bill. How are you?" Phelon greeted as if he had not seen him before.

Hanna looked at him with a start and did not reply. Again Phelon repeated the performance, and the third time was the climax. Hanna had had it. The story is he called a cab and went to a hospital and gave himself up. He recuperated in a nursing home.

Phelon had another dastardly trick, but he never actually knew how it turned out. He would be riding through some town like Little Rock, Arkansas. When the train would stop, he would look around for signs and spot the name of some honest citizen like "Harold Smith—Hay, Grain, Coal, Etc." Bill would jot it down.

Then when he arrived in Havana, where the team was training, he would begin sending the poor victim dirty post cards with affectionate greetings, signed by some girl's name. Here is a sample:

"Hello, honey. How have you been? Can't live without you. Have missed you so since we were together. All my love. Leona."

Probably this prank caused several divorces. There is no known record.

Phelon would go out to a ball game at the Polo Grounds where there might be 30,000 fans. He would look around at the crowd and write in his score book where it said "attendance," 29,684. Then his eyes would sweep the park again, and he would rub out his original figure and make it 29,686. He also frequently brought a Gila monster to the press box with him as a companion, which did not make him any more popular.

The guy is dead now. As far as I know, he died a natural death. This is surprising.

Another prankster was Charles E. Van Loan, a fine reporter and short story writer in the early part of this century. He was nationally known and widely read. We made a deal for him to cover the 1916 World Series, and because of his reputation, we got a fine sale. Now old Charley was a big guy, about six feet four, and a physical humorist. To give you an idea, he once tickled a colored porter washing up the lobby floor of a hotel in Reno, Nevada, before the Jeffries-Johnson fight. The young man was sensitive to such gestures and unintentionally slapped a perfect stranger, who happened to be passing, across the kisser with his mop—a big joke.

Van Loan arrived in New York from his home in California with his typewriter muscles in fine shape and decided to travel to Boston a day early to meditate and get a good sleep. The rest of us took the night train as usual, arriving about 7 in the morning. In our group of experts were Christy Mathewson, Hugh Fullerton, a hard-boiled, old-time pro sports writer, Clare Briggs, the cartoonist, and one or two hangers-on. We had connecting rooms in the Copley Plaza Hotel.

Van Loan greeted us in a friendly fashion by getting out of

bed and kicking Christy Mathewson playfully in the shins with his bare feet, a serious mistake, for the big pitcher had shoes on and kicked back. The contest wasn't even a tie. Charley pulled down his nightshirt and crawled under the covers. Then someone suggested a drink.

Finally, after spending the morning in convivial fashion, we adjourned to the press box to watch the athletes. Immediately after the contest Van Loan, Fullerton, and I went to the Western Union office to write and file our stories. I had about six ballplayers on my hands. Van Loan turned out one page and had three or four lines written on the top of the second sheet when he stopped. Beads of perspiration stood out on his forehead. He turned to me.

"John, I'm through," he said. "I can't write any more."

At first I thought he was kidding. "But you've got to," I insisted. "We have sold you all over hell's half acre."

He shook his head despondently. "I know it," he admitted, "but I can't do it tonight."

Fullerton overheard the conversation. He got right to the point. "You big yellow so-and-so," he said, "go on and write your story."

"Call me anything you like," answered Charley, "but I can't."

He couldn't either. So Hughie and I finished it off and sent it out.

When we got back to the hotel, we found our star had invited in some guests he had just met. Clare Briggs and he were acting as hosts and ghosts, signing my name to wine tabs, until I chased the bums out.

Matty, Fullerton, and I were sleeping in separate beds in the same room, and our slumber was disturbed at 5 the next morning by the entrance of old Van, moaning, groaning, and grunting. "Oh, I'm dying," he said.

Mathewson, usually a kindhearted man, woke up. "Well, if you are going to make all that noise and die, go in your own room and don't be waking us up at 5 o'clock in the morning," he said and turned over.

Then Hugh Fullerton came to. "What you need, Charley," he prescribed, "is a whisky peg."

This turned out to be straight whisky mixed with a raw egg and tabasco sauce. Hugh ordered two and drank one himself to prove the worth of his remedy. Van Loan swallowed his dose and became sicker. A little later Ty Cobb showed up and immediately took charge of the case.

"The best thing for a bad stomach in the morning is a big platter of vanilla ice cream," he said.

"But I don't want any vanilla ice cream," protested Van Loan.

"If you don't eat it, I'll shove it down your throat," threatened Doctor Cobb.

Our patient got sicker, so I decided it was time to give up on the amateurs and call the house doctor. As a matter of fact, it was more serious than I thought, and our star was not able to write a single story on the Series. Fullerton and yours truly did the job every night under his name.

After Van Loan got back home, we mailed him a check for the agreed amount—$1500 plus his expenses. He returned it to me with an apologetic note.

"Just send me a set of matched golf clubs," it read, "and we will call it square."

I picked out the best tools I could find and shipped them before he could change his mind. In all modesty, I might add we received a great many letters and several telegrams from subscribing editors congratulating us on the excellence of the Van Loan coverage. Fullerton and I kept the secret.

Several years ago, Grantland Rice told me that Bob Jones, as he likes to be called instead of Bobby, wanted to write some golf articles for syndication. This was before Bob had won the Grand Slam.

He walked into the office one day to discuss the matter. "Will O. B. Keeler help with this series?" I asked him. Keeler was the golf writer on the *Atlanta Journal* and had followed Jones on all his tournaments from the time he started as a boy.

"No," replied Bob. "If I can't write these articles myself, I don't want to tackle the job. I am not interested in a ghost. I brought four pieces along with me."

He reached into his pocket and pulled out several pages in longhand on the yellow sheets lawyers use. He handed them to me. They were first-rate, and we made a deal on the spot. The series went on for three or four years until he thought he had run out of gas and had covered the subject thoroughly. Then he decided to quit in spite of my urging otherwise. He was a fine contributor except he was inclined to be late with his copy. I had to wire him about release dates and deadlines. He recently presided at a dinner in Atlanta for the Ryder Cup players, and jokingly introduced me as one of the biggest nuisances he had ever met.

In reply I said, "Yes, and yours was the best golf series ever published."

Grant Rice, some years back, was at a big party at the Augusta National Golf Club, attended by the sports and aristocracy of the South, with a few scattered prominent guests from the North. Because of Grant's distinguished record as a sports authority, all sorts of questions were fired at him—who was the greatest football player, which was the greatest race horse, who the best baseball player, and so forth.

Finally, somebody said to him, "I would like you to name the finest sportsman and gentleman who ever competed."

Bob Jones was sitting across from Grant at the table and, of course, all of Bob's admirers present expected Grant to name the great Jones.

Grant paused, and then surprised the hell out of the gathering when he said, "My answer is Jack Dempsey. He would kill his own mother in the ring, but he was the greatest sportsman and gentleman outside, and one of the most generous fellows I ever met."

Grant explained afterwards that he had known Bobby Jones since he was twelve years old and admired him very much, but he realized that the group had built him up to this question. And, he admitted, that was the way he felt anyway about the old champion **Dempsey.**

One of Rice's great talents was writing verse. After his death, we found an unpublished poem which reflects his philosophy:

Over the Plate

Bill Jones had the speed of a cannon ball;
He could loosen a brick from a three-foot wall;
When he shot one across it would hurtle by
Too swift for even the surest eye.
No one could hit him when he was right,
As no eye could follow the ball's swift flight.
Bill should have starred in a Big League role,
But he stuck to the minors . . . he lacked control.

Jack Smith had the curves of a loop-the-loop;
It would start for your head with a sudden swoop
And break to your knees with a zig-zag wave.
And the league's best batters would roar and rave
At the jump it took and the sudden swerve.
Shades of the Boomerang, what a curve!

But Jack's doomed to a Bush League fate.
He could not get it over the plate.

Tom Brown had both the speed and the curves,
A combination that jarred the nerves.
He would steam 'em by 'till they looked like peas;
They would take a break from neck to your knees.
From the best to the worst in the league, by jing!
He had 'em all in the phantom swing.
But he missed the mark of the truly great.
Poor Tom, he couldn't locate the plate.

How is it with you, if I may ask,
Have you got control of your daily task?
Have you got control of your appetite,
Of your tongue and temper in the bitter fight?
Have you got control of your brawn and brain,
Or are you laboring all in vain?
It matters not what your daily role.
Have you got control . . . have you got control?

It matters not what you "may have," my friend,
When the story is told at the game's far end.
The greatest brawn and the greatest brain
The world has known may be yours in vain.
The man with control is the one who mounts,
And it's how you use what you've got that counts.
Have you got the bead, are you aiming straight?
How much of your effort goes over the plate?

Most all athletes liked and admired Grant Rice. He was a prosperous and generous sports writer. When Yogi Berra, the great Yankee catcher, was breaking into the Big League, he was poor and his sartorial ensemble was scanty. In fact, he had one thin suit.

Grant met him at the dog races at St. Pete one cool, spring night, and he had no overcoat, so he was shivering. Grant bought him a two-dollar ticket and the dog won, paying $115. Ever after that, Yogi was Grant Rice's great friend.

Another great sports writer was Bill Corum who at one time was president of the famous race track at Louisville, Churchill Downs. He died prematurely of lung cancer, and his funeral at Campbell's was a sellout, with standing room only. This writer was among the many mourners with Westbrook Pegler, Rube Goldberg, and Gene Tunney. Afterwards I asked them to ride downtown with me in my car. We started walking up Madison Avenue, and Tunney lagged behind, shaking hands and signing autographs. A retired champion has no peace, even at a funeral. Then he hustled up to me and said: "Have you room for one more?"

"Sure," I replied.

"I just ran into Quentin Reynolds and asked him to ride down with us."

Old Pegler blanched. Reynolds was the fellow who sued him for $175,000 in a libel suit and collected. Naturally, they are bitter enemies and naturally Gene was only kidding.

We began to reminisce about Bill Corum, and someone brought up an event in his life which was not included in the obituaries. It seems there was a young lady who was supposed to be in love with an actor, and they were playing house in an apartment down around Gramercy Park. However, Bill was filling in when her boy friend was out of town on the road. Then the show closed unexpectedly, so the actor headed for home, unannounced.

When he arrived, he found his rival ensconced and enjoying himself. Being quick-tempered, the actor produced a revolver and shot Bill Corum in the behind. Always a gentleman, Bill dressed and departed. When he reached the street, his wound became painful, so he approached a cop.

"I was walking down the block," he explained, "and some hoods got to rowing and shooting. A bullet hit me. Can you call an ambulance so I can get to a hospital?"

The policeman did. Bill was stripped and examined. He had been shot all right, but the surgeon was puzzled because there was no hole in his shorts. He survived, and so did the actor who got his girl back by this drastic method.

I also got my girl by making an impression, but of a somewhat different kind.

After I became a baseball writer on the *Herald*, I bought a diamond ring and a Chalmers car. All Big Leaguers had diamond rings. The combination made quite an impression, but the clutch in my automobile began to slip so it would only creep forward no matter how hard you stepped on the gas. As I was a night worker, I left the car at the repair shop one afternoon and arranged with the night watchman to pick it up after I finished my toil at midnight.

I showed up on schedule all right and started out of the garage, only to find it was slipping worse than ever and would make no forward progress. Then I discovered by putting it into reverse, it would back up. That is the way I made it to Yonkers where I lived then. I believe I still hold the backing record for the distance—15 miles in four hours, but I couldn't turn my head for two days my neck was so stiff. The news of my achievement got noised about, and I was known here and there as "the fellow who backed to Yonkers." Finally a young lady heard of it and expressed a wish to meet me, probably thinking I was some sort of a nut. She was right, but in 1918 she married me anyway, and still is the missus. The moral must be that if you wish to remain a bachelor either don't back an automobile to Yonkers or if you do, don't boast about it. I have never tried a repeat performance.

III. SELLING OTHER MEN'S BRAINS

GHOST-WRITING was my business until the syndicate got settled on a firmer foundation. I pinch-hit for Billy Sunday, the hell-fire and damnation evangelist who had reformed drunks strutting up the sawdust trail after he got through delivering his spell-binding sermons. I even wrote pieces for his wife, Ma Sunday, on occasions.

Meanwhile, the syndicate engaged a first-class reporter on the old *World,* named Joe O'Neill, to write a weekly short sermon for Billy, designed to appear on sports pages on Monday mornings. We got a lot of customers. But some days, after attending the revival meetings up where the old American League Park had been, Joe couldn't resist shopping at a few saloons on the way downtown. Frequently, I would have to fill in since he was vague as to whether he was writing for Billy Sunday or Nick the Greek.

Another tough man to keep track of was Finley Peter Dunne. He was a good writer and an entertaining fellow, ruined by the rich. He made his reputation writing Mr. Dooley in Irish dialect for the *Chicago Tribune* and later for Associated Newspapers. The series combined humor and philosophy. For example, one of the sage remarks by Dooley or Hinnissy was: "Trust your friends but cut the cards."

I met him after he moved on to New York and had gotten to know all the swank gents in the Racquet Club and other social centers. Among these were Bob Collier, whose father started *Collier's Weekly,* Harry Payne Whitney, and Payne Whitney. He fitted into this group well, because he amused them, and he was a good drinker, too good. They gambled for high stakes and engaged in other pranks.

One day they were all by the swimming pool in the stylish Racquet Club when a waiter appeared in full uniform, very fancy, in response to a call for a round of drinks. Apparently his appearance was tempting, and somebody caught him off balance and shoved him into the pool. Naturally he had to go to the drying room to be wrung out, so they didn't get a drink and rang for another waiter. Again it was tempting, and he too wound up in the tank. It turned into a regular game and shortly the aquarium was full of floundering waiters, and the club had run out of these servitors.

Of course, other members missed the usual excellent service, so that an investigation showed that the whole corps was soaking wet. When the cause was explained, the Board of Governors called a hasty meeting and bounced the playboys from the club. They decided to start one of their own where there were no restrictions. They sent out a scout who found a location in Fortieth Street. The name of the new club was the Meeting House. It had no rules and a peculiar system. The members were billed only at the end of the year. Nobody signed a check for food, drink, or service. Annually the total cost was split up, and each one paid his share. The only way to keep even was to spend most of the time there, which Mr. Dunne did.

Along about 1920, I got the idea of reviving the Dooley series, and I talked to him about it. At first, we took the old articles, and he revised them and brought them up to date. The enterprise proved to be a success, but pretty soon we ran out of copy. In the meantime, Peter Dunne had a serious illness, mostly due to his habits, and was laid up in the hospital. I went to see him frequently and we became great friends. I suggested he turn out some new pieces and made him a substantial offer. He agreed to do it. Now in the past, one of the problems in connection with this series was delivery. The author would promise anything and then disappear. I reminded him of this reputation, and told him one of the difficulties would be convincing the editors he would produce on schedule.

"Listen," he assured me, "the doctors have told me if I ever take another drink, I might as well swallow cyanide of potassium."

We got off to a brilliant start with a big sale. Everything went smoothly for about two months, when he missed the weekly piece, and it was impossible to find him. All his haunts, including the Meeting House Club, would deny he was there. Of course, we got kicks from editors who didn't believe us when we said he was sick. He hit his stride again for another four or five weeks before there was an interruption, and this was a royal one.

The Prince of Wales, the glamor boy of the period, had arrived in this country and got caught up in Long Island society. Simultaneously, Pete Dunne disappeared in the social swirl, and of course his literary efforts disappeared, too. He was impossible to find. Editors were wiring us complaints and cancellations. Finally, in desperation, I sent Dunne a telegram firing him. He never forgave me for that. It was the end of the Dooley series, except for one or two articles he later wrote for *Liberty Magazine*. Of course, he had started to drink again in spite of the cyanide of potassium threat. The doctor had apparently been right in his diagnosis, for it wasn't long afterwards that this genius, who wasted his talents, died. However, he lived up to his extravagant tastes to the end and could afford them, for Payne Whitney had thoughtfully left him $500,000.

Less thoughtful was Frank Munsey, publisher of the *New York Herald*. When he died he left the bulk of his fortune to the Metropolitan Museum of Art, although there were reliable reports he had never been inside the place while he was alive. His employees expected to share his riches, but none of them did except for a few favorites, and these were small bequests. For example, Bob Davis, an old hand, got only $10,000.

After Munsey's death William Allen White wrote of him: "He had the mien of an undertaker and the heart of a pawn-broker."

Mr. Munsey's first New York daily was the *Press,* a morning sheet devoted largely to sports. One of its features was information to fishermen about what time it was high tide and which way the fish were running. This sold a lot of papers to the nuts who got up at 4 o'clock in the morning to wake up the fish. Munsey was a great fellow for charts and graphs, so he had his general manager draw up one to show the trend of circulation. The curve indicated clearly there was an increase during the fishing season. The publisher studied it carefully and then asked for an explanation.

"Well, you see, boss," said his lieutenant, "this shows our circulation goes up in the spring and summer during the fishing season, because of the news we print for anglers."

"We'd better level it off," decided Munsey. "Let's cut out that kind of news."

He later bought the *Globe, Evening Mail, Morning* and *Evening Sun,* and the *New York Herald.* He also wanted to purchase the *Tribune,* owned by the Reid family, and made a buy-or-sell offer of $4,000,000. Much to his surprise, Mrs. Reid told him she would buy the *Herald,* so that the *Herald Tribune* is the only survivor today of all Munsey's papers.

Charles Lincoln was the managing editor of the *Herald,* and a damn good one of the time I write. He was also a friend of mine.

"If you want to sell features to the old man," he said to me one day, "flatter the hell out of him first."

Downtown in New York was the Hardware Club where Munsey used to eat lunch, and so did I. Occasionally we would put on the feed bag together. One day he invited me to go back to his office with him. He said he wanted to show me something, the color reproduction on a Fontaine Fox Sunday page which we sold him. Of course, I admired it, and then I waited for an opening.

"Mr. Munsey," I began, "how do you manage to accomplish all the work you do? It's remarkable."

His face lit up with a smile, so I knew the needle had gone in a little. "Oh," he said, "I am in this office every morning at 9 o'clock and am busy all day. I don't smoke which wastes time."

He had a rule in his city room that none of his employees could smoke, so they spent more time ducking out into the corridors and the can to grab a few puffs than if they could do it on the job.

"But," he went on, "when I get back to my apartment before dinner, I take off all my clothes, put on my nightshirt, and sleep for half an hour. Then my valet calls me, and I go to all the big parties to which I am invited."

"Sometimes when I get home from the office at night and am tired and weary, I lie down and sleep for fifteen or twenty minutes," I said.

"That's no good," he insisted. "You have to undress and put on a nightshirt."

I shook my head. "I'm sorry, I can't do that, Mr. Munsey."

"Why?"

"For two reasons," I replied. "I haven't any nightshirt and I haven't any valet. I'll get both as soon as I can afford them and you buy enough features."

We became as good friends as possible, and the flattery worked. He was a bachelor and lived at Sherry's, Fifth Avenue and Forty-fourth Street, then one of the stylish establishments of the town. He invited me there to see him a few times, and actually he was a damned bore.

Finley Peter Dunne had a friend in the newsprint business who asked to be introduced to Munsey. Dunne arranged a dinner party. After it was over his friend said to him: "Don't bother any more. Munsey is such a bore, I would rather not sell him paper."

I doubt if I've ever taken such a lighthearted attitude toward a possible customer, and, especially in those days, I was kept busy not only selling features but developing features to sell.

Of course I made a few edifying mistakes. One of them happened early in the First World War.

The German cruiser, *Emden*, had got loose in the Indian Ocean and began to raid and destroy enemy shipping. The captain, a daring seaman, would hit and run. Soon he had several British warships pursuing him, but he was able to elude them for some time. Finally one day he was cornered and outnumbered, so he put the *Emden* aground on an island and ran for it. Most of the crew escaped capture.

The first officer with a small group made the hazardous journey back to Germany using various disguises and ducking around remote corners of the world. It was a thrilling tale. At the time, we had a mysterious character in Boston who made a business of getting foreign papers, especially German and Scandinavian, and reading them. In this roundabout way he came across a first-person report of the *Emden* adventure. He sent it to us by mail.

At that time we had no leased wire which meant some delay in publication. We sold the story well and set a release date. The day before our report was scheduled to appear, the *New York Times* came out with the same dispatch on its first page. Its Berlin correspondent, Cyril Brown (called Squirrel Brown), had finally found it and cabled it. This break ruined our story, so it taught me a lesson which is never to hold a hot one to try to get a little more money.

I learned another lesson when my wife and I went to England in 1920. A friend of mine, Isaac Marcosson, a writer for the *Saturday Evening Post,* gave me a letter to Lord Northcliffe, the great English newspaper publisher. I didn't know whether the letter was any good or not, but on my arrival in London I sent it around and shortly Northcliffe's secretary called me at the Savoy to invite me for lunch the next day. Unfortunately, I had already made a date with Ralph Blumenfeld, then the editor of the *Daily Express* which was buying "Mutt and Jeff," so I declined reluctantly. I thought, well that's the end of his Lordship as far as I am concerned.

Not at all. A couple of days later he asked me for dinner at his home in Carlton Terrace. Harry Houdini, the magician, had crossed on the ship with us and was playing at a West End theater, so I sent my wife off for the evening with him.

There were only four of us at dinner, Northcliffe, his secretary named Price, a Spanish newspaperman, and myself. We talked about the *New York Daily News,* the first tabloid in the United States. It had just started.

"If I were your age," Northcliffe said, "I would start a tabloid in Chicago."

"I haven't got the money," I replied.

"Why not? I started the *Daily Mirror* with two thousand pounds."

"Yes, but you don't know Chicago. It is a tough town. The

circulation plug-uglies would knock your drivers off the trucks and throw your papers in the sewer."

Then he switched to Prohibition which was just starting in the United States as the Great Experiment. He was a 100 per cent against it.

"Have you ever known a real creative man who was a tee-totaler?" he demanded.

I thought for a minute and nominated Theodore Roosevelt.

"Oh, no," he insisted. "When I was in America in 1916, I gave him a lunch at the St. Regis Hotel in New York, and he drank plenty of champagne."

If I had thought of George Bernard Shaw, I would have had him.

After that first visit I saw him a few times. In 1924 we went to Liverpool with Grantland Rice and his wife to watch the British Amateur Championship played at Hoylake. North-cliffe, a great golf enthusiast, was staying at the same hotel. One day we were following a close match, and between shots I was talking to his Lordship about buying the Bell Syndicate budget, and I was making progress, I thought. Suddenly my wife stepped into a gopher hole, and by the time we got her on her feet and dusted off, Northcliffe had disappeared into the crowd. My sale went down the drain. It reminded me of Kipling's famous verse.

> High hopes die on a home hearthstone,
> He travels fastest who travels alone.

Actually, even on my own, I was far from being 100 per cent persuasive. For example, shortly after the First World War, I went to Paris armed with a letter of introduction to Georges Clemenceau, the French premier, from Melville Stone, then general manager of the Associated Press. In his early manhood Clemenceau had taught in a girls' school in

Connecticut, and Stone and he had become friends. He spoke English better than I did.

After he received the letter, Clemenceau graciously made an appointment to see me. He was a funny, bent little man who always wore gray gloves because he had eczema. I explained to him we would like to make him an offer for the American rights to his memoirs.

He thought a minute before he replied, and then said: "I have never kept a diary or made notes during my life, so what I have to tell would be inaccurate and dull. No, I will never try it."

He stuck to this and was one of the few world leaders who didn't produce his memoirs, although after the First World War ended, everybody wanted to buy somebody's memoirs. The Kaiser headed the list, and all hands were in hot pursuit. Bradford Merrill, general manager of the Hearst papers, who recognized my talents by this time, sent for me.

"We would like to have you make an offer for the Kaiser's memoirs on behalf of the Hearst papers," he said. "We may be able to get them cheaper if it isn't known you represent us."

"Do you know what's in them?" I asked.

He shook his head. "I'll cable Karl von Wiegand," he said. Von Wiegand was the Hearst correspondent in Germany.

A couple of days later Mr. Merrill sent for me and handed me the reply. Von Wiegand reported only three chapters of the Kaiser's memoirs were about the war. The rest dealt with social affairs and yachting at Kiel. We decided not to make an offer. Then shortly afterwards, Charley Lincoln of the *New York Herald* called up and invited me over to visit Frank Munsey and himself.

"We want to make an offer on the Kaiser's memoirs," he began, "and we would like you to act for us."

"Do you know what's in them? I have seen the chapter headings and brief synopses. I don't think they are worth bidding for."

Then I turned to Mr. Munsey and said, "Would you pay fifty thousand dollars for the New York rights?"

"No," he answered firmly.

That ended the conversation. The McClure Syndicate finally bought them at a very high price, and the memoirs proved to be a bust.

That was one time I guessed right. But in 1927, the year Lindbergh flew the Atlantic, I guessed wrong.

It was my last night in Paris. I went to dinner with Rube Goldberg and his wife and "Bugs" Baer and his first missus. We came out of a fashionable café, and a French photographer offered to take Rube's picture for two francs.

"For two francs," replied the cartoonist, "I'll draw your picture."

The Frenchman turned the offer down. Then a taxi driver stepped forward.

"If you will draw my picture," he said, "I will take you anywhere in Paris you want to go for nothing."

Goldberg accepted and made a sketch of his subject. We all piled into his cab. His name was Marcel, a very nice guy as French taxi drivers go. First we stopped in a low dive in Rue Blondell. There we met Floyd Gibbons, the famous correspondent who had lost an eye in the war and wore a conspicuous black patch.

"Isadora Duncan has written her memoirs and wants to see you," he said to me. "I hear they are pretty hot."

We all got into the cab again and were off for her flat in Montparnasse. She was aging then, a little on the fat side, and broke. She wore a long shawl draped around her shabby dress. We, of course, took Marcel in with us and introduced him as a retired dancer. She greeted him with enthusiasm. However, his reputation was somewhat tarnished a little later. We sent him out to get some beer, and as he came in with a trayful of glasses, he tripped over the door sill and spilled the whole damn business.

The apartment was as run down as the occupant. In a corner was a neglected phonograph which apparently hadn't been dusted for years, since it had a couple of sand dunes on top of it. Someone put on a record, and the old girl began to dance again. All her obesity disappeared, and she was the graceful star of years ago.

Then we got down to business. She showed me her manuscript.

"I'm poor," she announced. "For five hundred dollars cash, you can buy all American rights."

Now I happened to have more than that amount in my pocket, but I got cagey.

"I don't buy memoirs blind at 4 in the morning when I am full of champagne," I replied cautiously. "Let me take the manuscript with me. I'll cable you as soon as I arrive in New York." I was sailing that day.

She agreed. We all left, with Marcel still the pilot.

On the ship I read her manuscript. It was a good story with color and lots of romance. I sent her a message when I reached New York, offering her two thousand dollars. Two days later I got a notice from the French post office that the addressee had moved, leaving no address and without announcing her destination. The cable was never delivered. The next morning I read she had gone to the Riviera and was driving in a car wearing the same long shawl. It blew out, wrapped around a wheel, and she was pulled to her death.

The estate got all tied up with her brother and other relatives, and we never did buy her memoirs. It was one of my many mistakes.

Another was letting Will Rogers, the great comedian, slip through my fingers. He was playing at the New Amsterdam theater in the Ziegfeld Follies where he was making a big hit with his jokes, chewing gum, and rope. He discussed current events, and didn't hesitate to mention such characters as the Prince of Wales and President Coolidge. Ring Lardner took me around to his dressing room one Saturday afternoon. Rogers was pecking away at his typewriter. He said he wanted to write a newspaper feature.

It seemed to me he depended for his success on his props and personality, and I passed up this Sunday feature he was offering. Then he went on a trip to Europe, his first I think, and before he departed, he asked Adolph Ochs, publisher of the *New York Times,* if he could send back brief dispatches reporting his observations. It was agreed the *Times* would pay the cable tolls, and, for the first time, it began to publish a regular humorous feature. Soon, through a competing syndicate, the column was published in hundreds of papers. Here's a sample:

When President Wilson sailed for the Peace Conference in 1919, after the First World War, he was accompanied by Admiral Cary Grayson, who was his personal physician and a fine gentleman. Of course in his job of watching the President's health, the Admiral had done mostly desk duty in the White House. Shortly after the Admiral's arrival in Paris, Rogers sent back the following dispatch:

"Admiral Grayson stood his maiden voyage well."

I missed out on signing up Charlie Chaplin for an entirely different reason.

Bud Fisher and I had started a moving picture company to sell rights to distributors in each state for "Mutt and Jeff" in animated cartoons. We rented an office at 727 Seventh Avenue, hired a manager named Harry Grossman, and organized a studio in the Bronx to turn out the weekly product. Business boomed, as I believe this was one of the first animated cartoons.

Then one night Bud and I went to a prizefight in Madison Square Garden, accompanied by Charlie Chaplin, who was then at the peak of his career, and Winnie Sheehan, general manager of the Fox Movie Company. After the fight Chaplin, Fisher, and I stopped for a nightcap at the old Waldorf bar. The movie comedian told us his contract was about to expire, and we made a big pitch to hire him, offering to make him a partner in our company. He was impressed.

Every few minutes I would rush out to telephone Grossman to ask how much we would be safe in guaranteeing Chaplin and would return with a better proposition. We reached the point in the negotiations where we were looking for a late-working lawyer to sign an agreement. But then we made the mistake of moving to the Claridge Hotel bar where Chaplin was staying. We ran into Chaplin's brother Syd, who listened briefly to the conversation and then whisked Charlie off to bed.

The next day we couldn't get in touch with Charlie, nor the following day, nor the next—in fact, never. So a big deal fell through for want of a lawyer and because of bad luck in running into a brother who loused it up.

IV. THEODORE ROOSEVELT

WHEN the First World War started in 1914, Charles Lincoln was then the managing editor of the old *New York Morning World*. He sent for me. Getting right down to cases, he began:

"You know Theodore Roosevelt and Mr. Pulitzer [*World* publisher] had a bitter row when he was President, and we are not on very good terms. I want you to make him an offer to go abroad as a war correspondent with a guarantee of three thousand a week. The *World* will underwrite it with the understanding we will get the New York territory."

Up to that time I had never met Colonel Roosevelt, although I had long been an admirer of his. I recall once as a youth when Colonel Roosevelt was to camp on the parade ground at Van Cortland Park overnight, I rode six miles on my bicycle just to get a glimpse of him on horseback.

I called up Charles Scribner, the book publisher, and asked him to give me a letter to the former President. Armed with this, I took off for Oyster Bay with Guy T. Viskniskki, an associate.

"I doubt if he will do it," I said gloomily.

"Maybe we can dig up another idea if he won't."

"How about a series on the lessons this country should learn from the war?" I suggested.

Roosevelt received us in the famous trophy room at Sagamore Hill. I explained our proposition. He thought a minute.

"Sure, I would like to go," he replied, "but it would reflect on the dignity of this country and the position I have held."

43

"Why not change the label from correspondent to international observer? You could send back articles only when you wished."

He shook his head.

"With your experience, how about doing a series on the lessons this country should learn from the war?"

"That's a good idea," he answered. "You will hear from me about that."

"Would it be okay to sell the New York rights to the *World?*"

"I don't care who publishes them in New York," he said, "but I want you to protect Van Valkenberg in Philadelphia and Colonel Nelson of the *Kansas City Star.*"

We went back to New York, and I reported the results to Mr. Lincoln. He didn't seem to be particularly impressed. About a week later T.R.'s secretary, John McGrath, came into my office without previous warning and plunked four articles down on my desk. I was a little surprised since we had not talked terms. However, we reached an agreement without any trouble—a guarantee of $1000 an article against 50 per cent, whichever was better, for a series of twelve.

When I called on Mr. Lincoln, I walked in the door triumphantly. Much to my surprise and consternation, he turned the whole business down. I decided to try my luck with Hearst.

Bradford Merrill was general manager of the Hearst papers at the time, but he was in Europe, making deals for war correspondents, and a man named T. V. Ranck was his stand-in. Ranck listened carefully, and then shook his head no. It began to dawn on me maybe this wasn't such a hot idea after all.

My next target was Carr Van Anda, managing editor of the *New York Times* and one of the best ever to stick his head inside a newspaper office. It took me only ten minutes to make a deal. The *Times* gave a big display to the series which de-

lighted T.R. Frequently, it would run an editorial disagreeing
with his views.

"The *Times* and I have a joint debate every Sunday," he
said to me with a grin.

As a footnote to this anecdote, Morrill Goddard, the brilliant
editor in charge of the Hearst Sunday papers, called me up
and asked me to come to see him.

"Why didn't we have a chance at those articles by Colonel
Roosevelt?" he asked me.

"They were offered to Mr. Ranck, and he turned them
down," I replied.

"It was a Ranck decision," he added wryly.

We sold the series widely, successfully, and profitably. As a
result, T.R. and I became friends, and, when the articles were
published in book form entitled *America and the World War*
(published by Scribner's), he sent me an autographed copy
giving me credit for the idea. I am still the proud possessor of
this volume dated June 1, 1915. I also volunteered for the division T.R. tried to raise to fight in Europe, but Woodrow
Wilson refused to sanction it. I have a letter of discharge from
him. Here it is:

Office of
Theodore Roosevelt
753 Fifth Avenue
New York

Room 402

May 25, 1917

Mr. John N. Wheeler,
   The World Building
   New York City

My dear sir:

You have doubtless seen the President's announcement

wherein he refused to make use of the Volunteer Forces which Congress had authorized him to permit me to raise.

Prior to this announcement by the President, I had sent him a telegram as follows:

> "I respectfully ask permission immediately to raise two divisions for immediate service at the front under the bill which has just become law and hold myself ready to raise four divisions if you so direct. I respectfully refer for details to my last letters to the secretary of war. If granted permission I earnestly ask that Captain Frank McCoy be directed to report to me at once. Minister Fletcher has written me that he is willing. Also if permission to raise the divisions is granted I would like to come to Washington as soon as the war department is willing so that I may find what supplies are available and at once direct the regular officers who are chosen for brigade and regimental commands how and where to get to work."

To this the President answered as follows:

> "I very much regret that I cannot comply with the request in your telegram of yesterday. The reasons I have stated in a public statement made this morning and I need not assure you that my conclusions were based entirely upon imperative considerations of public policy and not upon personal or private choice."

Accordingly, I communicated with as many of the men who had agreed to raise units for service in this division as possible, and after consultation with about twenty of them I issued the statement which is herewith appended.

I now release you and all your men. I wish to express my deep sense of obligation to you and to all those who had volunteered under and in connection with this division.

As you doubtless know, I am very proud of the Rough Riders, the First Volunteer Cavalry, with whom I served in the Spanish American War. I believe it a just and truthful statement of the facts when I say that this regiment did as well as any of the admirable regular regiments with which it served in the Santiago campaign. It was raised, armed, equipped, drilled, mounted, dismounted, kept two weeks aboard transports and put through two victorious aggressive fights in which it lost one-third of the officers and one-fifth of the men; all within sixty days from the time I received my commission.

If the President had permitted me to raise the four divisions, I am certain that they would have equalled this record, only on a hundred-fold larger scale. They would have all been on the firing line before or shortly after the draft army had begun to assemble: and moreover they could have been indefinitely reinforced, so that they would have grown continually stronger and more efficient.

I regret from the standpoint of the country that your services were not utilized. But the country has every reason to be proud of the zeal, patriotism and business-like efficiency with which you came forward.

With all good wishes,

> Faithfully yours,
> Theodore Roosevelt

As a footnote to my friendship with Theodore Roosevelt, before the United States entered the war in 1917, I proposed to T.R. that we might be able to get money to start a national newspaper, of which he would be the editor. He was intrigued by the idea and finally agreed he would consider it. I went to Victor Lawson, publisher of the *Chicago Daily News* and a very wealthy man, with the proposition. He decided he would back it. Then I returned to talk to T.R.

"Mr. Lawson says he will go ahead," I reported.

"That's fine," he answered with a grin, "but let's wait a little.

You see, I am beginning to think my ideas are out of tune with those of the people. Maybe I am getting old."

Nothing ever came of it. The war started, and I went into the Army and off to France. In January, 1919, before I got back, T.R. died. He was 60 years old.

T.R. had the reputation of possessing a remarkable memory and seldom did he forget a name. He was also lightning fast in his mind. Here is an example:

When he was campaigning, unsuccessfully as it turned out, on the Bull Moose ticket in 1912, some crackpot took a shot at him in Milwaukee. He lay wounded, not too badly, when two ambulances arrived. He demanded to know from what hospital each came. One belonged to a city institution and the other driver answered: "St. Mary's."

"Is that Catholic?" asked Roosevelt.

The interne nodded his head.

"Take me there," he said.

Of course, he was considering the Catholic vote. It was a hectic campaign. James Gordon Bennett, then the owner of the *New York Herald,* was so bitter about T.R. running that he issued orders that Roosevelt's name was not to be mentioned in stories. He was to be referred to as the "Bull Moose" or the "Third Term Candidate." When the news that T.R. had been shot reached the office late one night as the paper was about to go to press, it posed a problem. Bennett, the publisher, was out of reach in Paris. Randolph Marshall was the editor in charge. Finally, Marshall made a decision.

"We'll call him Theodore Roosevelt even if I get fired tomorrow."

He did and didn't get fired.

Recently Clare Boothe Luce and I were talking about this and that, and the question of memory came up.

"I was reading Montaigne's essays the other night," she said, "and one dealt with memory. He contended that storing up facts, especially casual ones, in the mind is a waste of space. The active brain can be used for more useful purposes. Did you ever know anyone with a good memory who was smart?"

"I can name two candidates," I answered. "Theodore Roosevelt and Herbert Bayard Swope."

She had to agree with me, but even so dissented. "They remembered things which had to do with their professions," she contended. "What I'm talking about is the fellow who can tell you what three left-handed pitchers were in the World Series of 1922."

Well, I guess she has a point there.

V. RICHARD HARDING DAVIS

ONE of my boyhood heroes was Richard Harding Davis, a dashing, handsome fellow who made his reputation as a novelist, short story writer, and war correspondent. When he wasn't off somewhere attending a war, he could be found in the smart places of the town, always immaculately dressed. Charles Dana Gibson, a friend, used him as a model in his drawings.

There were many stories about Davis. He was sitting in a fashionable club in London one day when he decided to send an engagement ring to his fiancee, Miss Cecil Clark, in Chicago. He rang for a messenger boy, and shortly one showed up in his smart uniform.

"Here, Jaggers," said Davis, "take this package to Prairie Avenue in Chicago, U.S.A. Bring me back the receipt."

"Yes, sir," replied the boy, without showing any surprise.

He took a train to Southampton where he caught a liner for the U.S.A. By this time his unusual errand had begun to get some publicity, and a delegation of American messenger boys met him at the dock in New York. They had arranged a reception and a banquet for him that night.

"No, thanks," said the boy. "I am on duty and cannot waste time."

He took a train to Chicago, delivered the ring, and got a receipt. Then he about-faced and headed back for England. In due course, he reported to Davis that his mission had been accomplished. History does not estimate what the cost and tip were. It is too good a story to spoil with figures anyway.

Sad to relate the marriage ended in divorce, and our hero

several years later made Bessie McCoy, the musical comedy star, his bride. She was playing in a show called *The Three Twins* at the Herald Square Theater at the time. Davis was a regular nightly attendant at the stage door. This reporter happened to be in Philadelphia covering the New York Giants at the time, and was in the office of the *Inquirer,* when the first edition came off the press carrying the head:

THREE TWINS BURNED OUT AT HERALD
SQUARE THEATER, NEW YORK.

A conservative editor scanned it and changed it for the next edition to read:

TWO TWINS BURNED OUT AT HERALD
SQUARE THEATER, NEW YORK.

It was against this backdrop that I first met Richard Harding Davis. There was a revolution going on in Mexico as usual, and Paul Reynolds, a literary agent, called up.

"Would you like to make a deal to send Richard Harding Davis to Mexico?" he asked.

A meeting was arranged to discuss terms. It turned out Reynolds wanted $1000 weekly for the first four weeks, and after that, if Davis stayed longer, $500. We agreed to go ahead. Then Reynolds fumbled a little bit with his handkerchief and added, "You are a new and young syndicate. How do I know we will get our money?"

"You sign a contract," I proposed, "and we will put forty-five hundred dollars in the bank in a special account which can be used only to pay you. Is that satisfactory?"

Reynolds agreed it was, and Davis took off for Galveston, Texas. By this time, it looked as if the United States would intervene, because the Mexicans had fired on one of our ships in Vera Cruz harbor, as I recall it. One night I was at a party being given by "Cap" Huston, who later became one of the owners of the Yankees, when we got the flash:

"Funston has been ordered to Vera Cruz."

Funston was the commanding general, a fiery fellow with a great reputation for daring.

Davis filed his story. I recall it began:

"There was a dance at the Galvez Hotel tonight . . ."

Then he went on to describe vividly the scene that followed the announcement. He told about officers in dress uniforms dancing gaily with their wives or other ladies when the orders were called. Suddenly the men dropped their partners and disappeared. They quickly shed their stylish costumes, changed to khaki, and headed for the transports. Our correspondent was aboard, as he seldom if ever got left behind on an occasion like this.

The Mexican port was taken without any trouble and with very little shooting. As I recall it, an apology was demanded from President Huerta, a stubborn man when sober and very tough when full of brandy which he usually was. Davis filed a few stories and then became restless. One day he reported that Medill McCormick of the *Chicago Tribune* and he had arranged for safe conduct to Mexico City to interview Huerta. Before we could reply, he took off. In the meantime, the Mexican President had changed his mind or gotten full of cognac or both.

When the two correspondents arrived in Mexico City, instead of seeing Huerta, they were thrown into jail with no explanation. Knowing the Mexican soldiers were trigger-happy in those days, we appealed to William Jennings Bryan, then Secretary of State, to get them out. He refused to make a move, insisting they had gone without the permission of his department and were on their own. We finally sprung them with the help of the British Ambassador.

Here is a description I wrote shortly after the event in a book by Charles Belmont Davis, the writer's brother:

Richard Harding Davis went to Vera Cruz for a newspaper syndicate, and after the first sharp engagement in the Mexican seaport there was nothing for the correspondent to do but kill time on that barren, low-lying strip of Gulf coast, hemmed in on all sides by Mexicans and the sea, and time is hard to kill there. Yet there was a story to be got, but it required nerve to go after it.

In Mexico City was General Huerta, the dictator of Mexico. If a newspaper could get an interview with him it would be a "scoop," but the work was inclined to be dangerous for the interviewer, since Americans were being murdered rather promiscuously in Mexico at the time in spite of the astute assurances of Mr. Bryan. No matter how substantial his references, the correspondent was likely to meet a temperamental and touchy soldier with a loaded rifle who would shoot first and afterward carry his papers to someone who could read them.

One of the newspapers taking the stories by Mr. Davis from the syndicate had a staff man at Vera Cruz as well, and thought to "scoop" the country by sending his representative to see Huerta, in this way "beating" even the other subscribers to the Davis service. An interview in Mexico City was consequently arranged and the staff man was cabled and asked to make the trip. He promptly cabled his refusal, this young man preferring to take no such chances. It was then suggested that Mr. Davis should attempt it. By pulling some wires at Washington it was arranged, through the Brazilian and English Ambassadors at the Mexican capital, for Mr. Davis to interview President Huerta, with safe conduct to Mexico City. Mr. Davis was asked if he would make the trip. In less than two hours back came this laconic cable:

"Leaving for Mexico City tomorrow at 3 o'clock."

That was Richard Harding Davis—no hesitancy, no vacillation. He was always willing to go, to take any chance, to endure discomfort and all if he had a fighting opportunity to get the news. The public now knows that Davis was arrested on this trip, that Huerta refused to make good on the interview, and that it was only through the good efforts of the British Ambassador at the Mexican capital he was released. But Davis went. He had plenty of moxie."

As a result of this first successful deal, Davis and I became friends. When the big war started in 1914, he met me in the Lambs Club where we discussed plans. He agreed to leave immediately for Europe. By this time, Reynolds, the literary agent, had been eliminated as the middle man, and we settled the matter with a handshake—no written contract. As I recall it, Davis was to get $700 a week and pay his own expenses. He didn't skimp either.

"Send three hundred a week to Bessie," he told me, "and deposit the balance in my account with J. P. Morgan."

He sailed on the *Lusitania* on her first-night departure. I went to the dock to see him off. As we walked down the pier in the darkness, the great ship loomed up with all her portholes lighted. He looked at the spectacle and then said: "Windsor McKay stuff." McKay was an artist on the *New York American*, famous for his draftsmanship and the details in his drawings.

Shortly after he reached London, we had a cable from him saying Lord Kitchener was willing to accredit one American correspondent, who was approved by the U.S. State Department, to the British Army at the front. Davis asked us to try to get him accepted. This brought me face to face again with my old sparring partner, Chautauqua lecturer, and part-time Secretary of State, William Jennings Bryan. I called his office in Washington to make an appointment to see him.

"Wait a minute," came the reply. "The Secretary is right here and will talk to you."

I explained to him what I wanted, reminded him of Davis's reputation, and listed the important newspapers publishing his dispatches. Bryan hesitated only a minute and then replied, "You know he gave us a lot of trouble in Mexico. No, we can't accept him."

Reluctantly, we cabled this information to Davis in London. That night he dressed in white tie and tails as usual when in England. He had dinner and took in a show. Afterwards he went to the London office of the *Tribune* which was publishing his war dispatches in New York. A young whippersnapper looked at his costume and said sarcastically, "Don't you know there is a war going on?"

Davis turned on his heel and walked out. The next day he left for Belgium without any official credentials. Here he wrote what many believe was the finest story on the war. It was his description of the German Army marching through Brussels, but there is no use trying to paint the lily. Here it is as Davis told it in 1914:

> The change came at ten in the morning. It was as though a wand had waved and from a fete-day on the Continent we had been wafted to London on a rainy Sunday. The boulevards fell suddenly empty. There was not a house that was not closely shuttered. Along the route by which we now knew the Germans were advancing, it was as though the plague stalked. That no one should fire from a window, that to the conquerors no one should offer insult, Burgomaster Max sent as special constables men he trusted. Their badge of authority was a walking-stick and a piece of paper fluttering from a buttonhole. These, the police, and the servants and caretakers of the houses that lined the boulevards alone were visible. At eleven o'clock, unobserved but by this official audience, down the Boulevard Waterloo came the advance-guard of the German army. It consisted of three men, a captain and two privates on bicycles. Their rifles were slung across their shoulders, they rode unwarily, with as little concern as the members of a touring-club out for a holiday. Behind them so close upon each other that

to cross from one sidewalk to the other was not possible, came the Uhlans, infantry, and the guns. For two hours I watched them, and then, bored with the monotony of it, returned to the hotel. After an hour, from beneath my window, I still could hear them; another hour and another went by. They still were passing. Boredom gave way to wonder. The thing fascinated you, against your will, dragged you back to the sidewalk and held you there open-eyed. No longer was it regiments of men marching, but something uncanny, inhuman, a force of nature like a landslide, a tidal wave, or lava sweeping down a mountain. It was not of this earth, but mysterious, ghostlike. It carried all the mystery and menace of a fog rolling toward you across the sea. The uniform aided this impression. In it each man moved under a cloak of invisibility. Only after the most numerous and severe tests at all distances, with all materials and combinations of colors that give forth no color, could this gray have been discovered. That it was selected to clothe and disguise the German when he fights is typical of the General Staff, in striving for efficiency, to leave nothing to chance, to neglect no detail.

After you have seen this service uniform under conditions entirely opposite you are convinced that for the German soldier it is one of his strongest weapons. Even the most expert marksman cannot hit a target he cannot see. It is not the blue-gray of our Confederates, but a green-gray. It is the gray of the hour just before daybreak, the gray of unpolished steel, of mist among green trees.

I saw it first in the Grand Place in front of the Hotel de Ville. It was impossible to tell if in that noble square there was a regiment or a brigade. You saw only a fog that melted into the stones, blended with the ancient house fronts, that shifted and drifted, but left you nothing at which to point.

Later, as the army passed under the trees of the Botanical Park, it merged and was lost against the green leaves. It is no exaggeration to say that at a few hundred yards you can see the horses on which the Uhlans ride but cannot see the men who ride them.

If I appear to overemphasize this disguising uniform it is because, of all the details of the German outfit, it appealed to me as one of the most remarkable. When I was near Namur with the rear-guard of the French Dragoons and Cuirassiers, and they threw out pickets, we could distinguish them against the yellow wheat or green gorse at half a mile, while these men passing in the street, when they have reached the next crossing, become merged into the gray of the paving-stones and the earth swallowed them. In comparison, the yellow khaki of our own American army is about as invisible as the flag of Spain.

Major-General von Jarotsky, the German military governor of Brussels, had assured Burgomaster Max that the German army would not occupy the city but would pass through it. He told the truth. For three days and three nights it passed. In six campaigns I have followed other armies, but excepting not even our own, the Japanese, or the British, I have not seen one so thoroughly equipped. I am not speaking of the fighting qualities of any army, only of the equipment and organization. The German army moved into Brussels as smoothly and as compactly as an Empire State express. There were no halts, no open places, no stragglers. For the gray automobiles and the gray motorcycles bearing messengers one side of the street always was kept clear; and so compact was the column, so rigid the vigilance of the file-closers, that at the rate of forty miles an hour a car could race the length of the column and need not for a single horse or man once swerve from its course.

All through the night, like a tumult of a river when it races between the cliffs of a canyon, in my sleep I could hear the steady roar of the passing army. And when early in the morning I went to the window the chain of steel was still unbroken. It was like the torrent that swept down the Connemaugh Valley and destroyed Johnstown. As a correspondent I have seen all the great armies and the military processions at the coronations in Russia, England, and Spain, and our own inaugural parades down Pennsylvania Avenue, but those armies and processions were made up of men. This was a machine, endless, tireless, with the delicate organization of a watch and the brute power of a steam roller. And for three days and three nights through Brussels it roared and rumbled, a cataract of molten lead. The infantry marched singing, with their iron-shod boots beating out the time. They sang "Fatherland, My Fatherland." Between each line of song they took three steps. At times 2000 men were singing together in absolute rhythm and beat. It was like blows from giant pile-drivers. When the melody gave way the silence was broken only by the stamp of iron-shod boots, and then again the song rose. When the singing ceased the bands played marches. They were followed by the rumble of the howitzers, the creaking of wheels and of chains clanking against the cobblestones, and the sharp, bell-like voices of the bugles.

More Uhlans followed, the hoofs of their magnificent horses ringing like thousands of steel hammers breaking stones in a road; and after them the giant siege-guns rumbling, growling, the mitrailleuses with drag-chains ringing, the field-pieces with creaking axles, complaining brakes, the grinding of the steel-rimmed wheels against the stones echoing and re-echoing from the house front. When at night for an instant the machine halted, the silence awoke you, as at sea you wake when the screw stops.

For three days and three nights the column of gray, with hundreds of thousands of bayonets and hundreds of thousands of lances, with gray transport wagons, gray ammunition carts, gray ambulances, gray cannon, like a river of steel, cut Brussels in two.

For three weeks the men had been on the march, and there was not a single straggler, not a strap out of place, not a pennant missing. Along the route, without for a minute halting the machine, the post-office carts fell out of the column, and as the men marched mounted postmen collected postcards and delivered letters. Also, as they marched, the cooks prepared soup, coffee, and tea, walking beside their stoves on wheels, tending the fires, distributing the smoking food. Seated in the motor-trucks cobblers mended boots and broken harness; farriers on tiny anvils beat out horseshoes. No officer followed a wrong turning, no officer asked his way. He followed the map strapped to his side and on which for his guidance in red ink his route was marked. At night he read this map by the light of an electric torch buckled to his chest.

To perfect this monstrous engine, with its pontoon bridges, its wireless, its hospitals, its aeroplanes that in rigid alignment sailed before it, its field telephones that, as it advanced, strung wires over which for miles the vanguard talked to the rear, all modern inventions had been prostituted. To feed it millions of men had been called from homes, offices and workshops; to guide it, for years the minds of the high-born, with whom it is a religion and a disease, had been solely concerned.

It is, perhaps, the most efficient organization of modern times; and its purpose only is death. Those who cast it loose upon Europe are military-mad. And they are only a very small part of the German people. But to preserve their class they have in their own image created this terrible engine of destruction. For the present it is their servant. But, "though the mills of the Gods grind slowly, yet they grind exceedingly small." And, like Frankenstein's monster, this monster, to which they gave life, may turn and rend them.*

Davis had on the same correspondent's uniform he wore when covering the Boer War. It resembled that of a British officer. Instead of waiting for any further credentials, after finishing his masterpiece, he joined the German column. He kept going for two or three days before he was discovered by bigger brass.

* From Richard Harding Davis, *With the Allies*. Reprinted with credit to Scribner's and the Wheeler Syndicate.

Hauled up before the commanding general, he was charged with being a British spy. Why the Heinies would think, if he were, he would be wearing a British officer's uniform is a puzzle. Anyway, it looked as if he were going to be convicted and shot when a German major on the staff stepped forward. He spoke English and had lived in the United States and had heard of Richard Harding Davis, the writer. He put in a plea for him and finally persuaded the military court to let him go. However, the conditions were strict. Davis was to follow a certain route laid out on a map. If found anywhere else, he was to be shot forthwith. You bet he watched his course closely and reported to Brand Whitlock, the American Ambassador in Brussels.

After our correspondent had written his piece about the German Army marching through Belgium, I put in a request to the German Embassy in Washington to accredit him, since the Germans had been stuffy about correspondents. This was being considered when Davis came through with another story of the Germans' destruction of the cathedral in Rheims. It was a biting dispatch about the savagery and wantonness of the invaders. He had joined the French Armies and there was no more talk about going over to the other side.

Yes, he always had plenty of moxie.

Davis went back to the war for us in 1915 and 1916. The situation in France was static and the armies were deadlocked, so he moved along to Salonika, where the British had sent an ill-fated force. It was a dismal, cold spot, and several American correspondents were quartered there in the same big room. The group included John McCutcheon of the *Chicago Tribune* and William Shepherd of *Collier's*, reporting his first war.

One morning a young American burst into the room, covered with mud fresh from the trenches. After he had scraped off some of the caked clay, it was seen he was wearing a British uniform. He greeted the correspondents and then explained the reason for his arrival.

"I have had it," he began. "They gave me a pass for two days' leave. See that ship across the street at the dock? I found out she sails tonight at 6 for the U.S.A. I will be on it."

He was already pulling off his filthy uniform as he talked.

"One of you lend me a suit of civvies," he went on. "I come from a farm in Iowa, and I'm going back there. I've had my bellyful of this war. I joined up to see the sights, and I've seen all I want to. I was hit on the Somme, and, when I came out of Blighty, they sent me here, and I've been in those stinkin' trenches ever since."

He looked at the steamer with smoke pouring out of her stacks.

Davis turned to his fellow-correspondents. "Would you fellows mind going out for a little walk which will take at least half an hour?" he said.

By this time the visitor had stripped off his clothes. The others left. When they returned, the soldier was again in his dirty uniform. He went back to the front.

After Davis got home, he wrote a fiction story for the *Metropolitan Magazine* called "The Deserter," based on this incident. It was his last story for he died shortly afterwards.

There is another sequel. Months later, Shepherd met this same soldier walking down the Strand in London and recognized him. He was wearing the ribbon of the Victoria Cross, the highest British decoration for bravery.

"What do you think of me?" he asked. "When I was figuring on deserting out there in Salonika, they were fixing to give me this before a regiment drawn up on parade." He pointed to the ribbon proudly. "It was for something or other I had done on the Western Front," he explained modestly.

"Did you know Davis was dead?" said Shepherd.

"Dead!" exclaimed the soldier. "He talked me out of deserting and died thinking I was yellow, didn't he?"

Bill Shepherd later wrote this as a postscript to Davis's story.

I once asked Davis what was the secret of good writing.

"I don't believe there is any fixed formula to be followed," he answered, but added, "I recall when I was a young man and just starting I got a letter from Robert Louis Stevenson giving me some advice. Finally he said, 'Always remember the secret of good writing is rewriting and rewriting. It takes great pains.'"

Davis used to do all his writing in longhand on short yellow sheets of paper, using a pencil. Then he would throw away the ones he didn't like. I have seen the floor of his study carpeted with these discarded yellow sheets.

The last time I saw Richard Harding Davis alive we had dinner together at the Waldorf and went on to the old Madison Square Garden to a fight between Jess Willard, the champion, and Frank Moran. He complained of indigestion, and we stopped in the Prince George bar for a brandy. About a week later he was in his home in Mt. Kisco, telephoning John Purroy Mitchel, mayor of New York, when he had a heart attack, keeled over, and died. It is the way he would want to make his final exit.

VI. PANCHO VILLA AND OTHER SOLDIERS OF FORTUNE

EL PASO was a rip-roaring town in 1913 when I first visited it. My purpose was to sell features to the newspapers, but soon I fell in with some pleasant and exciting companions and began to relish the atmosphere. Several of my friends were soldiers of fortune who would shoot for hire and joined the side that paid the highest for a good machine-gunner.

First there was Sam Dreben, a husky colorful gent who had fought with several armies across the border as a machine-gunner. Damon Runyon wrote a poem about him called "The Fighting Jew." Tex O'Reilly was a part-time newspaperman and an occasional soldier of fortune. Tracy Richardson was one of the calmest, most cold-blooded men I have ever met. Gunther Lessing was the United States representative and lawyer for Pancho Villa, then flying high as a revolutionary leader. We were sitting around the bar in the Shelton Hotel one night when someone told me the story of how Villa beat the races—a sure-fire system you might call it.

After he had captured Juarez, the Mexican town across the Rio Grande River from El Paso, Villa went to the track one afternoon. He picked out a horse in the first heat and made a bet. The nag finished out of the money, so Pancho whipped out his old equalizer and shot the horse. He took aim but missed the jockey, who by this time was running faster than his mount had. After that lesson, Villa was watched carefully by one and all to see what his pick would be. Needless to say, he quit a big winner, and all the horses and jocks survived.

"I'd like to go to Mexico and write the story of Villa's life," I said one night, casually.

"If you mean it," answered Gunther Lessing, "I will get you a visa and free transportation."

"No," I replied. "I guess I don't want to ride on those lousy Mexican trains by myself for a couple of weeks."

"Make up a party," he said, "and you can have a private car."

We were in business. I telegraphed Bud Fisher, the cartoonist, who was marking time waiting for his contract with the Hearst papers to expire. I wired Charley Van Loan in Los Angeles, and he declined about as follows: "Lay off that Mexican hop."

Fisher accepted, and we decided to give him a good reception. The town was still decorated with flags and other bunting for the cattlemen's convention which had been held the week before. We dressed Tex O'Reilly as the mayor, which did not require much thought, since he already was wearing a ten-gallon hat. Sam Dreben, we decided, would be the Mexican consul. We picked up a six-piece band which had been left behind by the cattlemen.

When the Southern Pacific train pulled into the station, the musicians struck up with some appropriate tune like "Hail, the Conquering Hero Comes." All this commotion attracted no little attention as dapper Bud dismounted from the rattler. O'Reilly greeted him with a sweeping gesture and handed him the key to the city. Dreben was bowing low and jabbering Spanish in his ear. Fisher was duly impressed.

"What's it all about?" he asked me as we got into cars to drive to the Shelton.

"It's for you," I replied. "You are a bigshot."

He agreed. "Who's that guy?" he asked pointing to Dreben.

"He's the Mexican consul. Can't speak any English!"

That night we hired a private dining room. The "mayor"

made a speech of welcome. Dreben made a speech in Spanish which we all applauded loudly, although actually it was insulting. Finally, Fisher, who of course occupied the head of the table, was called upon. As he stood up, Sam Dreben took dead aim with a baked potato which was still in its skin, with butter. He hit the guest of honor in the kisser just as Fisher opened his mouth to burst into oratory. Then we introduced Sam all around, and Bud took it in good part. He had to. He was up against too many tough guys.

Hippolito Villa, Pancho's brother, had the gambling concession in Juarez, so we all decided to go across the river to see the town. Fisher was playing roulette when a Mexican standing beside him began to reach over and sneak chips off his pile. Bud cracked him over the wrist which touched off a little row. A cop grabbed Fisher, and Dreben punched the policeman and knocked him down. Three or four more came running, and soon Sam was in the sneezer. We located Hippolito Villa, explaining we were guests of his brother, and he sprung our friend promptly.

Meanwhile, Floyd Gibbons of the *Chicago Tribune* had arrived to cover his first war. We invited him to join our crowd which he did with alacrity.

We began to organize our expedition. Harry Stevens had the catering privileges at the Juarez race track, and he generously stocked our car with liquor of all varieties and quantities. Hippolito Villa started up the printing presses and furnished us with 11,000 pesos to finance the trip. We turned this over to Gunther Lessing as treasurer, not knowing whether it was any good or not. Our car was an ordinary, old-fashioned Pullman which had strayed across the border, and the Mexicans had neglected to return it. The smoking room had been converted into a kitchen where a colored fellow named Tom presided. We had everything except *soldaderas* who were part of the standard equipment of Mexican armies in those days. They traveled with the troops and among other duties acted as the commissary.

The first night out we got into an argument and decided to try Gunther Lessing on some trumped-up charge. He was found guilty by a crooked judge, Bud Fisher, and fined the 11,000 pesos. This sum was turned over to me.

Our first important stop was Chihuahua which we reached the next morning. With my bankroll, I thought I would see whether the money was any good. I asked a man where I could buy a Chihuahua dog, but he said he had never heard of the breed. They are for sale on Fifth Avenue in New York.

Then I saw a Mexican carrying a very tough-looking rooster under his arm. Our scouts had told us that Villa did not drink or smoke but was fond of cockfights, so I thought I would get a couple of birds to make a good impression when we met him. I tried to ask the owner, in my halting Spanish, how much he wanted for the rooster. He answered something, and I peeled off a 20-peso note. He shoved the gamecock at me before I could change my mind and hurried off. Probably I could have bought a whole barnyard full for the price.

We had three or four eating chickens tied by their legs on the platform of the car, the idea being to keep them fresh until Tom was ready to serve them. There wasn't any deep freeze in those days.

Proudly I fastened my gamecock alongside the chickens and explained to my companions what I planned to do. All agreed it was a brilliant idea. After about an hour, I decided to go out to see how my champion was getting along. Much to my chagrin, he was flat on his back, dead as a doornail. The eating chickens had killed him.

We first met Pancho Villa at Torreon. He then had an army of about 50,000 men. The soldiers traveled in boxcars through the courtesy of the Pennsylvania, New York, New Haven and Hartford, etc., according to the labels on the sides. The horses occupied the interior of the cars and the *soldados* and *soldaderas* rode on the roofs or on mats shoved underneath on the rods. The women built small fires and cooked frijoles and tortillas, the Mexican staple. Pancho himself traveled in style. He had a private car attached to the end of the train and just forward of this was a boxcar in which were a piano and barber chair. Also, a few dames were on the fringe.

He was one of the most remarkable men I have ever seen. Uneducated, he had animal cunning and amazing cat's eyes. No matter where you were in the room, he always seemed to be looking at you. He was genial enough when on your side, but a bad man if against you or suspicious. Shortly after we joined up, he announced he was going to shoot a prisoner the next morning at daylight and invited us to attend. We asked him to put it off entirely, but failing in that, we got him to agree to delay the matter until 10 o'clock to let us sleep a little later. The next morning, puffing on a cigarette, the man faced the firing squad and died bravely. Villa presented the prisoner's six-shooter to Bud Fisher. The victim's name was cut on the butt—José Ruiz. In later years, Fisher used the gun occasionally for target practice late at night in his apartment, which resulted in his moving fairly frequently.

On his staff, Pancho Villa had a Major Fierro, also known as "the butcher," who believed he was deadly with a gun. He was in a café in Torreon one night when he began to brag about what a good shot he was. There was a Mexican girl sitting across the room, a perfect stranger. She had high combs, according to the style of the country, in the back of her hair.

Fierro pulled out his pistol and boasted he would shoot the ornaments out without hitting her. He took aim, but was a little low, and the bullet struck her in the middle of the forehead. It killed her deader than a mackerel. There was little sympathy for the victim in the crowd, but the Villa followers thought it a great joke on the Major because he had missed his target.

Also traveling with Villa was his strategist, General Angeles, who had been educated at the French military academy, St. Cyr. Angeles urged his chief to attack and take Tampico, which would cut off the oil supply and money for Carranza's army. We were en route for this battle through Monterrey.

One night we stopped at a small town in the mountains, and Villa told us he had an American prisoner there who was going to be executed. We asked to see him. He turned out to be a young man named Miner Merriweather, who had gone to Annapolis. He was kicked out for getting into some kind of a fight with a midshipman named Bunce, who died as a result of his injuries.

Merriweather had come to Mexico as a soldier of fortune and joined with Orozco's Red Flaggers. He made the bad mistake of getting captured. Naturally, he was feeling very low when we saw him in the hoosegow because he realized what his fate would be.

We returned to Villa's private car. I was made spokesman.

"Why do you execute Merriweather?" I asked. "He is an American."

"He was fighting against me," Villa answered firmly.

"You say you want to be friendly with the United States. Do you think that is any way to accomplish it?"

"What else can I do?" he asked.

"Take him to the border and put him across with a warning that if he ever returns to Mexico, he will be shot forthwith."

All this conversation was conducted through an interpreter, Raoul Madero, who was on our side. Villa finally agreed.

Three or four years later, Merriweather came into the office to see me. "You fellows saved my life," he said. "I am most grateful."

There was a rule in the Mexican Army an officer could promote up to his rank. One night Fisher and I were talking to a Major who had gone to the University of Pennsylvania and spoke good English. We expressed some dissatisfaction about hanging around so long and having no rank. He reached into his pocket and drew out two bright-colored cords to put on our hats.

"You are now Captains," he said.

We saluted and felt pretty good until the next morning. The Major showed up with orders for us to join his command. We gave him back his insignia and resigned.

Things began to go badly for Villa all of a sudden. We were in a couple of small battles which didn't amount to much. As a matter of fact, half the time the enemy was out of range. Then Villa got word General Obregon was moving north toward Torreon. Obregon had once been a close compatriot, but Villa now hated him. Also, Villa had a girl back in Guadalajara, and it irritated him to think he might be cut off from visiting her. General Angeles argued with Villa, urging him to disregard Obregon except to send a few troops to fight a rear-guard, delaying action and to make the main attack against Tampico.

Villa paid no attention to him. He reversed his whole army and started back to fight Obregon. It was his first major mistake and proves romance and war don't mix.

Fisher and I realized Angeles was right. We visited Villa in his car one evening after fortifying ourselves with a couple of drinks, courtesy of Harry Stevens. By this time, we knew him pretty well, and I had already gotten most of the material for my story. We put it up to him straight.

"General, you are a great leader," said Fisher. "You are a soldier, but what you need are a couple of smart managers who can advise you. You should be on better terms with the United States Government."

Then I chipped in. "We know the newspapers. We could handle your publicity. Make Fisher and me your managers, and we can't lose. We will split Mexico three ways, and there will be plenty for all."

Of course, this statement was made with becoming modesty. Even so, Villa seemed somewhat abashed by it. He thought a minute and then said, "I fight my battles with the sword and not with the pen."

It was a fateful decision, for he wound up behind the eight ball, and Fisher and I lost a third of Mexico apiece.

Villa met his first real defeat in a battle at Celaya where he fought Obregon head on and got the hell kicked out of him. That was the beginning of the long retreat which led to the Columbus raid and the pursuit by General Pershing. When we saw how things were going, we turned tail and headed north.

We were all wearing Villa buttons and his colors on our lapels. One night the train stopped suddenly and, after a brief pause, began to back up. Someone said the Red Flaggers had halted it. We quickly changed our religion. Villa buttons went out the windows or down the john. It turned out, however, that the engineer had dozed off and run past a stop signal. He was reversing himself at top speed to avoid being hit by a locomotive coming from the other direction. We made the siding in time.

We spent a day in Chihuahua as the guests of Villa's legal wife. He had married her when he had gone to Mexico City for Francisco Madero's inauguration. The new President had insisted on it to make the occasion measure up to the best social standards. She was living in a large, ornate house with her young son. She had us all to lunch.

"What do you think of the joint?" I asked Bud Fisher.

"Looks like Nell Brinkley designed it and Hearst built it," he answered. Miss Brinkley was an artist of the day who drew pretty fancy stuff.

We finally got back to El Paso all in one piece, and I wrote the Pancho Villa story which was widely published. It told of his poor youth and how he had to take to the hills because he shot a wealthy Mexican who had ravished his sister. He organized his guerrillas, raided haciendas, robbed the rich to feed the poor—a kind of Robin Hood. Villa came to a bad ending, for he was double-crossed and ambushed after being granted amnesty.

Another whose life ended tragically was Sam Dreben, a great character who was with us on this trip. He had color. One night before we left for Mexico a bunch of us were together at the Paso del Norte Hotel in El Paso, and a Captain in the U.S. Army from Fort Bliss joined us. He tried to move in on my girl which was irritating, so I told him to lay off. One word led to another until I invited him to scram.

"I'll get you," he said as he walked out.

"That's bad," remarked Sam. "He has the reputation of being a very tough guy."

Two or three days went by, and Dreben never left my side. He had appointed himself my bodyguard. Then the Captain came around to the hotel and asked for me. Old Sam was there, too.

"I'm sorry for what happened the other night," he began. "It was my fault. I hear you are going to Mexico on a trip, so for insurance I brought you an Army pistol and dumdummed some bullets."

He handed me the gun. He had flattened out and scraped the noses of the bullets so these would spread if they hit a human target.

Once on the trip, Sergeant Dreben got pretty tight. He swallowed a drink and then took a bite out of the glass and crunched it up in his teeth. This seemed to be a dangerous digestive situation and called for a consultation. We decided to feed him great quantities of bread with the idea this would form sort of a cushion and keep the glass from cutting his insides. It worked, and he survived.

He went with Pershing later as a scout when the General was chasing Villa back across the border after his raid on Columbus. Then when World War I started, Dreben was offered a commission but insisted on going as a sergeant. In the meantime, he had struck it fairly rich in Austin Amazon copper and had married a very pretty blonde on whom he lavished everything.

He made a great record in the war and won many decorations. His first night back in America he spent with us in Yonkers. My wife had never met him before, but she was impressed with his ribbons.

"How did you get that, Sergeant Dreben?" she asked, pointing to one.

"We raided a German front-line position with eighteen men. We killed fifty-eight Germans and brought in two prisoners."

"How was that?" she asked.

He seemed a little apologetic. "You see," he explained, "I shot at one, missed, and only wounded him. I didn't have the heart to finish him. The bullet hit him in the jaw."

"You didn't!" exclaimed my wife.

"Upon my mother's honor, Mrs. Wheeler," he answered with a low bow. By this time he was pulling the caps off beer bottles with his teeth. He didn't bother with the opener.

"The other fellow," he went on, "pleaded for his life and showed me a picture of his wife and children. Also, he had some rations with him. I was hungry, but afraid to eat the stuff for fear it might be poisoned. Just then I saw a French soldier. I handed him a piece of the bologna.

" '*Bon, pour manger*,' I said to him.

"He swallowed some of it, and I watched him for about fifteen minutes. When his eyes didn't blink, I figured it was all right and finished off the rest of it."

Next day, Sam, Damon Runyon, and I went to see Harry Stevens, the same man who furnished liquid supplies for our Mexican junket and who now has all the catering privileges at the New York race tracks and ball parks. Stevens disappeared from his office and came back shortly with a check for $500 which he offered to Dreben. Sam refused it.

When he returned to El Paso to a great reception, he found his wife had been true to the home guard while he was in France fighting for his country. Not only that, but Dreben had given her the power of attorney which she had used freely and cleaned out the till.

He later married a Dallas girl and moved to Los Angeles. Shortly afterward he died of an overdose of salvarsan, which a nurse had given him by mistake. He would rather have been finished by a good enemy bullet.

Another of our cohorts in Mexico was a slight, soft-spoken fellow named Tracy Richardson. He was an expert machine-gunner and would fight for anyone who offered him the highest pay. After the European war started, he joined up with the Princess Pats and was badly wounded. When he recovered, he went into the U.S. Air Force.

After the war, the soldier-of-fortune business was sort of slow, so with the assistance of General Wild Bill Donovan I got him a job in a Prohibition unit. This turned out all right since, when his outfit would make a raid and he found some particularly good booze, he would slip me a few bottles.

He was a great man to have on your side. Every April the newspaper publishers hold their annual convention in New York at the Waldorf, and during the dry days our syndicate used to rent a suite of rooms where our customers could relax and also get a free drink. One night a group of us, including Richardson, gathered in these quarters. After the big dinner, Bill Curley, one of the top Hearst editors, and Joe Bannon, circulation manager, dropped by. Another guest was Mr. Murphy, managing editor of the *Baltimore Sun*. Bannon, a tough talker even when in a dinner jacket as he was, began boasting. "I got my start," he said, "robbing Hoist [Hearst] and immigrants."

Murphy, without really meaning any offense, began to imitate his pronunciation, and the Royal Blood of Ireland, as Bannon called himself, bristled and boiled.

"I may not have gone to Yale or Harvard," he said, "but I know more than you do."

When he discovered Bannon's belligerent attitude, Murphy retreated, and, as the host, I stepped between to make peace.

"Come now, Joe," I said. "He didn't mean anything. Don't get mad."

He turned on me. "And a dime a dozen for your kind, too," he declared. "I can tear you apart."

"Well, I'm still standing here all in one piece," I answered.

Then in the mirror Bannon saw Richardson circle around behind him. So did I. My opponent calmed down.

"That fellow has a knife," he said as he got his hat and coat and left without saying good night.

After he had gone, I said to Richardson, "Did you have a knife?"

"No," he replied, "but I had this." And he showed me a blackjack.

"It was a nasty situation," he said. "He had a revolver in his pants pocket. If he had made a wrong move toward you, I was going to let him have it."

"It's just as well you didn't," I said. "If you had, I would have spent the rest of my life dodging around alleys trying to duck his plug-uglies."

Joe Bannon and I later patched everything up and became friends. He is now retired and living in luxury in Florida, circulating in the best circles, and is still known as the Royal Blood of Ireland.

Good old Tracy Richardson is probably dead, since I haven't heard from him in years. In fact, I'm surprised he lived as long as he did. He was afraid of nothing.

Neither was Alexander McClintock, a soldier of fortune who made his record in the First World War with the Canadians before the U.S. became a participant. He was badly gassed, and his back was creased with shrapnel at Ypres. He was sent home to recuperate, and that is when I first met this colorful fellow. Guy Empey had just written a best-seller, *Over the Top*, about his experiences. I got McClintock to do a series for us. This was widely published, and George Doran later brought it out as a book.

While still recuperating, McClintock went up to Plattsburg's second camp to get an officer's commission. I enlisted at the same time. As a token of appreciation, McClintock gave me a pistol he had carried when soldiering with the Canadians. He also gave me some advice.

"If you get a chance, join the artillery," he said. "You are just as liable to be killed or wounded, but you frequently land near a French wine cellar."

Since I knew as little about the infantry as any other branch, when they called for volunteers for the artillery, I followed McClintock's advice.

Toward the closing days of the camp, he came to see me and asked me to lend him the revolver he had given me. His company was having some sort of service practice with live ammunition, and because of his experience, he was to play a leading part. As it turned out, he never returned the revolver.

Meanwhile, because of the success of his book, Lee Keedick made him an offer to go on a lucrative lecture tour. McClintock was granted a sick leave by the Army to accept the proposition. Now McClintock stuttered slightly when sober, but this was accentuated after drinking. In order to get up his courage for his first lecture appearance, he took on a few, and the lecture was a flop for the simple reason the audience couldn't understand what the hell he was saying. The rest of the tour was canceled forthwith.

Bud Fisher and I went off to France to fight the Germans and "save democracy," so the balance of this story I got after my return. It seems McClintock had his leave and nothing much to do, so he took up regularly with Peggy Hopkins Joyce, to whom Bud Fisher had introduced him. She was interested in money and jewelry, and he soon ran out of both during the romance. Then he overstayed his leave, and the Army was looking for him as a deserter. Broke and despondent, he called on Miss Joyce in her apartment. He explained he had reached the end and was planning to commit suicide if she didn't help him.

"Don't do it around here and get blood all over the carpet," she said. "Go to a Turkish bath and do it."

In her defense, I might say she probably never expected him to make good on his threat. But he did. He went to the Murray Hill baths and there blew his brains out with the pistol he had given me at Plattsburg—a sad ending for a brave man.

VII. IN THE ARMY

ALTHOUGH I was slightly above the draft age when the U.S. went into World War I, I decided to join up, because I didn't want some nosy dame coming around pinning a white feather on my coat, which was the custom in those days. I didn't return a great hero, although I spent more than six months at the front in France and got shot at plenty.

Following the Plattsburg training, I became a lieutenant in the Field Artillery, as McClintock had advised. When we arrived in France, we were sent to Camp Meucon. Shortly afterwards, I was ordered to proceed to a little town called Chateaubourges, near Rennes, with 125 men on a remount detail. The purpose was to collect horses for the artillery brigade. After traveling all night, we reached our destination at 7 A.M., and I lined my men up, saluted, and reported to the commanding officer who was a Major.

The Major immediately called General Hearn by long-distance to ask why he hadn't sent him at least one Captain to impress the French. This made no hit with me. The Major also had on more junk than Peggy Hopkins Joyce wore as jewelry in her best days. He had a compass, an identification tag on one wrist and a watch on the other, and some odds and ends dangling. All soldiers were compelled by regulations to have identification tags around their necks so the one on the wrist was fancy.

I hadn't been there long before the Major began to recognize my talents and made me his adjutant. He put on a great

show. If a soldier was on fatigue duty without his blouse and
his shorts showed above his pants, he would throw him in the
guardhouse. He kept the place pretty well filled up and frequently drove by it. On such occasions, as required, the sergeant would yell, "Commanding officer—turn out the guard."

Usually any normal guy would say, "Never mind the guard."

But not our boy. He also had sentries marching up and down
in front of headquarters, a French château we had appropri-
ated, as well as at the billet of the officer of the day. He was a
hell of a spit-and-polish fellow. But pretty soon he got stuck on
a girl in Rennes and devoted more time to her than to the
horses, so he left me to keep the store.

We shipped more than 2000 horses through this little town,
at least half of them stallions. Our men, accompanied by
French officers, would fan out over a radius of 100 miles to
requisition the animals. These would be brought in by road
and lined up in the town square to be checked against descrip-
tive lists. It was quite a ceremony. Then we would load them
on little French cars for Camp Meucon—a job when you are
handling studs. One day the commanding officer came back
from a visit to his dame to find all the sentries off post and the
guardhouse empty. He called me in and started to give me
hell.

"What does this mean?" he demanded. "Don't you know
anything about military discipline?"

"Yes, sir," I replied, "but we needed men to go get horses
which, after all, is our job here. This is a war for keeps you
know." Then I went on: "I had a friend who was in the
Canadian Army, and he told me when they first got to the
front, a lot of their officers were shot by their own men. Their
soldiers turned out to be a quick-tempered bunch."

"What do you mean?" the Major asked.

"Well, as soon as they got under fire, they took shots at all the officers they thought were sons-of-bitches before they aimed at the enemy."

This remark reformed him, and he was a changed man. When we came to transferring the command, I had a problem. Our statistics showed we were seven horses short. We stabled the critters at several farms around the fringe of the town. I didn't want personally to get stuck for seven horses, so I arranged a plan with my assistant, Lieutenant Henry Berg. I explained my route while my successor was counting the animals.

"As soon as I leave the first farm, take seven and put them on the last one. Then the figures will come out even."

It worked, and the total added up right. What the hell ever became of those seven missing horses I don't know or what the next man did about them.

By this time General Hearn had made me ammunition officer for the division, in which capacity I acted while at the front, and I have a letter from him commending me for my services. The Major was put in command of the first battalion. I never saw a guy who could get his command post so far underground. His mother must have had mole blood. Anyway, one day he was out on a reconnaissance tour with the Colonel who was a little deaf when the Germans began shelling the area. One burst somewhere near them and the Major high-tailed it for a trench. The Colonel followed and jumped on the Major's shoulder, dislocating it.

This "wounded" officer was around for a few days with his arm in a sling, whining about his condition, when he was sent back for reclassification and finally returned to the United States. After we got back following the Armistice, the Major met us with a wound stripe on. Later the regiment had an officers' dinner at Reisenweber's restaurant. He foolishly attended and got a good razzing.

The regiment asked me to bring Ring Lardner to liven up the situation. It was during Prohibition. When he arose to speak, he pulled a bottle of whisky out of his pocket.

"Has anybody got a corkscrew?" he asked. One was produced, and he took a swig.

"You boys probably wonder why I was not in the Army," he went on. "Well, my feet were too flat to be a soldier and not flat enough to be a cop."

Colonel Frank Knox, later Secretary of the Navy under Roosevelt, was in command of the horse section of the ammunition train, so in my official capacity I saw a good deal of him. We became friends. After the Armistice, we were sent back to Montbard, a small town near Dijon. The war being over, there was no need for ammunition, so General Hearn made me the brigade supply officer. It was a cinch job with practically nothing to do. I was billeted with a French family with two good-looking daughters. When they showed me around the house, I wanted to acquaint myself with the facilities.

"*Ou est le cabinet?*" I asked with a doughboy accent.

"*Le cabinet?*" one of them queried puzzled.

"*Oui, mademoiselle.*"

She showed me clothes closets and other nooks. I kept shaking my head. Then her eyes brightened.

"Oh, the water closet," she exclaimed and took me to the bathroom.

I began to get restless, hanging around that town, so I set out to wangle orders to go home. By now, the General and I were on very good terms. We ate in the same mess, and he had recommended me for promotion several times. He sent off a letter to Chaumont, A.E.F. headquarters, outlining my record and asking for orders for me to return to the United States. Shortly these came through. I knew the journey was a slow process, and I figured if I was accompanied by more rank, I would make better time. I tipped Colonel Knox off, since I knew he wanted to get back, too, and it worked.

We were ordered to report to a camp in southern France where we were put up in the hospital waiting for orders to move. We had to report at the barracks every morning, and one rainy day I spotted a familiar figure doing close-order drill. He was Grantland Rice. We rescued him with the Colonel's help, and he moved into the hospital with us. I had made a bet with Knox that the war would be over by Christmas which I had now won. The pay-off was to be a gourmet dinner for four when we got back to New York. One evening after dinner, the Colonel and I decided to include the Rices, and we whiled away the time by writing out the menu. It was a wet one, so at the end I put one word "Stretchers."

"Let me keep that," suggested the Colonel. "I want to save it so I won't forget."

We three made it together to St. Nazaire and finally aboard the transport. Knox was the ranking officer, and he made Rice and me his adjutants. Then unfortunately he got seasick, and Rice and I ran the ship as far as the troops were concerned. We also found a Major named White. He had discovered a soldier on board who used to be cook on J. P. Morgan's yacht. Major White had also thoughtfully laid in a supply of old cognac before embarking. Every night after taps we would foregather in his cabin and enjoy ourselves. When the Colonel recovered, we invited him.

"Hey," he exclaimed as he sipped some brandy, "I thought I told you fellows not to bring any liquor aboard. It's against the rules."

"We didn't," I replied, and being a broad-minded man, he let it go at that.

On the long voyage, an epidemic of flu broke out, and we

lost a lot of men. Grant and I did the best we could under the conditions, but it was a sad experience, making out the final papers and burial at sea for some. All were so eager to get home again.

About two weeks after our discharge, Colonel Knox announced the missus and he were going to give us the dinner I had won. I remember I stopped in the old Waldorf bar on my way uptown and met John McGraw, manager of the New York Giants.

"Have a drink," he invited.

"No, thanks," I answered. "I won a bet on the war and have a big night ahead of me. I want to be in shape."

Colonel Knox was a changed man. When he got home from the wars, he was wearing a big red mustache like a cavalry-man. Now this was gone. His missus was a prim little New England woman with a whim of iron. We went in to dinner dry, and the oysters came. Then the steak and the dessert. No booze.

"Maybe you mislaid that menu," I whispered behind my hand to the Colonel.

He blushed a little. "Mrs. Knox is very much against liquor," he explained.

We later went out to a café where Rice and I were the hosts, and we took charge. There was a change.

A final experience in the Army is worth telling. During the battle of Mont San Michele, I was in the front-line command post by myself, trying to keep the supply of ammunition flowing. My Army automatic was hanging on the wall while I concentrated on figures.

Suddenly a man in a dirty, muddy German uniform walked in. He raised his hands as a sign of surrender and said, "*Kamerad.*" I immediately frisked him, but if he had challenged me first, I am not sure how much resistance I would have put up. I led him into General Hearn's quarters—proudly —and said, "General, look what I captured!"

The prisoner was a pleasant-enough guy, and said he was a Belgian who had been forced into the German Army when it marched through that country. He insisted he had been trying to sneak through the lines and surrender ever since, as soon as he could find a kindly guy who would not shoot him. He picked me out, which is a little flattering. He was sent back to a stockade, apparently happy.

VIII. GENERAL PERSHING

In 1931 I was put in charge of the North American Newspaper Alliance, and one of my first assignments was to negotiate with General Pershing for the serial rights to his memoirs. My bosses authorized me to offer as high as $275,000, a very high price then. The deal was finally closed for $270,000.

The memoirs contained several highlights. The General had insisted on a separate American Army, and he reported the rows he had had with our allies, the British and the French, to accomplish this. They wanted to brigade our troops with theirs.

One anecdote sticks in my memory. After the U.S. had entered the war, the General had gone abroad with an advance army of officers. He was invited to lunch at Buckingham Palace. After the meal, King George V took him by the arm and led him over to a window. The King pointed sorrowfully to a statue of Queen Victoria which had been badly damaged by bombs dropped from Zeppelins.

"There's what the Kaiser has done to his grandmother, God damn him," remarked the King with feeling.

This was in the original manuscript, but the General, who sought a lot of advice, wanted to take it out. I argued against it.

"That is no reflection on the King," I said. "In fact it makes him look like a man."

So it stayed in for newspaper publication and was printed just that way when the memoirs appeared in the dignified

New York Times. But the General, with his long military training and inhibitions, couldn't swallow it for the permanent
record in the book and cut it out.

After the memoirs were published, General Peyton C.
March came to me with his version of the war. He had been
Chief of Staff in Washington. There was no love lost between
Pershing and March. "Black Jack" was a spit-and-polish
soldier. As soon as our troops got to France, he put Sam
Browne belts on the officers. The boys liked to wear them.
But let an officer put his foot on United States soil, and he had
to shed this trimming, according to General March's orders.

By this time, newspaper editors had had a pretty good dose
of first-hand reports by the top brass, so I offered General
March $3000 for two chapters dealing with a dramatic inci-
dent—a row between General Pershing and General Leonard
Wood, who commanded a division in the United States. Wood
had gone to France on what was known as a "Cook's tour,"
unattached. Pershing didn't want him and had sent a memorandum to Washington, marked confidential, to the Chief of
Staff, General March, and to the Secretary of War, Newton
Baker.

Wood was a controversial figure who mixed politics with
the military and almost got the Republican nomination for
President in 1920. He hoped to be ordered abroad with his
division. Pershing pulled no punches in his memorandum. He
criticized Wood's personal conduct while in France as well as
his ability as a commander. Pershing concluded by saying he
would order Wood home as often as Wood was sent over and
added that the only way to keep Wood abroad was to relieve
Pershing of his command of the A.E.F. It was a strong dose.

We mailed the copies out in advance, and someone must
have slipped one under the table to General Pershing. He
called me from Washington highly indignant, which means

he was plenty warm under the collar. He could heat up good.

"John," he said, "you can't publish this. It contains a confidential memorandum of mine. March has no right to use it."

"Why don't you call up General March and tell him?" I suggested. "I can give you his number in Great Neck."

"No, I don't want to talk to him," Pershing snapped and hung up the telephone.

So I called March. "General Pershing is raising hell," I said, "about publishing his memorandum on General Wood. He claims it is confidential, and you have no right to use it."

"It is properly a part of my papers, and you can tell him so," replied crusty, stern old March.

"Why don't you call him up and say so?" I suggested. "I can tell you where you can reach him right now. I was only a lieutenant in the war, and I don't want to get caught between a couple of full Generals."

"I won't talk to him," he snapped back and hung up.

I telephoned Pershing and reported my conversation and the unsatisfactory outcome. I urged him not to worry, since publication would not hurt him. He finally agreed.

The last time I saw the old General was about two years before he died. George Pattullo, a writer and war correspondent who was a friend of Pershing, and I had gone to Washington. We called the General and he invited us to have lunch with him the next day at 1:30. Having some chores to do in the morning, Pattullo and I separated and agreed to meet at the hospital.

"Don't be late," cautioned Pattullo. "The old man is a stickler for punctuality."

Around 1:15 I grabbed a cab and said to the jockey, "Walter Reed Hospital and don't let anybody pass you. I have a date with General Pershing and can't afford to be late."

The driver poured on the coal, and we made it on time.

When we knocked on Pershing's door, a sergeant answered, looked us over, and said, "The General is in bed."

"Oh, well, don't bother him," I replied. "Just tell him Mr. Pattullo and Mr. Wheeler stopped."

"Wait a minute," he said and disappeared. Soon he was back.

"The General says for you to come in."

He showed us into a drab living room. It was a very hot day, even for Washington. In about fifteen minutes Pershing walked in, still straight but feeble, with a cane in one hand and a bottle of bourbon in the other. He had on a very high stiff collar and tie, morning coat and striped pants. We put our coats back on. After he shook hands, he said, "This looks like an occasion. Let's have a drink."

It was so warm, I didn't really want it, and Pat was on the water wagon. Our host passed the bottle. I poured a modest dose. Pattullo just covered the bottom of his glass. Then the General took a tumbler and filled it nearly full of straight whisky.

"Well, here's a go," he said, and swallowed the whole drink without taking the glass down from his mouth. Now is when he collapses, I thought. Not at all. He perked up, and we had a delightful lunch.

We talked about the war. Pershing had been appointed to West Point just at the time that Fred Bonfils, later one of the publishers of the *Denver Post,* had resigned. I told Pershing about a book by Gene Fowler called *Timber Line,* which was the story of the *Post* and its proprietors.

We finally said good-by, reluctantly. The old man seemed happy when we left. I sent him a copy of *Timber Line,* and Pattullo, who is wealthy, dispatched him a case of bourbon.

About six weeks later I met General Julius Ochs Adler who had been a patient in Walter Reed.

"How is General Pershing?" I asked him.

"Well," he replied, "he hasn't been so good lately. Some friend of his sent him a case of bourbon."

I would like to add as a footnote that when I first knew Pershing, he drank very sparingly, but during the last years he was a lonely man, an old soldier fading away.

My relations with General Pershing were always somewhat cold and distant. Although he would call me "John," I always called him "General." My first recollection of him was when I was a soldier in France, and I would be trudging along a muddy road, frequently in the rain, and a big limousine with the four stars of the Commander-in-Chief would barrel down the highway. I would stand aside, come to attention, and salute, but there would be no response—except mud splashed on my already dirty uniform.

However, one night while we were negotiating for his memoirs, I stopped to see him at the Waldorf, and we had a very pleasant discussion of his book and other matters. We seemed to have gotten on a cordial basis, enough so that as I was leaving I said to him, "General, how would you like to come home and have dinner with us tonight?"

"No, thanks, I can't," he answered abruptly, without any explanation or excuse.

When I reached my apartment I said to my wife, "General Pershing almost had dinner with us tonight."

"Why didn't you bring him?" she asked.

"Well, I asked him, and he said no."

That's the closest I ever came to a social affair with this austere man, except the final lunch at Walter Reed Hospital.

Irvin Cobb at the Illustrators' Ball. Drawing by Wallace Morgan,
well-known illustrator. (Wallace Morgan)

IX. SCORING A BEAT

BY the time I got on the *New York Herald* payroll the day after I finished college, the publisher, an eccentric character named James Gordon Bennett, had taken up permanent residence in Paris. He had a sound reason for moving. He had been engaged to a young lady named Miss May. He called on her one night somewhat inebriated, and forgot to ask where the bathroom was, using a piano leg in the parlor instead. For this social *faux pas,* her brother, Jim May, announced he would horsewhip Bennett on sight. The publisher took an early boat for Europe, buying a one-way ticket.

Another kind of one-way ticket was purchased by Charles Chapin, city editor on the old *Evening World* while Irvin Cobb was a reporter there. Chapin was a good newspaperman but thoroughly disliked by his staff. It was said that if he could fire a reporter who had a family and was broke on Christmas Eve, he was delighted.

One morning Cobb was coming to work and he got in the elevator with another reporter who said to him, "Did you hear Chapin is sick today?"

"Well, I hope it's nothing trivial," Cobb answered.

Chapin got his one-way ticket by shooting his wife. He had meant to make it look like suicide, but, unfortunately, as he pulled the trigger his wife turned over in her sleep and the bullet hit her in the back of the head. Chapin was convicted and sentenced to life in Sing Sing, where he died 20 years later.

All in all, those were glamorous days in New York for a young reporter. The *Herald* desk got a tip on a story in Philadelphia at the University of Pennsylvania. It seems that a fellow with a beard, named Curtis, had started a secret organization called "The Order of the 15." It was coeducational. The members met regularly and talked about occultism and its high priests. However, behind it all was a more simple and appealing idea. After those in the group had qualified, each sought an affinity, and when found, they threw the rule book away. Some of the young buds of Philadelphia society had joined enthusiastically.

"I want you to go over there," said the city editor, "and try to get in this order. Dress yourself up like a college boy and do your best to make it. Don't come back without the story."

It didn't seem like a bad assignment, so I got out my college cap and peg-top pants and took up residence in a boardinghouse on the fringe of the campus. I managed to contact Curtis and took him to lunch. He was a scrubby small guy with whiskers and little sex appeal as far as I could see, but who was I to know? We talked about Annie Besant and Madame Blavatsky, and I thought I was making a good impression. I had read some books in preparation.

Because of my interest, I suggested I would like to be tapped for "The Order of the 15." Curtis seemed to look at me with favor and asked me if I ever had dreams or visions. I assured him I did. We arranged another meeting, and he sent me some pamphlets to study, together with a list of the members. I found one who was a dentist, so I thought I would call on him, pretending I had a toothache. When I reached his office he was out and the receptionist had gone to powder her nose. I took the liberty of looking through his desk drawers and found there was going to be a meeting of the Inner Circle the following evening at 8 in Spring Garden Street.

The next night I found the address and rang the doorbell with assurance. Curtis himself answered. I greeted him as a candidate.

"Good evening, maestro," I said, sticking my foot in the crack of the door as a precaution. "I had a vision that the Inner Circle was meeting tonight, and that I should come and join."

He looked at me a minute and then replied, "We don't want you around here. You are a fake. Go back and tell whoever sent you to stop bothering us."

I withdrew my foot, and he slammed the door. That left me standing in the rain for two hours waiting for the meeting to break up. From the shadow of a doorway across the street, I saw the members departing. One girl set off by herself. I followed. She boarded a streetcar, and so did I. We rode to Germantown together. When she got off, I trailed her to a nice-looking suburban home which she entered with a key. Giving her ten minutes, I rang the bell, and she answered.

"Who are you?" she demanded.

"I want to talk to you about 'The Order of the 15,' " I explained.

"But I haven't anything to say," she answered.

Again I stuck my foot in the door. "Are you married?" I asked.

"Yes, my husband is asleep upstairs. I will call him."

"You had better not," I told her. "I am a reporter from the *New York Herald*. If you will tell me the facts, I will protect you. Your name will not be used. Does your husband know about this?"

She shook her head. She was a nice girl and good-looking, too. We went into the living room and closed the door. She told me the whole story—how it was organized, how she got hooked into it, where and when they met, etc. I bade her good night, went back to the boardinghouse, and wrote it up. It was a good beat. It also broke up "The Order of the 15." Curtis got kicked out of the University, as he should have been. And the source of my story was protected, and no one was any the wiser as to how I got it.

There were certain members of the *Herald* staff who were regarded as expendable. I was one. A fellow named Ulrich was another. I remember an evening the night city editor, named Marshall, got a telephone tip that Jack Johnson, the heavy-weight champion, was over in a black-and-tan joint on Thirty-fifth Street, drunk and beating his white wife. The boss looked around.

"Let's see who I can spare best," he said. "Oh, Charlie, go over to Baron Wilkins and ask Johnson why he is beating his wife. If you live, come back and write the story."

Ulrich straightened his toupee, grabbed his cane, put on his hat, and walked out. In a couple of hours he was back, still in one piece.

"Boss, there is no story," he announced. "Johnson wasn't beating anybody, but it was disgusting sitting around there with Jack and his white wife. Why, I could hardly drink my champagne." This last crack brought a laugh.

Enrico Caruso was the Babe Ruth of Metropolitan Opera. He was a genial guy with a golden voice. Before the management found out about it, he used to go to Italian restaurants and get full of spaghetti and vino and give away hundreds of dollars' worth of music. Naturally the joints were crowded and the owners cleaned up.

He got himself into a little trouble, innocently enough, and also picked up considerable publicity. One warm spring day, when the buds were beginning to blossom and the sap was coming up in the trees, he decided to go to Central Park. He wandered into the monkey house and maybe he got the idea from one of the apes. Anyway, there was a lady who had a walk like Marilyn Monroe. The tenor couldn't resist and

Baseball writers covering the New York Giants, 1908. *Left to right, seated:* Sam Crane of the old Evening Journal; Fred Lieb, old New York Press; Damon Runyon, New York American; Bozeman Bulger, Evening World; Sid Mercer, old New York Globe; Grantland Rice, Evening Mail; Walter Trumbull, The Sun. *Back row, standing:* John Wheeler, John Foster, old Telegram. *On the ground, in front:* Harry Stevens and his grandson. *(New York Giants)*

To JOHN N WHEELER
WITH ALL GOOD WISHES
Richard Harding Davis
SALONIKA   DEC. 1915

Richard Harding Davis in the trenches at
Salonika—December, 1915—probably the last
photograph made of this famous correspondent. *(The Wheeler Syndicate)*

Group of Mexican troops including Raul Madero (in uniform), brother of Francisco Madero, former President of Mexico; Bud Fisher, with the cowboy hat; Wheeler, looking like a dude. Rough character, second from left, is Madero's bodyguard.

General Villa's private railroad car.

Photograph of Ring Lardner acting as lion tamer on moving picture studio lot.

Before a golf game (photo taken at the White House): *Left to right*:
President Harding, Grantland Rice, Ring Lardner, and Henry
Fletcher, Undersecretary of State. *(Harris & Ewing)*

Three lousy golfers: Deac Aylesworth, then president of NBC; Roy Howard, head of the Scripps-Howard Newspapers; and the author. *(Golf Illustrated)*

Captain Eddie Rickenbacker and John Wheeler arriving Mexico City after first flight of Eastern Air Lines. *(Eastern Air Lines)*

Helen Reid at state dinner given at the Lotus Club, 1954. *Left to right*: General Leon Johnson, now Deputy Commander of NATO and Congressional Medal of Honor winner; Hugh Baillie, then president of United Press; Mrs. Reid; Wheeler; and Jimmy Doolittle, famous general who raided Tokyo. *(Courtesy of the Lotus Club)*

John Wheeler

pinched her in the behind. She hollered for the cops, and the next thing Caruso knew, he was in the sneezer for his friendly gesture which wouldn't have meant anything in his native Italy. As I remember, he was finally turned loose, but not before the papers had printed columns about the matter, and the vindictive lady had got a lot of publicity for her backside, which was nothing to write home about as I recall her photographs.

Of course, Caruso was rich, and the Black Hand got an idea about sharing his wealth. They sent him a mash note threatening to put a bomb under him unless he came through with $50,000 on the line. This item also attracted considerable attention in the press. He refused the demand, and the next night he was to sing at the Brooklyn Academy of Music. It was suspected the bomb would go off either in the opera house or en route. Again Marshall surveyed his staff to see which reporter was expendable and put the accolade of approval on me.

"Wheeler," he said, "go to Brooklyn with Caruso tonight. If they throw a bomb at him, cover the story."

"Where from—the hospital?" I asked.

"I don't care where," he conceded.

The great tenor took the subway as the safer means of transportation. He was accompanied by several newspapermen and detectives. He seemed unconcerned about the threat. He hummed, and you could hear him above the rattle of the cars. He went through with his performance without a hitch. I stood in the wings watching furtively for a suspicious character and getting ready to duck. We escorted him to the old Knickerbocker Hotel where he was then living. He never paid and never got bombed. He finally went back to his native Italy to die in Naples where he was born.

Another expendable reporter was Lawrence Mott, a big

strapping fellow who was a cub on the *New York Telegram*, also owned by Bennett and operating from the same building as the *Herald*. Mott lived in White Plains. His father was wealthy and the head of the Mott Iron Works, so the son didn't worry about money. He used to drive to the office every morning in a Packard car with a chauffeur. He was supposed to report at 8 o'clock. One day he was late, and Bill Summers, the city editor, jumped him.

"What happened to you?" demanded his boss. "You're supposed to be here on time."

"I'm sorry," Mott explained, unashamedly, "but my valet forgot to call me."

This became a classic in the newspaper business. The guy was then being paid about $22 weekly.

One of the first big balloons was called *The America* and was based at Lakehurst, New Jersey. It was to make an ascension, and Mott was sent to cover this event. He came back with the story, and reported to Summers.

"How did it go?" asked the editor.

"Oh, fine," he answered. "In fact I liked it so much I bought the balloon."

What he ever did with it, I don't know.

Finally, this screwball fell in love with a chorus girl playing at one of the New York theaters. The fact he was already married didn't interfere with the romance much. He planned to go to Tahiti or some place where they could loll in the sun and strum guitars or whatever they play there. Of course, any guy is going to get tired looking at the same dame in a grass skirt in a tropical climate every day, no matter how pretty she is. I knew one top magazine editor who tried it and finally came back to the United States and blew his brains out.

Anyway, Mott and his girl took off for distant places. His father hired a former *Herald* reporter, Hector Fuller, to follow them and bring back his son alone and alive. Fuller started out with plenty of dough and chased the couple until he caught up with them somewhere in the Pacific. Then instead of trying to bring them back, he joined them, and the trio went joyfully the rest of the way around the world together. The father was busy answering cables requesting more expense money.

The romance fell apart after their return. Mott retired as a newspaperman. Fuller got some kind of a greeting job with the city.

Those of us who stayed in the newspaper business generally took to heart George Ade's comment: "Early to bed and early to rise and you meet very few prominent people."

Sometimes this paid off, as I myself found out at 4 one morning.

There was a handsome fellow named Jack Bustanoby with a beautiful wife. He ran a high-class French restaurant at Broadway and Sixtieth Street. The building was four stories high, and they had an apartment on the top floor. Just below their windows was a triangular electric sign which flashed off and on, advertising the joint. As they were retiring one night, the couple got into a violent argument, and the wife decided to commit suicide in her Lady Godiva costume. She opened the window and hopped out, but got caught on the electric sign which lit her up good. Naturally, this attracted a crowd of gapers, including this reporter.

When she got stuck, she changed her mind about ending it all and began to scream for help, so several thoughtful onlookers turned in an alarm for the fire department while she hung on. By this time the crowd had naturally grown to large proportions. A brave and lucky fireman put up a ladder and climbed it carrying a blanket, which he wrapped around her. Amid cheers he carried her down to safety. News of the event

I understand increased the number of applicants for this branch of the service next day.

When the First World War started, before we joined the Allies, the Germans were short many essentials so they sent an unarmed merchant U-boat over here commanded by Captain Koenig. The U-boat arrived safely in Baltimore, where I went to try to arrange to send a first-class correspondent, Henry Reuterdahl, back on her. As a result, I met a man named Hilken, the North German Lloyd agent, and Sir John Hammer who was a Swede and in the picture some place. For all I know he may have been a spy.

He invited me to a party at the Astor Hotel in New York which turned out to be a pretty gay affair, especially for a bachelor like me. Among the guests was a handsome fellow in the uniform of a Captain in the Swedish Air Force. With him was a beautiful blonde doll. It turned out the Captain had to catch the midnight train for Buffalo, so I took over after he departed.

"I'll tell you something," the doll began, "if you promise not to put it in the newspapers."

I assured her the secret would be safe.

"That man who just left is the Crown Prince of Sweden traveling over here incognito, and we were married today, but don't tell anyone."

"Then you are the Crown Princess of Sweden, incognito?" I asked, impressed. She agreed.

About 1 o'clock in the morning we all adjourned to a Swedish restaurant under the old Columbia Theater building, appropriately called Scandia. Things went along pretty smoothly for a while until the regular musicians left for home. Then the Crown Princess decided to play the piano, escorted to the stool by another gent in our party.

Across the room seated at a table were four customers, husky guys, the biggest one looking something like Jess Willard, the old champion, only with a walrus mustache. Meantime, I was in a serious discussion with one of my other companions about the war and who would win it. Pretty soon the lady returned, blushing and indignant. She addressed me.

"See those men over at that table," she said, pointing to the group I had already sized up. "They threw lumps of sugar at me, and I want you to go with me to get an apology."

Crown Princess or no Crown Princess, my yellow streak began to show. "Why don't you ask that fellow, who was up at the piano with you, to get the apology?" I suggested. "Can't you see I am busy here talking?"

"No, I want you," she insisted.

Reluctantly, I got up and faced the quartet with her at my side. I picked out the smallest guy.

"This lady was playing the piano and trying to entertain you," I said. "How do you show your appreciation? By throwing lumps of sugar at her which is very dangerous and might hurt her if you hit her in the head. She wants an apology."

He graciously admitted he was sorry, which was good enough for me, and I started back.

"No," insisted my companion who spoke good English. "I want one from that big guy."

"I didn't throw any sugar, and I ain't goin' to apologize," he replied. I was willing to let it go at that. Behind me, I heard a female voice.

"You won't apologize, you big S.O.B.," she said. "Well, take that!"

She threw a glass of Swedish punch she had in her hand right into his kisser. It is very sticky stuff and was dripping down on his mustache. He got up and started for me. I was covering up as best I could and hoping to escape through some handy exit when suddenly my Crown Princess picked up a chair and conked him from behind. He went down and out, cold, which caused no little excitement in the joint. We threw water on him, and he finally came to, but he was through with fighting for that night. She had probably saved my life.

Impressed, I invited her to go to Jack's restaurant, a famous all-night place. We walked in, and at a table by himself was Frank O'Malley, one of the great newspapermen of his day. He had been drinking at least a little.

"Sit down with me," he said.

"Frank," I replied, "I want you to meet the Crown Princess of Sweden."

"Crown Princess, I am damn glad to know you. Shake hands with the King of Greece."

He stuck his hand out. We stayed until about 7 in the morning when I took the lady home. I didn't remember the address and neglected to get her phone number, which now seems like a mistake, so I never saw her again. Maybe she really was the Crown Princess. Anyway she could swing a mean chair.

It was through this acquaintance with Sir John Hammer we got the exclusive story of Captain Koenig. After the *Deutschland* returned safely to Germany, there was a great scramble for the rights to his report of the hazardous round-trip voyage. One day I met Sir John Hammer in the subway.

"Have you read Captain Koenig's story in *Dagens Ny-heters?*" he asked.

I had to admit I hadn't. "Where can I get copies?" I asked him.

He told me of a store up on Third Avenue. I shanghaied a fellow named George Phyle, a Swede of my acquaintance, and locked him in a room with a few sandwiches and several bottles of beer. I told him to get busy translating the story and to hand me the installments as he finished each. It worked.

We began a big promotion campaign which resulted in a large sale to the newspapers. There were no effective copyright laws with the Germans during this period. We rushed our series out, beating everyone else including the Hearst papers whose editors thought they had made a deal and paid for the exclusive rights.

Another time the Hearst papers thought they had an exclusive but didn't, had to do with "Bugs" Baer, one of the great humorists and a brilliant day-to-day paragrapher. If it hadn't been for Bugs, a lot of vaudeville and television comedians would either be in the poorhouse or would have starved to death.

Bugs had a contract with the Hearst papers but had difficulty in getting along with the general manager. I had just taken over running of the North American Newspaper Alliance in 1931.

The two of us cooked up a scheme which worked fine for nearly a year. Bugs agreed to do a daily feature on the news of about 300 words. It was called "Wiregrams by Graham Wire." Only Damon Runyon, Baer, and myself knew who the author was. We put it out as part of our wire service, and it was widely published. The *New York Evening World* carried it on the front page in some editions.

This newcomer attracted the attention of the Hearst editors. Bradford Merrill, the general manager, called Runyon in to do an errand for him.

"Go find out who that Graham Wire is and hire him," said the boss.

"Yes, sir," answered Runyon, respectfully.

After about a week, Runyon went to Merrill and reported Mr. Wire didn't want to work for Hearst. Two or three offers failed, of course, because "Graham Wire" was already under contract to the Hearst papers. As far as I know, the secret has been well kept until this day, and now it doesn't make any difference.

A similar story concerns Walter Winchell. Winchell had been a vaudeville hoofer with Gus Edwards when he began doing a column for *Variety*. Then Bernarr MacFadden started an evening tabloid called *The Graphic* and hired Walter as a regular writer. Winchell's frank and lively column soon caught on. He printed racy news you couldn't find in the other gazettes.

For example, he ran an item about Lois Long, who wrote for *The New Yorker* and was married to Peter Arno. He announced she was expecting, but the lady had been to her doctor a short time before, and he had assured her she was not pregnant. However, when she read Winchell she returned to the specialist for further examination, and he confirmed the report. As I recall, a son was born.

Joe Moore for several years was the general manager of the Hearst papers, but he decided to resign and buy the *Morning Telegraph*, which was and still is a horse-racing sheet. Moore had an idea he could make a daily *New Yorker* out of it, and hired a lot of expensive talent. It was a tough stable of temperamental types to manage.

Moore wanted Walter to do a column for his Sunday paper, but Walter was under contract to the *Graphic*. Since Moore knew I was fairly friendly with Winchell, he asked me to invite Walter to lunch at Moore's apartment. Just the three of us were there, and it was a very hush-hush affair. The columnist was then drawing $300 weekly for his daily stint on the *Graphic* and Moore offered him $100 a week for a single Sunday column to be done under another name. Winchell snapped it up. He called himself "Beau Broadway."

Only the three of us were in on the secret. I made no cash

as the go-between. The column turned out to be a flourishing success, even better than the *Graphic* pieces. To make it look authentic "Beau Broadway" blasted the hell out of Winchell every Sunday, and Walter would take a crack at "Beau" in his daily column.

Since then, Walter Winchell has engaged in other feuds. I remember that before Westbrook Pegler and he were in the same syndicate stable, they carried on a running battle in their columns, each making nasty cracks about the other.

In those days Pegler and I were friends and neighbors in Ridgefield, Connecticut. We are neither now. Walter called me up one day.

"You see Pegler often," he said. "Why don't you tell him I am not a bad fellow, and you have known me for some time. I will lay off if he will."

It happened that afternoon I was going to play golf with Bruce Barton and Pegler. I told Pegler about my telephone conversation and suggested the public might not be too much interested in personal rows.

"Oh, gee," replied Peg, "I have just mailed the worst column I have ever written about him."

He was then working for the *World-Telegram,* and since Pegler's column didn't appear on Monday as scheduled, I thought it had been killed by Lee Wood, the managing editor, who frequently did not see eye to eye with his columnist.

"I will tell Walter I made good," I boasted to Peg.

"You'd better wait a day or so," he advised.

He was right. The essay was printed the next afternoon. I believe he called Winchell "a gents' room journalist." There was no peace between them until both joined up with Hearst.

One of the most colorful writers was Charlie Dryden,

mainly a Chicago operator, who did more to develop a humorous slang type of baseball writing than anyone else in the business. He was a real wit. He loved to sneak something past a copy reader with a double meaning. I could give a couple of examples, but censorship makes me pause.

Dryden was working on a San Francisco paper during the off-season as a general reporter. In those days they had cable cars pretty much all over town. Now I believe there is one line surviving. A Chinaman was crossing Market Street or some main thoroughfare when he pulled a quarter out of his pocket and it slipped down the slot. Two bits were worth nearly as much as a dollar today. The Chink leaned over the opening to peer down for his lost coin. His pigtail slipped into the slot and wound around the cable. Off he went. Emergency squads were called out, but the Chinaman flashed by before help could reach him.

He was rapidly giving out when a resourceful barber grabbed a pair of shears and waited for the Chinaman to come by. The barber fell in step and managed to snip off the pigtail. The victim dropped like he was dead. Finally he came to and bawled the barber out for sacrificing his pigtail, a mark of respectability. No thanks for saving his life. Dryden's account of this incident is still regarded as a classic. The quarter was never found.

After Gene Tunney retired as the undefeated heavyweight champion of the world, Bill McGeehan and he decided to take a trip to Europe. Bill, a brilliant fellow who also ran a column in the *Herald Tribune,* was a pretty good drinker when off duty and sometimes when on, too. One of their first stops was Scotland where the British Amateur golf tournament was to be held, at old St. Andrews, I think. Jess Sweetser, then a young fellow, had entered, but a couple of days before the start he was taken down with flu or pneumonia and was running a high temperature. He called a doctor who advised him to withdraw.

When Sweetser announced his intentions, McGeehan said to him, "I always knew all you Yale guys were yellow."

It made Jess so mad, he went ahead and played through the whole contest a sick man. He won his final match with a raging fever. He was carried aboard the steamer at Southampton on a stretcher and had to go to Arizona for six months to recover his health. He was the first American-born amateur ever to win this British championship. Of course, he is now proud of it, and I am glad to report his health is excellent. I saw him a couple of weeks ago. Should Bill McGeehan get an assist for this in the box score?

Gene Tunney, who has a sly wit, mentioned that trip at a Dutch Treat lunch recently. We were talking about the second Dempsey fight, and the long count in the seventh round when Jack knocked him down.

"You know I went to Ireland afterwards, and a Dublin reporter began asking me a lot of questions," he said. "I told him Jack was tired—I could tell that—so when he flattened me, I thought I might as well let him rest as long as I could. I didn't get up until I had to. He printed this explanation in his paper as genuine."

Equally trusting was a young man named John Igoe who started out as an artist. Tad, the cartoonist, changed his Christian moniker to Hype after hypodermic.

Igoe wanted to be a boxing writer, since he admired fighters very much, and I helped to get him a job in the sports department of the old *Morning World*. One of his first assignments was to cover a heavyweight championship match in Milwaukee, and he started out with a liberal advance in cash against his expense account. One evening with some convivial companions, Hype got the idea he wanted to buy a Shetland pony for his girl.

After some research, he found a gent with one of the animals for sale. Igoe paid $50. Then he took the pony around with him while he did some more shopping at saloons and tried to figure out where he could stable the animal for the night. Finally he went back to his hotel. He saw a fellow standing on the sidewalk who looked trustworthy.

"Would you hold my pony for me for ten dollars?" he asked the man.

"If you pay me in advance," answered the stranger.

Hype foolishly did. Then he went inside to confer with the night clerk. He explained his predicament.

"For ten dollars can I take a Shetland pony up to my room?" he asked.

"For ten dollars," replied the man, "you can take an elephant up to your room." Igoe slipped the clerk a tenner.

Igoe returned to the sidewalk to find that both the pony and the horseholder had disappeared without a trace. He never did see either again. However, when he put an item on his expense account—"purchase of a Shetland pony, $70"—he had one hell of a time making it stand up. In fact, he didn't.

"Why do you need a Shetland pony to cover a fight?" demanded his boss. "Do you have to ride him to the ringside?"

As a reporter, Irvin Cobb believed in the direct approach. So did I. In the syndicate business I have always told our salesmen:

"After you have made the best pitch you can, ask the man whether he is going to buy or not. He will have to give you a yes or no answer, and you will know where you stand."

While Cobb was working on the *World* and Joseph Pulitzer, the publisher, was still alive, Pulitzer got into some kind of a jam with his newspaper. William Travers Jerome was the district attorney, and Mr. Pulitzer hired expensive lawyers and detectives to try to find the answers to certain questions bearing on the matter. The newspaper publisher ran into a blank wall. Then he called in Cobb.

"Do you know Jerome?" he asked.

"Yes, well," answered the reporter. "I covered the Thaw trial."

Mr. Pulitzer handed him a memorandum with three questions on it. "See if you can get the answers to these," he said.

Cobb left the *World* building and rode up to Jerome's office in the Centre Street trolley car. Dismounting, he went in to see the district attorney.

"Judge," began Irvin, "my esteemed boss, Joseph Pulitzer, wants some information. He would like to have the answers to these three questions."

The D.A. glanced at the memorandum.

"Go back and tell him," he said, "the answer to the first one is yes, to the second no, and I am skipping the third for now. You might add if you or someone like you had come and asked me direct instead of hiring lawyers and detectives, he would have saved time and money."

Cobb got on the Centre Street trolley and rode back. He went to see Pulitzer in his tower office and reported the results.

"Good God," exclaimed the publisher. "And how much were your expenses?"

"Ten cents," answered Cobb. "Five up and five back on the trolley."

Along these lines, I believe a personal experience might fit in. Jack Benny, the comedian, had been with the National Broadcasting Company, but when his contract ran out, there were rumors he was shifting to Columbia. These could not be confirmed. David Sarnoff, then head of NBC, sent Niles Trammell, one of his best executives, out to the Coast to negotiate, and he was making progress, but the boss thought a lawyer would do better, so he dispatched John Cahill, a brilliant member of the bar. In the meantime, there was speculation about whether or not Benny had signed with CBS. I picked up the telephone and dialed the number. I asked for William Paley, head of the network. Much to my surprise I got him on the other end of the wire.

"Mr. Paley," I said, "I run the North American Newspaper Alliance. We would like to publish the true facts about the Jack Benny deal."

He told me the whole story—that the comedian had signed a contract—and we published it exclusively through our service. The next day it appeared in the *New York Times*, one of our clients. The following morning a member of the staff of CBS public relations department called me.

"Where did you get that story which appeared in the *Times*?" he demanded. "Of course, there is no truth in it."

Then he continued at considerable length, explaining how we had put out a false report. I let him hang himself before I interrupted.

"Do you have a man named Paley working there?" I asked him.

"Why, yes," he replied. "He's the boss."

"Is he reliable?"

"Sure."

"Well, he's the one who gave me the story," I replied.

A few years later I had the pleasure of sitting next to Mr. Paley at the annual Associated Press lunch. I told him this anecdote, and he was very much amused.

"Yes, I agree with you," he concluded. "The direct approach

is best. But how did you manage to get me on the telephone?"

"I asked for you," was my reply.

Kent Cooper, the great general manager of the Associated Press, has been a friend of mine for years. One night the dignified directors were having a dinner to listen to their recently returned Russian correspondent, Eddie Gilmore. Mr. Cooper invited me, which put me in the top drawer for the evening. After the clambake, Gilmore, another A.P. correspondent—Cassidy, Deac Aylesworth, then president of NBC, and I stopped in a tavern on the way home.

Eddie got telling about his problems. While in Moscow, he had fallen in love with a Russian ballet dancer and wanted to marry her. One angle was he already had a wife, but she had agreed to a divorce. However, Stalin was no cupid and had threatened to send the girl to Siberia if she didn't drop the American correspondent.

"What are you going to do?" I asked him.

"I am trying to get Wendell Willkie to help me," he replied. Willkie, after his defeat in 1940, had made a trip to Russia and met Stalin and the other bigshots.

"You see," Eddie continued, "he said he would send a cablegram to Stalin asking him to keep my girl in Moscow until I get back." It was a sad story, so we had another drink and went on home.

The next day, I called up Mr. Willkie, whom I had met during the campaign. "Can I come down to see you this afternoon?" I asked him.

He agreed. I told him about Eddie Gilmore and his problems.

"Oh, that's all straightened out," explained Willkie. He showed me a couple of cablegrams—his to Stalin and the Russian dictator's reply in which he agreed to the marriage.

"May I have copies of these?" I asked. "I want to publish this story."

"Sure," he answered, and rang for his secretary to make duplicates.

The next time I saw my friend, Kent Cooper, he hollered murder.

"That's the last dinner you will get invited to by me," he announced. "Deac and you take Gilmore down to some gin mill and beat us on our own story."

I am glad to report the marriage turned out all right, and Mr. and Mrs. Gilmore are now living in London where he is head of the A.P. bureau.

Claude Pepper, United States Senator from Florida, made a trip to Russia in September, 1945, and got one of the first exclusive interviews with Josef Stalin. It was an important statement, in which the Soviet dictator expressed the friendliest feelings toward the United States and the great desire of the Russian people for peace in the world.

The Kremlin has a habit of releasing these interviews to the press in general if they are not published promptly. We received a cable from the Senator saying he was sending the story by diplomatic pouch, which certainly meant a delay of several days. We finally caught up with the Senator in Cairo and urged him to cable it, which he did. It turned out to be a very excellent, exclusive story, and included a surprising quote, as follows:

> "Now that our common enemies have been defeated by our joint efforts," Stalin said, "your country and mine must find a new, common ground for co-operation in the peacetime."
>
> I asked if he was confident that such a new basis for co-operation would be found.
>
> "It may not be easy," he answered, "but as Christ said, 'Seek and ye shall find.'"

This was rather surprising coming from a Russian, who was an acknowledged atheist. The dispatch was widely published and appeared with a two-column head on the front page of the *New York Times*—October 1, 1945.

In 1948, Pan American Airways invited me on a trip with some other newspapermen to South Africa to pioneer a new route. The executives wanted to see if it would work and figured journalists were expendable. We reached Johannesburg all right, and then took off for Capetown about 8 one evening. The distance was approximately 1000 miles. We arrived over the South African capital in due course, to find the only airport fogged in. Captain Warren circled for an hour or so, hoping the wind would change, and then headed back for Johannesburg. I was sitting with Dave Ingalls, a vice president of the line and himself an old-time pilot.

"Have we got enough gas?" I asked him nervously.

"Pan-Am always has enough gas," he answered confidently, but the Captain had his engines cut down and didn't fly like a man who had plenty of fuel.

Anyway, we landed at the airport, which is about twelve miles out of the city, to spend the night. Some of us elected to try to sleep in the plane and others in the terminal. Either was equally uncomfortable. I stuck to the ship, and the Minister of the Interior was in front of me. He may have been a hell of a good cabinet member, but he was the damndest snorer I have ever encountered in a long career of research.

We flew to Capetown the next morning, weary and bleary-eyed. The great prime minister, Field Marshall Jan Smuts, invited us for lunch in the house of parliament and later to his residence, the beautiful place given to the government by Cecil Rhodes. We had some drinks, and then our host talked frankly and bravely about the world situation and made some rather startling statements. One impressed me.

"You know there are things worse than war," he remarked in talking about the threat of the Russians and communism. "We should say to them—'So far and no further.' "

Everybody thought these comments were "under the rose," and no one made any notes. At the conclusion, I asked, "Mr. Prime Minister, is this all off the record?"

"No," he replied. "Print anything you want."

Hugh Baillie, then president of the United Press, and other wire service men tore out of the place as if there had been a flash fire to file stories. The next day I saw Roy Howard, the publisher.

"I could have cut your throat yesterday," he began.

"Why?" I asked him.

"Because you were the only one who had sense enough to ask Smuts if his talk was off the record. Bernie Baruch had given me a letter to him, and I had spent two hours with him after lunch getting an exclusive interview. Your question loused it up good."

"Why didn't you tell me? I would have kept quiet. The North American Newspaper Alliance had an exclusive from him about two weeks ago, so I wasn't too much interested."

Hugh Baillie mentions this incident in his book *High Tension*.

Possibly this should not be introduced in a chapter on news breaks, but here goes. Large newspapers recognize death is the final exit for all of us and keep stored in their files obituaries of fairly prominent citizens which are brought up to date from time to time. We have access to the *Times* morgue, so out of morbid curiosity, I sent down to see if there was one on me. Sure enough, the messenger came back shortly with a neat envelope with my name on it. The essay wasn't very long and turned out better than I deserved.

It gave me a tempting idea. This was to rewrite the piece with a more favorable slant and substitute it. However, I resisted the temptation and returned the original as it stood. And so it will run, I imagine.

Brisbane's Park Row Pups. This sketch was drawn by Tad, the popular cartoonist. The characters are Bugs Baer, Damon Runyon, and Windsor McCay. (Tom Dorgan)

X.   RING LARDNER

In the winter of 1919 five or six of us were in the square bar of
the old Waldorf. Ring Lardner was just reaching his peak. He
had recently returned from Europe where he had been on an
assignment for *Collier's Weekly*.

"When my contract runs out with the *Chicago Tribune*,"
said Mr. Lardner without even clearing his throat, "I would
like to go to work for you." He meant the Bell Syndicate,
which I had started three years before.

A naturally silent guy, this was a long speech for him. I was
taken a little by surprise. Besides his *Chicago Tribune* column,
he was nationally known as a humorist and writer of the "You
Know Me, Al" baseball stories in the *Saturday Evening Post*.

"Sure," I answered. "We certainly want to make a deal.
How about a contract?"

"How about another drink?" he replied.

The conversation drifted off onto something else, but not
before I ascertained his current agreement expired at the
end of July. The next day he left for Chicago, I heard nothing
further from him for a couple of months, but an ugly rumor
slipped into the office that the McClure Syndicate was en-
deavoring to hire him. This disturbed me somewhat, so I sent
him a telegram which read about as follows: "Understand a
competitor is trying to make a deal with you. Would like to
take Century today to talk terms and sign a contract."

Before I could pack my bag, I got this reassuring reply: "If
you knew anything about contracts, you would realize we
made one in the Waldorf bar before five witnesses, three of
whom were sober."

That was the only agreement we ever had, and it worked for more than fifteen years while he wrote a weekly humorous column for the Bell Syndicate and later turned out the "You Know Me, Al" daily strip.

A book was published about Ring Lardner a few years ago. The author, Donald Elder, who had never met him, made him a morose, dour character all his life. The profile was out of focus. While never garrulous, Ring was gay until illness and depression overtook him during the latter years of his life.

When we first met, he was a traveling baseball writer for a Chicago paper, and I was acting in the same capacity for the old *New York Herald.* He was well liked by Frank Chance's Cubs.

Ring made up a song called "I'm a Little Prairie Flower," which required the help of ballplayers. This whiled away many a weary hour on a train. It went like this:

> I'm a little prairie flower,
> Growing wilder every hour,
> Nobody ever cultivated me.

Then the boys would take up the conversation where it had been interrupted, all hands watching Lardner. After several minutes he would scratch his ear, and they would holler, "I'M WILD!"

It went very good after a few drinks, and I introduced it into the 307th Field Artillery mess following the Armistice. The boys still remembered it at an officers' dinner recently and requested I sing it.

After Ring had made his first big hit in the *Saturday Evening Post* with his "You Know Me, Al" stories about the busher, he came on to New York and Philadelphia to see George Horace Lorimer, then the great editor of the weekly. I met him late one afternoon in a speakeasy. I had with me a lady whom I afterwards married, and she was breathless about Lardner. We asked him to have dinner with us. He explained he had a date with an artist who was illustrating his stories.

"Mr. Lorimer thinks we ought to get to know each other better," he said.

I suggested he call up and say he was sick or had missed his train or something. He agreed and disappeared. Shortly, he returned.

"It's all right," he said.

"What did you tell him?" I asked.

"I told him I had already met an artist," he explained.

When he first came to Chicago looking for a job he had a note to Hugh Fullerton, then working in the *Chicago Tribune* sports department. The veteran greeted him cordially and said, "Let's go across the street to Stillson's and get a drink."

"I don't drink," answered Lardner solemnly.

"You're going to be in a hell of a fix around here then," answered Hughie.

"Well, that's what the guy, who gave me the letter, told me to say."

They crossed the street to the well-known oasis. Ring later became one of its best customers. He also got the job.

One night Fullerton, Lardner, Walter Eckersall, the famous quarterback, and two or three others, including this reporter, were sitting around Stillson's. We were trying to persuade Fullerton to have dinner with us.

"No, I can't," he explained, apologetically. "My wife's giving a party."

"If I call her up and she says it's all right, will you stay?" asked Ring.

Hughie readily agreed. Soon Ring returned to the table, smiling confidently.

"She not only says it's okay," he reported, "but she wants you to stay."

Fullerton got suspicious and went to the telephone himself. He came back pretty indignant. It seems Lardner had said to Mrs. F., "Hughie is down here dead drunk. Do you want us to keep him or send him home?"

Naturally, she favored keeping him there. However, Fullerton showed up for her party.

In the old days Comiskey, owner of the White Sox, used to have a kind of a court jester, named Joe Farrell. Ring and he became great companions, since both had the same tastes. By this time, Lardner had built up a big reputation as a wit, for first he was running a column on the sporting page previously presided over by Hughie Keogh, a hard man to follow, and currently he had moved to the editorial page with the title "A Line o' Type or Two." This column had been conducted by Bert Leston Taylor, one of the best.

One bright enchanting Chicago evening, Ring, Farrell, and I were together doing a little shopping in saloons. Our star was frequently recognized in these gin mills, and a small knot would gather around waiting for him to be witty. To please the customers, Farrell would say, "Ring, tell them that story you told me today."

Then with a straight face Ring would begin a tale about two little girls named Pat and Mike. It would drag along and be pointless, but at intervals Farrell would burst into uproarious laughter and clap Ring and others on the back. Really, there was nothing to laugh at, but the audience didn't want to appear dumb, so they would join in. It seems the two brats had a Lithuanian nurse who looked after them in her way. One night the house caught fire and burned down. Poor little Pat and Mike and the Lithuanian nurse were all burned to death. When Ring finished this harrowing tale with a straight, sad face, Joe would respond with guffaws of laughter, and the uninvited chorus would join in. It was a sardonic demonstration of the ridiculous and how easy it is to make people laugh if you have a reputation as a humorist.

When we lived in Ardsley-on-the-Hudson, Ring and his missus came to spend a week end. We had some guests for dinner, one being Neal Smith who laughed easily. After a sumptuous repast, a Jap in our employ passed the cigars. Lardner refused one.

"They are Corona Coronas," I said proudly.

"I heard you the first time," he answered.

Mr. Smith rocked with laughter and broke one of my wife's best antique chairs in doing so.

As he went up to bed, Ring took along a copy of the *American Magazine*, then edited by John Siddall and depending on the success-story formula for circulation—about the guy who started in the gutter and wound up a millionaire. It seems Ring had neglected to include pajamas in his bag, so I loaned him a pair. Next morning he looked a little weary.

"How did you sleep?" I asked him at breakfast.

"I sat up all night," he replied.

"Why?"

"I couldn't put on your pajamas. The label said 'Varsity,' and I never went to college."

"Did you read the *American Magazine?*"

"I read George Ade's story and Hughie Fullerton's and Cornelius Vanderbilt, Jr.'s., until I got sick at my stomach. Then I tried to sleep sitting up."

Ring used to cover many world-rocking events for us as well as doing his weekly column. These included heavyweight fights for the championship, national political conventions, World Series, international yacht races, etc.

In 1920 we had an all-star cast of characters lined up to report the Republican gathering in Chicago and the Democratic meeting in San Francisco. Our starters were Lardner, Jimmy Montague, Irvin Cobb, and Sam Blythe, a political pundit of that day who wrote regularly for the *Saturday Evening Post*. Bud Fisher, the cartoonist, went along for the ride. It was a tough, temperamental bunch to handle and maintain harmony.

This was before F.D.R., and thrift was regarded as a virtue. I hired one drawing room to be occupied by Bud Fisher, Irvin Cobb, and myself. The first clash came the evening of our departure. Cobb was living in Ossining and got on the train at Harmon, about 40 miles from New York. The other boys had been hitting it up a little already, even though it was during Prohibition. After dinner Irvin and I decided to go to bed while Fisher and Lardner adjourned to the club car forward. I suggested that my famous writer occupy the lower berth, and I would take the upper, leaving the comfortable sofa for Fisher.

Along about 3 in the morning I was awakened by all the lights being turned on. Bud had found the drawing room with some difficulty. He was addressing his remarks to Cobb.

"Well," he demanded, "who decided to make you the star and give you the lower berth? So you are Irvin Cobb, are you? I never met you before tonight but, if first impressions are worth anything, mine of you is lousy."

"Shut up, young fellow, and go to bed," grumbled Cobb.

I kept quiet, pretending I was asleep and letting out a little snore once in a while as a convincer. I didn't want to get mixed up in it. Finally things quieted down. When I woke the next morning, Fisher was asleep on the couch with his high collar, tie, and all his clothes still on. I found out later they had entertained the conductor in the club car, inviting him to have a few drinks which he declined on the ground he was on duty.

"I make more in a week than you do in a year," boasted Fisher. Then they tried to get the conductor to bring the engineer back for a snort and let the fireman take charge.

They were three hectic weeks since Cobb and Blythe didn't like each other and neither did Fisher and Lardner. Ring had heavy going all the way through. He finally made a remark which came back to plague him many times and which he lived to regret. One night he said, "Irvin Cobb likes to spend an evening at home with his books, of which he has one complete set."

Cobb heard about it later and never forgave Ring. It's too bad since Lardner didn't really mean it. He was sarcastic when drinking but fundamentally kind.

Grantland Rice was a great friend of Ring's. The Rices and the Lardners decided to take in the Mardi Gras in New Orleans one season. Ring hated pretense and got bored with the fancy doings and maybe a little tight. One Southern gentleman of the old school attached himself to Lardner. He was an awful bore, boasting about his ancestors and what aristocrats his relatives had always been. He climbed his family tree hand-over-hand. Ring was silent and patient for a long time. Then he turned and said very seriously, "If you are interested in my forebears, I was born in Niles, Michigan, of colored parents on both sides."

The New Orleans gent took one look at Ring's high cheekbones and swarthy complexion and disappeared.

"Well, I finally got rid of that sonofabitch," remarked Ring.

When Warren G. Harding was President of the United States, he invited Grantland Rice and Ring Lardner to the White House for lunch and to play golf. After the meal, the President said, "Rice, I know why you came over here—because you expect to get a good story, but, Lardner, why in the world did you come?"

"Because I want to be Ambassador to Greece," Ring answered solemnly.

"Good God," exclaimed the President, surprised. "Why do you want that?"

"My wife doesn't like Great Neck," he replied.

"Well," remarked Harding, "that's a damn sight better reason than most of these gents who stop over here have."

They adjourned to the golf course. Rice was a good player. Ring had an erect stance with a tendency to hit a low hard ball with a hook. The President had a habit of playing a shot and then rushing ahead, not waiting for the others. Ring socked one which whistled by Harding's noggin and struck in the branches of an apple tree over his head, knocking down leaves, twigs, and fruit. The President looked around surprised and a little puzzled, evidently expecting an apology.

"Well, I did the best I could to make Coolidge President of the United States," said Ring. Harding laughed long and loud.

Ring was never a great orator and, in fact, usually spoke so quietly it was difficult for his audience to hear him. Before the 1919 World Series, he was paid $500 to make a speech in Cincinnati to some noisy gathering. After it was over he realized that most of the audience had missed his remarks, so he wrote it as a column for the newspapers—with an explanation.

However, he could make a droll talk well worth listening to. The following was one at a banquet just before John T. McCutcheon, the well-known *Chicago Tribune* cartoonist, was married in 1917:

> I am entirely unaccustomed to extemporaneous speaking. So I trust you will overlook halting phraseology and whatever

shortcomings there may be in this remarkable address on the ground that I am talking with absolutely no preparation. In fact, I had no idea I would be called on until last Monday afternoon. It was then that Mr. Dawes telephoned me and asked that I be ready with a few words. I assured him that speech-making was far out of my line. "All right," he said, "I suppose we will have to get someone else." So I yielded.

Mr. Dawes said he would count on me for ten minutes. But I cannot talk ten minutes. I am not a camel. When I am through, the elapsed time will have been a trifle over five minutes, including pauses for laughter.

It is customary to save the star speaker for last. I must explain why the order tonight is reversed. The social event of the season, the social event of the era, is taking place in Riverside, and unless I catch the 9:47, they will think I came only for the meal, particularly since they all know that I will have had my appetite whetted by attendance at a banquet.

I regret exceedingly that I will be unable to stay for the other speakers, R. H. Little* of the Stratford and Judge Landis** of the Post Office Building, but I can heartily recommend them both. I have heard Mr. Little talk. I have heard Judge Landis talk. Who hasn't?

Mr. Dawes is to be felicitated on his choice. He selected Mr. Little. I don't know why. Perhaps because he is a life-long friend of Mr. John T. McCutcheon. I was selected because I, like Mr. McCutcheon, get my stuff in the paper every day. The same holds good for Judge Landis.

Were he not absent from the city, you undoubtedly would also have the pleasure of hearing George Ade, Chicago's second humorist.

Possibly there are those among you who know something of our guest of honor, Mr. McCutcheon, and his work. For the

* Richard Henry Little—columnist and star correspondent for the *Chicago Tribune.*

** Judge Kenesaw Mountain Landis.

benefit of those who do not, I will say that he is the *Chicago Tribune's* cartoonist and is generally rated the greatest cartoonist in the world outside the Hearst papers. Personally I can tell you little about his pictures as I seldom get to the first page.

The *Tribune's* business manager informs me that in his judgment, if any, the present enormous circulation of that newspaper is chiefly due to two men. One of them is Mr. McCutcheon.

Up to something like two or two and a half years ago, Mr. McCutcheon's personal life was without a blemish. Then he began making illustrations for the *Cosmopolitan.*

This present function is in honor of Mr. McCutcheon, just as is that melodious song in the Follies "Good-by, Dear Old Bachelor Days." For Mr. McCutcheon, day after tomorrow, will launch on the marital sea from which no traveler returns the same. That reminds me of the story of the two Irishmen, Mike and Morris. The story would be out of place here. Mr. McCutcheon's absence from the first page will be felt keenly, will be mourned by everybody except liquor traffic. As a substitute for his cartoons we will probably run some pictures by Sidney Smith,* with some ideas by myself. In behalf of the proprietors of the *Tribune,* I will say, without their consent, that while the paper is loath to lose Mr. McCutcheon's services, even for a few weeks or months or whatever it is, the said paper's grief will be tempered by the knowledge that when he comes back to work, in his new condition of life, his cartoons will have in them what they heretofore lacked—human interest. Mr. McCutcheon is, like Robinson Crusoe, going away to a desert isle, but not being a copy cat of Robinson, Mr. McCutcheon won't have his Man Friday. Mr. McCutcheon will take his Woman Saturday.

Ring was stubborn, especially when fortified with a few drinks, and he hated long-winded, supposedly funny stories,

* *Chicago Tribune* comic artist, who drew "The Gumps."

either dirty or clean. He had a formula which sometimes worked. When a "wit" would come up to him and say, "Ring, have you heard this one?" he would invariably answer "yes" before the raconteur could get any further.

Well, one night after the theater, he settled in the Lambs Club for the evening, which ran along until daylight. Even the veteran sun dodgers began to urge him to go home—or at least to leave. They gave him all sorts of reasons, but he shook his head.

"No," he decided, "it wouldn't look right to go out on the streets in daylight with a dinner coat on. It would ruin my reputation."

He sat stubbornly through the next day with various members spelling one another as the honor guard. Finally, along about 3 A.M. of the second morning, some bum comic, whose name escapes me, came in and walked over to the table. Not knowing the situation, he greeted the lingering guest.

"Hello, Ring," he said. "Have you heard this one?"

"Yes," he replied and got up and put on his hat and coat and departed.

"Good God," remarked one of the weary bystanders, "why didn't we think of that forty-eight hours ago?"

Another Lambs Club anecdote: Bugs Baer and Lardner had begun the evening struggling to turn out Ring's column. Fatigued by their efforts in the old *World* building, they started uptown, stopping on the way in several saloons to do a little shopping. Finally, they reached Forty-fourth Street and the Lambs about 2 A.M. They walked in and up to the desk.

"How much do we owe here?" demanded Bugs.

The man looked up his records. "Nothing," he replied.

"Well, we're not members then," he said. "Come on, Ring." They walked out.

Lardner was a real pro when it came to writing stories. He found it hard to satisfy himself, and that and his failing health are what served to make him morose in his later life. After turning out the "You Know Me, Al," pieces for years, he got tired of this same pattern and wrote a fiction story called "The Golden Honeymoon" about an old couple in St. Petersburg, Florida.

George Horace Lorimer was then the editor of the *Saturday Evening Post,* and he turned it down. He advised Lardner to stick to his baseball yarns.

Ray Long, editor of the *Cosmopolitan Magazine,* promptly and enthusiastically bought the story, paying more than Lorimer would have. It was immediately recognized as a masterpiece.

Lardner was the master of the surprise answer or the unexpected word. Two examples:

He was driving in the Bronx with his sons one day shortly after he moved to New York. He got lost in this confusing section. Here is how he told it:

"Daddy, are we lost?" one of my sons asked me.

"Shut up," I explained.

Another example of the unexpected response occurred at my house in East Hampton a good many years ago. Wallace Irwin, the writer, and his wife, Tish, were our guests, and the Lardners joined us on Sunday afternoon. Now Mrs. Irwin is about six feet two inches tall, while Ring ranged up to around six feet one. We had a pleasant visit, swapping stories and quips.

After our friends left, I turned to Ring and said, "What did you think of Tish Irwin?"

"First time in my life I have ever seen a woman's nostrils," Ring answered without a smile.

Sol Hess and Ring Lardner were friends in the old Chicago

saloon set of which Mrs. Potter Palmer was not a member. Shortly after Ring got his first automobile and was practicing driving in the crowded Loop area, he ran into the fender of a car with a woman chauffeur. She wasn't tongue-tied. She jumped out and became a curbstone orator, bawling Lardner out good. He remained solemn and silent. This show naturally attracted a lot of citizens who stopped to listen and advise, having time on their hands. Hess happened to come along and pushed his way through the group.

"Hey, Ring," he shouted, "is there anything I can do for you?"

"Yes, get the hell out of here," he answered. "Ain't the crowd big enough already?"

Once when Lardner was invited out to dinner, he didn't want to go so he wrote a note of explanation. It said, "I'm sorry I can't come. It's the baby's night out, and I have to stay home to take care of the nurse."

Irvin Cobb, Bob Davis, famous editor of Munsey magazines, Captain Joseph Patterson, publisher of the *Chicago Tribune, New York Daily News,* and then *Liberty Weekly,* and this writer went for a week end at the Wyandanch Club made up of sports, fishermen, and hunters, in Smithtown, Long Island. On our way back we stopped to see Ring Lardner who was living in Great Neck.

Now when I went to work for Captain Patterson in 1924, I was told only one man in the organization addressed him by his first name. This was William Fields, the general manager and an old friend. As I got to know my boss better, he called me "Jack," but I stuck to the rules as long as I was on the job.

We arrived at the Lardner mansion in good form and our host greeted us with a kind of solemn and sour expression. The maid came in with a trayful of drinks while Irvin Cobb told a

couple of funny stories to keep the ball in the air. Finally
Lardner turned to Captain Patterson and said slowly and
emphatically, "Joseph, as I never dared to call you until you
fired me."

"I didn't fire you, Ring," answered his guest.

"Oh, yes, you did, Joseph," he replied insistently.

"No, I didn't," answered the Captain.

"Oh, yes, you did, Joseph!"

Lardner was a stubborn opponent, especially when he had
absorbed a couple of drinks, so the Captain finally gave up
and changed the subject.

Several years ago I wrote an article about Lardner for
Collier's Weekly. Later a book was published by A. S. Barnes
called *Collier's Greatest Sports Stories*. These were selected
by Tom Meany, and my contribution was included, so I take
the liberty of quoting excerpts from it as follows:

> One of the many names I am called in the appended article
> is "a stickler for accuracy." If ever I am asked to write an
> article about the writer of this one, you may rest assured I will
> not call him that. His anecdote concerning Hugh Fullerton
> and me is true in every respect except that it happened to two
> other fellows. And the one about Eddie Collins* never taking
> a drink—well, the answer to that is that the Collins boy lives
> in Lansdowne, a suburb of Philadelphia, where even Baby's
> first bottle comes from the "Haig Brothers" dairy.
>
> I could go on and point out a dozen other trivial errata, but
> the article itself seems long enough without being aggravated
> by a comprehensive introduction. In fact, when she to whom,
> when we are alone, I refer as Mrs. Lardner for lack of a more
> poignant name—when she, I say, read the manuscript, she
> suggested that it would be less of a strain on subscribers if
> *Collier's* were to run it serially.

---

* Collins was the great second baseman of the old Athletics.

What I will, and do, call Mr. Wheeler is redundant. You take, for example, the sentence where he refers to a "half-stewed comic artist." Aren't there twice as many words there as necessary? Has anyone ever heard of a comic artist who wasn't —but I too am getting verbose.

Ring Lardner.

Ring Lardner scares most of the people who meet him. Usually it is his countenance, of polished Syracuse limestone, Numidian marble, and onyx—one of the finest examples of the early Egyptian dynasties. But sometimes it isn't.

A friend of Ring's collects celebrities. One Sunday afternoon Ring stepped in and was rushed up to the head of the receiving line. The introduction was made.

"This is Prince Jazzbo of Jazzbonia."

"What of it?" replied Lardner, without changing his expression.

Yet I have seen a half-stewed comic artist scare Lardner, so what matchmaker is going to figure that out?

I asked Ring to tell me something about the songs he has written. In his reply, notice the exact date he gives. He is a stickler for accuracy always. The second song he mentions was composed in the 1919 World Series—the one that had a slight smell about it.

"Dear Sir:

"On the night of June 30, 1919, the night before the first Volstead law went into 'effect,' the correspondents who were in Toledo for the Willard-Dempsey 'fight' were entertained at the home of Herman Saxon, a Toledo theatre owner. He had a bar and a piano and everything.

"That night I made up words and music of a song refrain called 'Toledo Blues' (we were pretty tired of the assignment by that time), and it was learned and sung by a chorus composed of Tad, Tiny Maxwell, Jimmy Isaminger, Harry Witwer,

Rube Goldberg and all the rest of the stews. The words were:

> I guess I've got those there Toledo Blues,
> About this fight I simply can't enthuse,
> I do not care if Dempsey win or lose,
> Owing to the fact I've got Toledo Blues.

"But there is another one you may remember, written by me, in collaboration with Jim Crusinberry, Tiny Maxwell, and Mick Flatley, to the tune of 'I'm Forever Blowing Bubbles' and sung at a roadhouse in Bellevue, Ky., just outside of Cincinnati, during the 1919 World Series:

> I'm forever blowing ball games,
> Pretty ball games in the air.
> I come from Chi.,
> I hardly try,
> Just go to bat and fade and die.
> Fortune's coming my way,
> That's why I don't care.
> I'm forever blowing ball games,
> For the gamblers treat me fair.

"Three of the Cincinnati players were in our party and seemed to enjoy the song.

                                                        "R.W.L."

Once a magazine editor requested an article by Lardner on Success, and Ring produced a piece showing how he had undertaken to be a song writer and, figuring his time at 50 cents an hour, had lost something like $10,000. This is one of the few things Lardner has ever done that got a rejection.

Since his great success as a writer the highbrows have taken up Lardner, and he is invited to all sorts of literary and social functions, some of which he likes and some of which bore him to death. He is a curious mixture of the sensitive intellectual and the highly human; many of his best friends were lowbrows, ballplayers, bartenders and prizefighters, active or retired—the bartenders being most retired.*

Maybe you have heard of Ring as a humorist.

Well, if you meet him, don't expect him to grab you by the lapel and begin: "Did you hear the one about the Scot who was learning the Charleston?"

In one of his newspaper articles Lardner was discussing a ham-and-egg fighter loudly touted by his manager as a heavy-weight prospect. Ring outlined the fighter's daily routine:

"Young Dorval is in training all the time. From 6 to 7 in the a.m. he does road work for a paving concern. From 7 to 12 he eats his breakfast, usually a wolf or bear and the inevitable sweet potatoes. From 12 to 1 he reads a sentence. From 1 to 3 he manicures himself all over. From 3 to 4 he practices ex-pression, and from 4 to 5 cheek breathing. A good many boxers pick out the wrong features to breathe through, features that may get stopped up."

Two or three years ago he sent out Christmas cards. They were typed on a penny postcard, the product of his own type-writer, and read as follows:

> We've got so many aunt-in-laws
> Who seem to think we're Santa Claus
> That we just can't afford to spend
> No Money on a casual friend.
>
> And what did you give us last December?
> Nothing, so far as we can remember.
> So all you get is Merry Christmas
> From Mr. Lardner and the Mrs.

Mr. Lardner's idea of a Christmas card for 1927 follows:

> We combed Fifth Avenue this last month
> A hundred times if we combed it onth,

---

* This was during Prohibition.

> In search of something we thought would do
> To give to a person as nice as you.
>
> We had no trouble selecting gifts
> For the Ogden Armours and Louie Swifts,
> The Otto Kahns and the George F. Bakers,
> The Munns and the Rodman Wanamakers.
>
> It's a simple matter to pick things out
> For people one isn't so wild about,
> But you, you wonderful pal and friend, you!
> We couldn't find anything fit to send you.

And speaking of the Mrs., a newspaperwoman once asked a lot of authors to contribute to a symposium. The big idea was to show how their wives had helped them. Most of them said their wives had been swell helpmates and great pals; they would be in the gutter now except for the support of the little woman.

Now, Lardner thinks Mrs. Lardner is the ace of the world; nevertheless he wrote as follows:

"I was never one to keep a diary, and so must depend on an unsteady, Volsteady memory for the things my wife has done for me. In 1914 or 1915, I think it was July, she cleaned my white shoes. In 1918 she told the man at the draft board that she and three kiddies were dependent on me for support. In 1921 and again in 1923 she brought in some ice, White Rock and glasses.

"She dusted my typewriter in 1922. Late one night in 1924 we got home from somewhere and I said I was hungry and she gave me a verbal picture of the location of the pantry.

"Once a man named Morris called me up and she told him I was out of town.

"Once I bid a no-trump, and she took me out in spades and we were set three tricks.

"Once we were in the car and got stalled, and she suggested

that the car must be out of gas. Another time I quit cigarettes, and she felt sorry for me.

"When I was away from home attending high school she did all the plowing and fed the shote.

"Once we went on a trip, and it was going to take us all night to get there and we had a section of the sleeping car, and just as I was nearly crazy trying to guess whether I should take the lower or upper berth she solved the problem by crawling into the lower berth. Once a waiter was going to put two lumps of sugar in my coffee, and my wife stopped him. She didn't touch him or call him a name, but she just said, 'Only one lump!' And he did not put the other lump in. He was panicky. And back in 1910 I asked her to marry me right away; but she wouldn't do it until 1911."

"To what do you attribute your success?" I asked Lardner, to make this account of him official.

"To Home Run cigarettes and a family with extravagant tastes which always needs money," was the unqualified answer.

The final note in this Ring Lardner chapter is a sad one. During the last years of his life he was morose, due to failing health. He found it harder and harder to turn out stories. The following letter, addressed to Bugs Baer, is probably the last one he ever wrote.

La Quinta
[Friday, February 24, 1932]

Dear Bugs:

This is to tell you what you already know, that I fleed the city without making you come and see me at the hospital. As is customary in such cases, the final week brought a rush (four or five people) of visitors I didn't want and left me no time for those I did. But I assure you my loss is your gain. I was no treat as a host and bayed at everybody who came into the room.

Please accept my congratulations on Old Gold's acumen in choosing John Medbury instead of you as its master of ceremonies. Have you heard him? If not, tune in on some Australian nutwork. His stuff is even funnier on long wave lengths. It's a damn shame Roy Moulton died. He would have been the boy.

Perhaps you received one of the enclosed. I ought not to be spending money on night letters but I couldn't resist this guy as follows: "My own birthday is March six stop Please have Mr. Hearst write two-column front page editorial about it for release in papers of March first with slogan quote Buy American presents for Lardner unquote."

I don't even know who Henderson is, but I know that *Cosmopolitan* turned down a story of mine because of full inventory or small budget or something. This story established several records. It was intended to run about 4,300 words and ran 7,500. It took me from June until late January to write it. The *Post* got it on a Friday and returned it the following Monday (What to do with a 7,500-word story if the *Post* won't take it?) Bill Lengel said he liked it and would recommend it to Burton, but was pretty sure it didn't have a chance. He was right. *Collier's* said it was too long and tenuous and the required cutting would ruin it. In desperation I sent it to Mencken, who prints them all lengths and pays nothing. He "liked it," but said it was too much of a "Symphonica domestica" for the *Mercury*. He also said "Have you thought of the women's magazines? They are the only ones making money. Oscar Graeve of *Delineator* would grab it at first glance." Well, I didn't believe it, but I sent it to Graeve and he took it, paying me three times as much as Mencken would have given me and a quarter of the *Post* price, and saying the story was so absolutely unsuitable for *Delineator* that he didn't have the heart to turn it down. I don't even know whether *Delineator* is a daily or a semi-annual.

Have I bored you enough? No? Well, I was reading Van Loon's *Geography* on the boat and the deck steward made some remark about it. I, being very democratic, told him my son had given it to me for Christmas. He said, "That's a para-

dox, because I'm going to give it to my son when I get home."
So now you know what a paradox is.

Love to the household pets.

R.L.

Dear Jack—No date on letter. Signed with initials only. But
year is easily fixed by a bit of research. Strangely enough, my
masseur, Carl Dahlgren, was at La Quinta when Ring was
there. Carl says Grant Rice visited Ring at the time.

This is the story of a career. Why not send a copy of this to
all those glorious pals of Ring's who generously threw a
drowning man both ends of the rope?

B.B.

P.S. Copied exactly including punctuations. B.B.

As a sequel to Ring Lardner's description of his efforts to
sell his last story, there follows one from Oscar Graeve, then
editor of *Delineator*:

February 9, 1933

Delineator
Butterick Building
New York
Editorial Offices
Dear Mr. Lardner:

I didn't find "Poodle" our type of story at all. So we shall be
very glad to use it.

About price, I think seven hundred and fifty is about the
best I can offer. Mr. Mencken is wrong. We haven't much
money. We're working on a very limited budget. (And that's
much, much more than Henry would have paid you.)

It's our policy—or lack of it—to publish occasionally a story
or an article that isn't at all typical woman's magazine stuff. So
that's why we welcome "Poodle." Personally, I think it's pretty
grand. I think we will have to cut it a little. But don't let that
worry you. I'll do it myself and I am one of the most judicious
of cutters, guaranteed painless to the author.

It's a little late to tell you that I've always been one of your fondest admirers. I've positively gloated over some of your stories. I think "Some Like Them Cold" is unforgettable.

So it's no wonder that I'm glad to have you in *Delineator*.

Very sincerely,
(Signed)
Oscar Graeve,
Editor.

Mr. Ring Lardner
La Quinta, California

Incidentally, this last Lardner story was not published until after his death—in 1933.

XI. BUD FISHER—CARTOONIST

THE first time I saw Bud Fisher was in a little office on West Forty-fifth Street, New York, in 1913. Bill MacBeth, a sports writer on the old *American* and a friend, had told me the cartoonist's contract with Hearst was running out shortly, and Fisher wanted to make a move. "Mutt and Jeff" was the best-known and most widely published comic of that time.

Fisher was a dapper, cocky little guy who was not impressed by my approach. After I told him we would like to make a contract with him, he got right to the point.

"How do I know I am going to get my money?" he asked brusquely.

"You know Ty Cobb, don't you, and John McGraw and Christy Mathewson? Ask them if they get paid. They write for us."

"What do I care about those dumb ballplayers?" he replied.

Then he invited me to go up to his apartment at Riverside Drive and Ninety-sixth Street. He introduced me to his wife, Pauline. I thought she was one of the prettiest and most charming girls I had ever seen. We continued to mumble along about a deal. Finally, I said, "Suppose we put the first year's guarantee in the bank in your name? Would that satisfy you?"

For the first time his eyes brightened and his ears pricked up. "Sure, it would," he answered.

Well, to make a long story longer, we finally signed a contract by which he got 60 per cent of the revenue and a guarantee of $1000 weekly. He had been drawing $300 a week from Hearst.

But it wasn't all as simple as that. For the only time in my life a bank turned me down on a loan. I haven't asked for one since. My proposition was that I would show them contracts with reputable newspapers which would exceed $1000 weekly. I asked for a loan of $50,000, the money to remain in the bank except for the payments to Fisher, and we would deposit all the revenue.

"Never heard of such a proposition," said the banker as he turned to answer the telephone.

Florence White was then general manager of the *New York World,* a wonderful gentleman who later became a friend of mine and a valued adviser. The *World* had previously tried to hire Fisher away from Hearst and might have done so except for a slight slip. Bud, still single at that time, was stuck on a girl named Peaches who happened to be in his apartment alone one afternoon when the telephone rang. She answered it.

"Is Mr. Fisher there?" asked a female voice.

"Who wants him?" demanded Peaches.

"Florence White," came the reply.

"Well, he doesn't want to speak to her," she snapped and hung up the telephone. Of course, it was Mr. White's secretary calling Bud. It cost the cartoonist several hundred dollars a week, temporarily.

When the bank turned me down, I approached Mr. White and asked him if the *World* would underwrite the contract, provided I could show him agreements with big newspapers which would cover the guarantee. He agreed. After I told Bud Fisher about it, he accepted the proposition, and we signed a contract. This was the beginning of a friendship which proved to be pretty turbulent through the years. However, before he died in 1954 he made me the executor of his estate, so our relationship lasted until the end.

As soon as the Hearst people found out Fisher was going to

quit, the art director started a man named Ed Mack drawing imitations of "Mutt and Jeff" which Hearst expected to syndicate as soon as Bud's contract ran out. This started a suit that made new law and in which we won a complete victory.

Fighting the Hearst organization was no easy job. No holds were barred. The *Sunday American* had already printed a comic section with the imitation "Mutt and Jeff" page in it before we got our injunction. Fisher and I armed ourselves with certified copies and proceeded to serve these personally on distributors and news dealers who already had received the comic section to stuff into the paper. The *American* appeared in the metropolitan area without any Sunday comics for the only time.

When we won the lawsuit and stopped the Hearst syndicate from putting out an imitation, Bud, who was always an opportunist, hired Ed Mack as his assistant, in which capacity Mack continued until he died.

Bud Fisher was one of the old school of cartoonists who were known as sun dodgers because they hated the daylight. Other members were Tad Dorgan, Hype Igoe, and Tom Powers. Fisher once wanted to be a prizefighter and never got over the idea he was one, although at the time of his only professional appearance, a punch on the jaw knocked him out and convinced him a cartoon career was better.

He first tried his luck in San Francisco, but had trouble getting a job on a newspaper. In consequence, he dug up an idea which he managed to sell to several merchants. He would draw a cartoon of the proprietor of a shop and stick the cartoon in the show window. The cartoon would carry some such caption on it as: "Meet Joe Peck—the best hatter in town."

Charles P. Young was managing editor of the *San Francisco Chronicle* at that time, and he finally gave Fisher a job drawing layouts in the art department. Then, in 1908, Fisher began doing a race-track tipping strip with only Mr. Mutt in it at first. Jeff joined the team later.

Tad Dorgan and Bud used to travel the saloon trail together. The former had lost most of his right hand in an accident while a boy in San Francisco, so he was a one-punch guy. If he missed, he was through.

One night the two were in a joint called Marshall's when Tad excused himself because he suddenly decided he didn't like some of the other customers. He walked down the aisle swinging without warning, and soon surprised patrons were spinning off their chairs. The proprietor knew the two cartoonists and quieted things down without the help of the police. But several of the angry victims waited outside.

Tad telephoned Joe Bannon, then circulation manager of the *Journal,* saying he needed assistance. Joe dispatched several gorillas, who worked in his department, as an escort. Fisher and Dorgan departed in triumph and unscathed. But they made the mistake of going to a saloon called Dowling's at the corner of Seventh Avenue and Forty-third Street. They were enjoying a glass of beer there when three or four of their late adversaries, following their trail, entered, spotted them, and attacked. Tad let go one punch, missed, and ducked.

"The next thing I knew," reported Bud, "a couple of them had me bent backwards over the bar and were pushing me up and down and punching me. I looked around for Tad, expecting him to help me. He was at the free lunch counter, picking up an olive here and a sardine there, paying no attention to me and pretending I was a stranger. Finally, the bartender pulled them off before I got killed."

On one or two occasions, I was the victim of Bud's impetuous belligerency. We were with Ed Barrow, later with the Yankees as general manager, and Guy Viskniskki in the old Waldorf bar one evening doing a little shopping. Fisher decided to invite a couple of girls for dinner, so he called up and told them to wait for us. Time moved on, as it does in bars, and it got to be 10:30.

"We'd better cancel the dinner date," I suggested.

"Oh, no, they'll wait," Bud answered with his customary assurance.

In my old Chalmers car, we drove up to this apartment house in West Forty-fourth Street where one of the young ladies lived. We missed Barrow, but thought nothing of it at the time. As we walked into the hall, a big, burly janitor stopped us, demanding to know what we wanted. We explained we were calling for Miss Dixon and started for the elevator.

"Go on and walk up," he said, refusing to budge. So I did three flights, leaving Fisher alone. Naturally, I did not get a very friendly reception after I had rung the bell, for Miss Dixon had retired for the night, and the other young lady had departed. Also Miss Dixon began to bawl me out as I deserved.

"Oh, I've got a better fight than this downstairs," I said, and she slammed the door.

I didn't know how true my remark was, for when I descended, I found Fisher and the janitor in a red-hot argument. The janitor welcomed me with this remark: "As for you, you big sonofabitch, I'll throw you out, too."

I turned one loose and caught him just right. Down he went and Fisher jumped on top of him, grabbed him by the lapels, and punched him as he kept pulling his head up. The janitor began to holler for help and soon tenants were rushing from doors in various costumes, and some woman screamed, "They are killing Pat."

"Bud," I urged, "we had better get the hell out of here."

We did and walked down to a corner saloon to freshen up. Soon we heard a rumble like an approaching stage mob, and

Pat, the janitor, walked in, bleeding a little, with a cop, followed by several other supporters.

"There they are," someone shouted, pointing to us. The cop put a hand on each of us and started hustling us toward the door.

"Where are we going?" I asked.

"To the West Forty-seventh Street police station," he answered.

"Why not ride? I have a car."

The cop agreed. The lieutenant behind the desk greeted us and took our names. When he recognized Bud Fisher, he looked at the policeman and said, "Why did you arrest these men? I don't see any complainant. You fellows had better get out of here."

Naturally there was no complainant as Pat was walking. But as we headed for the door, Pat came in with his followers and registered a complaint, so we were stuck. The friendly lieutenant agreed to hold Fisher while I went out and hustled some bail. When I returned I found Bud in the back room playing dominoes with the cops. He had won two dollars.

The next morning we had to appear in a Magistrate's Court, but Pat was too sick to show up, and we were released, but that was not the end of it. Pat hired a slick lawyer and sued us for something like $100,000 for the damage we had done to his person. We managed to dodge subpoena servers for about two years, and then one day a smart one caught us. We finally settled for $500.

Ed Barrow turned up in a park in Brooklyn, a policeman tapping on his feet with his night stick. He could never explain how he got there.

When Fisher was working for Hearst, a man named S. S. Carvalho was the general manager and a very fine gentleman. In fact, he testified during the litigation that he had assured Fisher if he ever left the *American* he would have the rights to "Mutt and Jeff," and this helped us to win the case.

But even before the lawsuit Bud was trying to get out of his contract to accept a better offer from the *World*. Mr. Carvalho was away on a vacation when the cartoonist, who usually delivered his drawings by messenger, visited the old offices in William Street. An old gentleman, named E. H. Clarke, was acting as general manager. He spotted Fisher smoking a cigarette. There was a rule against smoking because of the inflammable nature of the shabby structure.

"Young man," Clarke said, "do you work here?"

"Yes," answered Bud.

"Don't you know we have a rule against smoking?"

Bud nodded his head, taking a long drag on the cigarette and blowing out the smoke. "What are you going to do about it?" he asked.

"Well," came the stern reply, "we usually discharge our employees who violate the rule."

"Mister," answered Fisher, "I don't know who the hell you are, but if you will fire me and make it stick, I will meet you here at 3 o'clock this afternoon and give you five thousand dollars in cash."

Fisher's life was full of crises, most of which he made himself. He was a strange contrast of shrewdness and stupidity about his own affairs. By his guts and independence, he probably did more to make the cartoon business for his more cowardly confrères than anyone else who has ever been in it. Yet he squandered his own life and was a very unhappy man.

The greatest crisis came when Pauline and he separated. He blamed his mother-in-law, which was only an excuse. His wife moved to a hotel. One of the big theatrical producers of that day was in love with her and wanted to marry her. The producer decided to hire Val O'Farrell, an ex-cop who ran a

detective agency, to follow Bud and get the evidence necessary for a divorce, and while marking time, arranged for
Pauline to play a week at Hammerstein's Victoria vaudeville
theater. Fisher, seeing the billing, went to the show one night,
and then proceeded to the stage door.

"How about going over to the Knickerbocker Hotel and
having a drink and something to eat?" he asked Pauline.

Being beautiful and weak, she accepted. They had supper
and some champagne together and some memories. One word
led to another until they proceeded to the desk and registered
as Mr. and Mrs. Bud Fisher. The detectives had been following them, so the first lady they caught the cartoonist with was
his own wife. Of course, the reconciliation didn't last long and
the romance with the producer also blew up. She went back to
Baltimore to live. Whenever I would visit that city, I would
look her up. She still had her charm and beauty, but they were
fading, helped along by some snorts of bootleg gin.

In the meantime, Fisher had gone to Europe. He had
planned to return on a Cunard boat, but became restless in
Paris and decided to switch to the *Leviathan*. Captain Hartley, a dashing sea dog, invited him to sit at his table, and
Fisher found himself next to a lady with an accent, named the
Countess de Beaumont. When they reached New York, they
announced their engagement on the dock.

This sudden romance surprised me, since Bud had known
many women. I called him up, and he confirmed it and even
brought the Countess into the office to meet me. Of course, I
had to approve. If I hadn't they would have wed anyhow
and agreed I was an S.O.B. They sailed back on the return
voyage of the *Leviathan* and were married on the bridge by
Captain Hartley.

But it didn't take. I believe they lived together about four
months and were legally separated in 1924. She received $400

a week alimony until Fisher died in 1954. Then, as his widow, she claimed and got 62.5 per cent of the estate which amounted to about $1,000,000, although quite a sum was chewed up in taxes. Bud hadn't paid any for four or five years before his death, so there were interest and penalties. He didn't believe in income taxes.

To show what kind of a girl Pauline was, when Fisher was engaged in litigation with the Countess, and she was trying to get his eye teeth, Bud's lawyer, a man named Charles Kelley, asked me to call Pauline in Baltimore and try to persuade her to come to New York to give some routine testimony. Incidentally, when Fisher and she split up, she settled for a paltry $25,000. I got her on the telephone and explained what I wanted.

"Listen, John," she said, "I'm not going to lie too much for Bud."

She was willing to lie a little for old times' sake. I assured her we didn't want her to commit perjury. She came and testified—a swell girl.

Her ending was sad and unhappy. She went downhill fast, and one morning was found dead. She had told me about a man living in Washington who was in love with her but was married. His wife knew nothing about the romance until the tragic ending. He looked at Pauline in her coffin and was so shocked he fell over and died beside it. This was the first his widow knew Pauline and he were even acquainted.

How Fisher got into horse racing is typical of his character and stubbornness. We were living in Yonkers at the time. One Saturday afternoon Bud, Herbert Bayard Swope, and I went to the Empire City track. After adding up my winnings, I invited them back for a drink at my house. On a recent trip to London, we had hired an Irish girl to come back and work for us. She had some idea that, if she could get to America, she wouldn't have any trouble marrying a millionaire. She is still single, as far as I know. Anyway, she wasn't any Marilyn Monroe to start with.

Her name was Kathleen, and she had been a bartender, too, in the Savoy Hotel. She began to mix up cocktails for my guests. Fisher remarked he was leaving for Saratoga the next day for the summer meeting.

"I will give you a letter to George Bull, the secretary," said Swope, "to see that you are properly taken care of at the track."

Whereupon, Swope sat down and wrote a very effusive note, saying Bud was America's greatest cartoonist and his drawings appeared in the *New York World*. He asked Bull to provide him with press badges, clubhouse privileges and any others available. In fact, Swope requested Bull to do everything he could for Fisher but pick winners. Fisher thanked him and stuffed the note in his pocket. Then they left for New York in style, in the cartoonist's big Rolls Royce, very friendly and full of Kathleen's potent cocktails.

It was a few days later I heard the sequel. Fisher was living at Riverside Drive and Eighty-sixth Street then. Swope had a date with his wife at the Ritz at 7:30 and was already half an hour late and impatient.

"Bud," he said when they arrived at Eighty-sixth Street, "I want to take your car to meet my wife."

"No," replied the artist, "I have to send it for my mother. I will get you a taxi."

This ruffled Swope. "No, thanks," he answered indignantly. "I can take care of my own taxi."

He started off. It was a very hot night in midsummer. He couldn't find a cab, but he did pass a Western Union office. By this time he was burned up. He stepped inside and wrote the following telegram to George Bull: "If Bud Fisher presents a letter to you from me, pay no attention to it. He is well able to take care of his own race-track privileges."

When Bud presented the letter, Bull showed him the wire.

The spunky cartoonist was not one to take this slap and lie down and roll over. He composed a reply to Swope as follows: "You ought to challenge Harry K. Thaw for the egomania championship of the world, but out of sportsmanship give him a handicap." (For the benefit of younger readers, Thaw was a rich crackpot who shot Stanford White and later went to Matteawan State asylum for the insane.)

Fisher promptly got this shot in return, signed Swope: "I acknowledge you are an authority on egomania, but what the hell do you know about sportsmanship?"

That exchange set off a feud which lasted for a couple of years. Fisher immediately went out and bought two or three racehorses so he would get an owner's badge. This eventually proved an expensive undertaking, for the size of his stable grew over the years, and he wasn't too successful. Once he was in Europe, and the trainer ran out of money, so we advanced it to the tune of $10,000 a month.

However, he had some winners. He owned a filly, Nelly Morse, named after his mother. He was on a ship on his way back from Europe when his trainer, Alex Gordon, entered her in the Preakness without Fisher's knowing it. She won, so when Bud landed he found a check for $50,305 waiting for him, as I recall the amount.

Meantime, the feud with Swope simmered. I would go to the track occasionally and be with one when the other would come along. They passed each other like strangers. One day after a year or more I got fed up. It was during Prohibition, and Fisher and I met in the bar after the last race. Fisher had an ornate flask which didn't contain cologne water.

Swope strode in. I walked up to him. "Listen, Herbert," I

said, "I'm tired of you two fatheads putting on this kind of a silly show. Why don't you shake hands and forget it?"

"It's all right with me," he said. We went over to Bud.

"How about giving Herbert a drink?" I suggested.

Bud pulled out his flask, and they shook hands. Then Mars Cassidy, the starter, came up. Swope introduced Fisher to him. "How about a drink for Mars?" he said.

"Sorry," answered Bud, "but I'm all out."

We rode back in Fisher's Rolls Royce. On the way we got a flat tire, and while waiting for the chauffeur to change it, the cartoonist pulled out his flask.

"Let's have a drink," he said.

"Thought you told Cassidy you were empty," said Swope.

"Sure, I did. What's the use of wasting my liquor on him when he's half a mile across the track and don't know which horse I'm betting on?"

Fisher afterwards named a horse for Swope, and he turned out to be a pretty good kind of a colt. He once named one for me, too, but the horse got a sore throat and had to have a tube put in it after his first start, so he couldn't run again, which probably saved me a lot of money.

In a previous chapter, I mentioned the prisoner's gun given to Fisher by Pancho Villa. Now occasionally, when Bud was feeling good, he would get out this souvenir and have target practice in his apartment. He was living in an old-fashioned place, since torn down, called the Alps. One evening I stopped to see him. It happened to be my birthday, so we celebrated a little, and along about 2 in the morning we got to arguing as to whether the United States was prepared for war. This was before we entered the first one.

Bud got out his old equalizer, loaded it, and took aim at a dried coconut on the mantle. He hit it squarely and then selected other targets. Of course, the shots could be heard all through the quiet building, and naturally the tenants complained. Pretty soon the superintendent called up and told the tenant there would have to be less noise in his apartment.

"You're too damn strict around here," answered Fisher. "It is getting so you can't shoot off a pistol in your own place at 4 in the morning without someone complaining. I will move out tomorrow."

"You bet you will," said the man. And he did.

A little later, Bud was occupying a sumptuous apartment on fashionable Riverside Drive. One of his guests was a very pretty girl, named Gertrude something, who was fond of Bud. Another was a man named Eddie Harden, who made a precarious living by always agreeing with Bud and getting small handouts. It was a very hot summer night, and Gertrude was in the kitchen cooking some scrambled eggs and bacon. Fisher produced his six-shooter and began firing at various targets, but not his guests. Suddenly he turned to Eddie.

"Lie down, and I'll pretend I shot you," he said. He smeared some ketchup on Eddie's white shirt to make it look like blood.

Naturally Gertrude rushed in when she heard the shooting.

"My God, I have shot Eddie," Bud announced. "You get out, and I will call the police."

She didn't give in that easy. "No," she insisted, "I will put a bottle by his hand and swear he attacked you, and you fired in self-defense."

The argument continued well into the night, and then we all fell asleep, including the victim on the floor by an open window. In the morning we couldn't wake him, for he was a sound sleeper.

"Maybe we did shoot Eddie last night," said Bud.

We spent a few anxious minutes until Eddie finally came to with a hard cold.

Another episode I recall began at a gathering place in New

York called Doyle's pool and billiard parlor, run by the genial Jack Doyle. This was the headquarters for a lot of newspapermen of that period. One of the members of the crowd stopped in on his way home from the psychiatric ward in Bellevue. A companion began to question him about his experience and his mental balance. He reached in his pocket and produced a document.

"This certifies I am sane," he announced proudly, showing it around. "Can you show anything like that?"

"I guess you got me there," replied his friend ruefully.

Golf pool was a favorite pastime, and Tad, Bud Fisher, and some of the other boys used to gamble at it and play until 4 and 5 o'clock in the morning. I was never very good. There is an old saying that a good pool player is the sign of a misspent youth.

I had a date with an eye doctor at 10 one morning, and realizing he would put drops in my eyes so I would have to sit blind for a time, I suggested to Bud Fisher that he go along. I wanted a companion. He cheerfully agreed. We went to Doyle's for a little entertainment, and along about 2 in the morning, I said to Bud, "Come on. We had better go home and get some sleep. We have to get our eyes measured for glasses tomorrow morning."

"Oh, to hell with that," he answered. "I want to be fitted with cheaters so I can see when I am tight."

Next day, when the nurse put the belladonna in our eyes, Bud entertained the rest of the room with such remarks as: "There goes my bankroll. Somebody just took my watch."

Notwithstanding, the glasses worked fine for years.

XII. HERBERT BAYARD SWOPE

No account of my friends would be complete without devoting more space to Herbert Bayard Swope, one of the most colorful of newspapermen. When I first broke in, he was already a legend in the business. He had preceded me on the old *Herald* and moved to the *Morning World* for a better opportunity. He was always a dapper dresser and a fast talker. He had the charm to get in with bigshots and come out with the story.

E. H. Harriman, the great man who put railroads together like children do blocks, was a hard fellow to reach and then to get him to talk. He was reporter-shy. Swope went out to his home in the country. It was a magnificent mansion with all the frills and accouterments of the rich. Not only did the reporter talk his way in, but he made such a favorable impression, he was asked to stay for dinner and spend the night. In the course of the proceedings, he got his interview.

Now it turns out that up to this time in his career, Herbert had had very little to do with valets. One was assigned to him when he got ready to retire. He remembered he had a hole in his sock his wife had forgotten to mend, so he thought he would hide it. When he woke the next morning, the gentleman's gentleman was on hand. The first thing Swope noticed was that not only was the sock missing but all his clothes were gone as well.

"What temperature would you like your bath?" asked the valet.

This was a puzzler as the house guest had never taken the tub temperature before. But he met the situation, as he did many.

"Oh, tepid, tepid, tepid," he replied.

When he finished his ablutions, he stepped out and could find only hard-surfaced little hand towels which he thought was strange, but he blotted himself with these until he was fairly dry and then opened the door. There stood the valet with an enormous Turkish towel spread to greet him. His clothes were returned, pressed, and the hole in his sock had been mended. Swope later became quite an authority on valets—including his own.

Although he won the first Pulitzer Prize ever awarded for his brilliant work as a correspondent in Germany during the First World War, probably his most spectacular achievement was in the Lieutenant Charles Becker case.

This was in 1912. Charles Becker was head of the so-called "Strong Arm Squad" which was organized to handle gambling and other forms of vice in the Broadway and Tenderloin districts. Herman Rosenthal was a gambler who had operated and prospered by paying off the police.

Rosenthal and Becker had had a row when the gambler thought the cop had become too avaricious and had refused to pay the amounts demanded. The story was that Rosenthal was going to expose the graft and kill the racket even if it put him out of business, he was so bitter about the unfair demands which he had refused. Lieutenant Becker then raided his establishment in revenge.

Rosenthal was scheduled to testify next day before the grand jury which was looking into the situation, as there had been rumors round and about that Becker was not "clean as a hound's tooth." The gambler was dining at the Metropole Hotel in Forty-third Street just off Broadway a little before midnight, and the police lieutenant was on his way home from Coney Island where he had been attending a prizefight. A man came up to Rosenthal's table.

"There's a friend outside who wants to speak to you," he whispered.

Unsuspecting, the gambler walked to the front door, and the four gunmen waiting there let him have it, jumped in a car, and were off. News of the murder spread rapidly through the Tenderloin. Swope, who was in the neighborhood, heard of it and, like a good reporter, rushed to the Forty-seventh Street police station. He began to question the lieutenant in charge and the other cops, who seemed to be covering up. Then he called Charles Whitman, the district attorney, at his home and got him out of bed. Swope reported what had happened.

"What do you think I should do?" asked the district attorney.

"Get your clothes on and come down to the police station as soon as you can."

As a result the number of the murderers' car was traced, and its occupants located in the Catskills where they were hiding out. Their names were typical of their profession— Gyp, the Blood, Lefty Louie, Dago Frank, and Whitey Lewis. They were arrested, tried, and all four went to the electric chair. Becker was not connected with the murder during their trial, and, as a matter of fact, they didn't know whom they were working for.

However, two other characters came into the plot—Bald Jack Rose and Bridgie Webber—cheap gamblers who had acted as go-betweens. For the first time Becker's name was mentioned. Rose turned state's evidence to avoid the hot seat, and Webber, with Sam Schepps and Harry Vallon, shortly followed suit. There were two sensational trials, and Swope

was all over the case and had the rest of the reporters in town
tin-canning after him. I know, for I was working for the
Herald. The first time there was a hung jury, and the next
time around, the former police lieutenant was convicted and
sentenced to the electric chair.

There were many ramifications to this case, but the details
have been told so often these are not important here. The
testimony exposed the graft in the police department and the
hookup between powerful members of the force and operators
of gambling houses and brothels. The result was a general
cleanup—for a while anyway. It was generally agreed that if
Swope hadn't routed Whitman out of bed, the number of the
murder car would have been covered up. As a result of his
handling of the case, Whitman was elected governor of New
York.

By the time Becker in Sing Sing had lost his fight for a re-
prieve and was scheduled to be electrocuted, Swope had become city editor of the *New York World*, and an old-time reporter Joe O'Neill, a Catholic, was assigned to cover the last
act in the death chamber. Father Cashin was the prison chap-
lain, and Becker was a Catholic. After the condemned man
had gone to meet his Maker, I heard that Father Cashin had
sent a message to Swope through his reporter, Joe O'Neill. He
said, "Go back and tell Herbert Swope no mistake has been
made."

Not long before Swope died, he and I were reminiscing
about the old days. I asked him whether this story was true.

"Yes, it is," he answered. "I had known Father Cashin for
years, and he didn't want me to have anything on my conscience."

Another of Swope's great reportorial achievements was
accomplished at the Paris Peace Conference after the First
World War. When it came to the signing of the treaty in the

Hall of Mirrors at Versailles, it was decided only one American correspondent could attend. Swope was heading the *New York World* group. Lots were drawn to see who the lucky U.S. man would be. The winner was a dignified reporter of the *New York Times*—Richard Oulahan.

The *Times* had another correspondent, E. L. James, known to his friends as Jimmy. He had covered the war on all fronts and was a rough-and-tumble type with no inhibitions. He later became managing editor. He had a Cadillac car, same as that used by the Army brass, with a correspondent's insignia.

"Let's try to crash the gate tomorrow," Swope suggested. "You know General Pershing, don't you? Ask him if we can follow him to Versailles."

The General agreed, not realizing what the plan was. Jimmy dressed in his correspondent's uniform, and Swope showed up appropriately appareled in striped pants, a morning coat, and high hat. The procession started with their driver right in behind the four stars of General Pershing. When they reached the guard at the gate, he stood aside and saluted, admitting both vehicles. James and Swope swept up to the front door where it was taken for granted they were in the American Commander's party. They were escorted to front seats from which they got a good view of the whole show. They both filed their stories early.

When the other members of the press heard about the ruse, they posted a petition on the bulletin board in the Hotel Crillon, proposing the expulsion of both Swope and James from their organization for conduct unbecoming the profession of journalism. The first two names signed were those of Edwin L. James and Herbert Bayard Swope. Then someone tore the paper down, and the whole matter was forgotten in the Crillon bar.

Herbert Swope was never a bush-leaguer about anything he did. During the Peace Conference, Damon Runyon, one of the correspondents, was taken sick with pneumonia.

"I'll get you a doctor," volunteered Swope. "Not one of these French quacks."

Shortly he returned with Admiral Cary Grayson, President Wilson's private physician, in full uniform. It almost startled Runyon out of his illness.

"Did I get you a doctor?" asked Herbert.

"Yes, and you sure brought me a good one," agreed Runyon.

Swope had all the other correspondents on the run because he knew both Colonel House, the President's alter ego, and Woodrow Wilson. He would frequently say he was going to see one of these gents, but no one believed he was telling the truth. He was. He was also one of the few reporters who ever got an interview with the President in the White House by telephone.

He was a persistent and interesting talker. He had no weaknesses in carrying on a conversation. Now you take Albert Lasker, who built up a pretty fair reputation in the Middle West. He had a habit of pausing for breath and saying "ah" to hold the floor. A nimble opponent could leap in at this point.

Only once did I see Swope defeated. "Hurry Up" Yost, the old Michigan football coach, used a monotone and wouldn't pause for an earthquake. He had two subjects—football, naturally, and the Army after World War I. He was at Grantland Rice's house one fall evening, and the Swopes and Wheelers were also guests. Several times Herbert tried to break in, but Yost kept right on going. Finally, along about 11 o'clock, Swope became discouraged, picked up a new fall hat he had just bought, and was waiting to say good night.

"On that play," continued Yost, "Eckersall was back, and he could either run or kick."

To demonstrate, he reached for Swope's new kelly, grabbed it, and kicked it across the living room. Herbert slunk over, picked it up, and departed without another word.

Bill Hawkins of the Scripps-Howard papers gave a dinner for Wickham Steed, a distinguished British editor. Swope arrived with a boil on his neck so painful he couldn't turn his head without swinging his whole body. Among the other guests was Isaac Marcosson, who had a pretty fair local and European reputation as a talker. Some matchmaker arranged for a bout between Herbert and Ike in Hawkins' suite after the dinner. A select few were invited to attend, including this reporter. There were bets, and Marcosson was the favorite because of Swope's affliction.

It was no match. After about five minutes, Ike gave up, jumped out of the ring, and retired. He couldn't last with the champ.

At a large dinner party, when Herbert wanted to attract the attention of all at the table, he would pick out some lady about four or five places away from his and say, "Pinna, you are a very intelligent woman."

This naturally interested and perhaps surprised her. She would stop talking and listen. So would the rest—to find out why she was intelligent. I tried it one night. However, the lady I selected as my target was cockeyed and paid no attention to me. She evidently didn't care whether she was intelligent or not.

Woodrow Wilson used to call Bernard Baruch "Dr. Facts." It was derived from his standard answer whenever any serious problem confronted him, which was: "Let's look at the facts."

Herbert Swope first met Baruch when the latter was chairman of the War Industries Board during the First World War. They became close friends, and Swope guided Baruch in his public relations and helped him with his speeches. When

Baruch was head of the Atomic Energy Commission, he started his remarks to the United Nations on the perils of the nuclear bomb with a famous line: "We have to choose between the quick and the dead." According to good authority, Herbert Swope was the real author.

After World War I a group including Baruch was sitting around, and someone suggested that many famous men resembled animals—Churchill a bulldog, Wilson a horse, and so on. They finally came to Baruch. Swope spoke up.

"Don't say the obvious—that he is like a silver fox. He resembles the Indian elephant which is smarter than the African. When the former comes to a bridge, he tries it out first with his trunk, then he puts his front feet on it to test it. Next he turns around and leans his hindquarters on it. After all this, he sends another elephant over first. That's Bernie."

Mr. Baruch joined in the laughter.

Herbert Swope had two serious operations shortly before his death. The first was for hernia, and the second a few months later proved to be fatal. When his secretary called me to say he was in the Doctors Hospital, I sent him some red roses and put in a card which said: "Love from Marilyn Monroe."

I thought he would catch on, for I realized he knew M.M. The sequel was characteristic even though he was very sick. When I got home that night my conscience began to trouble me, so I called the hospital and asked for his nurse. She assured me her patient was getting on fine. Nurses always say that.

"You may speak to him if you want to," she said.

My friend came on the telephone.

"Did you get some red roses from Marilyn Monroe today?" I asked him.

"Why, you so-and-so," he responded. "And I wrote her a note thanking her."

"Maybe she will take the hint," I suggested.

It was to be the last time I spoke with him.

The news of his death made page one. Unfortunately, by the time it was published, this great newspaperman did not know about the good play it got.

XIII. SIR WINSTON CHURCHILL

THE first time I saw this great world figure was in New York
along about 1933. He was more or less in the political doldrums
and had come to the United States on a lecture tour.

One Sunday evening he decided to call on his old friend
Bernard Baruch, then living on Fifth Avenue. Churchill wasn't
quite sure of the street number but thought he would recognize the house, so he took off in a taxicab.

When he arrived in the neighborhood, he decided to dis-
mount on the west side of the avenue by Central Park. He
started across the street. It was Sunday night when traffic
was light. He was used to the British custom of driving to the
left and was careless. While he was looking the wrong way, a
car belonging to a young man from Yonkers came along at
moderate speed. The driver saw a bulky figure crossing the
avenue in the shadows and slammed on his brakes—too late.
Hit by a stunning blow, Churchill went down in a huddled
mass.

It was touch and go for several days. The great man's injuries were critical. But finally his indomitable spirit prevailed,
and he recovered.

I suggested to him he write an article for the North American Newspaper Alliance describing his sensations during this
dangerous experience. I offered him $1500 and he accepted.
I thought what he had to say would interest many readers,
since most people have contemplated being hit by a car, and

163

some have actually experienced it. As usual, Sir Winston did a masterful job. The story speaks for itself so I quote it here:

By Winston Churchill
North American Newspaper Alliance

New York.—I had finished dinner and was inclined to go to bed, but an old friend of mine rang up and suggested that I should go around to his house. He was Bernard Baruch, who was the head of the War Industries Board during the two years I was Minister of Munitions.

I did not know the exact number in Fifth Avenue of my friend's house. I knew it was somewhere near 1100, and I thought it probable I could pick it out from the windows of a cab.

We soon arrived, as I supposed, at about the 900's, and I told the cabman to stop where he was on the Central Park side of the Avenue—I would walk across the road myself and inquire at the most likely house.

I no sooner got out of the cab somewhere about the middle of the block and told him to wait, when I instinctively turned my eyes to the right, being a Londoner. About 200 yards away were the yellow headlights of a swiftly approaching car. I thought I had just time to cross the road before it arrived, and I started to do so.

Suddenly, upon my left, I was aware of something utterly unexpected, and boding mortal peril. I turned my head sharply. Right upon me, scarcely its own length away, was what seemed a long dark car, rushing forward at full speed. There was one moment—I cannot measure it in time—of a vast glare, of a man aghast.

I certainly thought quickly enough to achieve the idea, "I am going to be run down and probably killed." Then came the blow. I felt it on my forehead and across my thighs. But besides the blow there was an impact, a shock, a concussion indescribably violent.

Mario Contasino, the driver of the medium-sized automobile, was on his proper side of the road and perfectly entitled to make the best speed he could, when suddenly a dark figure appeared immediately in front of him. He applied all his brakes and at the same moment, before they could act, he struck a heavy body. Three or four feet from the right-hand wheel lay a black shapeless mass.

He heard a loud cry:

"A man has been killed!"

Meanwhile, I had not lost consciousness for an instant.

Somewhere in the black puddle toward which the passers-by are running there is a small chamber or sanctum wherein all is orderly and undisturbed. There sits enthroned a mind apparently intact and unshaken. Before it is a keyboard of levers or buttons directing the body. Above, a whole series of loudspeakers report the sensations and experiences of the empire controlled from this tiny headquarters. This mind is in possession of the following conclusion:

"I have been run over by a motorcar in America. Here is a real catastrophe. Perhaps it is the end."

The reader will observe from this authentic record that I experienced no emotion of regret or fear. I simply registered facts without, except for a general sense of disaster, the power to moralize upon them.

But now, wave upon wave of convulsive, painful sensations seemed to flood into this small room, preventing thought, paralyzing action, impossible to comprehend.

I had, for instance, no knowledge of whether I was lying on my back, or side, or face. How long this period lasted, I cannot tell. I am told that from the time I was struck down to when I was lifted into a taxicab was perhaps five minutes.

A policeman is bending over me. He has a book, quite a big book, in his hand.

"What is your name?"

"Winston Churchill."

"What is your age?" asked the officer, adhering to his routine.

"Fifty-seven," I replied, and at the same moment this odd

enough thought obtruded itself upon my mind: "How very old to be knocked down in the street by a motor-car. I shall have a very poor chance of getting over it."

I was lifted by perhaps eight or ten persons to the floor of a taxicab. All was in order in my inner sanctum, but I had not, until then, ventured to touch the keyboard of action.

I now saw, as I lay on the floor of the cab, both my hands, very white and covered with blood, lying across my breast. So I decided to give them an order to move their fingers, and at the same time I pulled the levers which affect the toes. Neither hands nor feet took the slightest notice.

I now became for the first time, seriously alarmed. The impression, "Crippled for life," registered itself in the sanctum.

So we rumbled on. And then a most blessed thing happened. I began to experience violent pins and needles in both my upper arms. They hurt intensely, but I did not mind, because at the same time I found my fingers beginning to move in accordance with my will. Almost immediately afterward the toes responded to my orders. Then swiftly, by waves of pins and needles, almost agonizing in their intensity, warmth, life and obedience began to flow back into the whole of my trunk.

By the time we pulled up at the hospital, I had the assurance that, although I might have an arm or a leg or two broken and was certainly bruised and shaken, the whole main structure of my body was sound.

At last we arrive at the hospital, and soon I am on a bed.

Reassuring words are spoken. I see a beloved face. My wife is smiling. In the background there rises the grave, venerable countenance of Bernard Baruch. So I ask:

"Tell me, Baruch, when all is said and done, what is the number of your house?"

"Ten fifty-five."

"How near was I to it when I was smashed up?"

"Not within ten blocks."

Such, in short, were my experiences. I certainly suffered every pang, mental and physical, that a street accident can produce. None is unendurable. There is neither time nor strength for self-pity. There is no room for remorse or fears.

For the rest—live dangerously! Take things as they come! Dread naught! All will be well!

After he had been paid, he invited me to call on him at his suite in the Waldorf. By this time he had almost completely recovered, but had canceled his lecture tour. I expected to stay about fifteen minutes, but we kept talking and drinking a little. The visit lasted two hours—two of the most interesting and informative hours I have ever spent. We spoke of many things that were worrying the world at that time. When I left, it seemed like we were old friends. Subsequently he wrote several articles for us, until he became a world figure.

A prominent publisher was summoned to 10 Downing Street when Winston Churchill was Prime Minister—at 9:30 in the morning. The publisher described this official residence as a rather plain and somewhat shabby house. He was escorted to Sir Winston's room where he found the Prime Minister propped up in a brass bed with a tray in front of him, reading the papers. On the table beside him was a glass with a whisky and soda in it, and he was smoking one of his famous cigars. He turned to the American publisher and said, "Would you like a whisky and soda and a cigar?"

"No, thank you," was the reply.

At the time my friend did not smoke cigars nor imbibe so early in the morning. However, he got thinking about the opportunity and realized he would have to explain to his grandchildren someday that the great man had offered him a drink and cigar and he had declined. So he said, "Sir Winston, could I change my mind about the whisky and soda and cigar?"

"Certainly," replied the Prime Minister. He rang for a man who furnished both.

My friend finished the drink and cigar with some difficulty and told me his stomach curdled for a couple of days thereafter, but at least he had something to tell his grandchildren.

After the last war, I tried to make a deal with Sir Winston for his memoirs. He made an appointment to see me at 5 in the afternoon in his suite at the Waldorf. He was dressed comfortably in his siren suit. His only companion was Frank Clarke, a friend and shipping magnate from Canada. Since I hadn't had a drink, I knew Sir Winston hadn't either. We sat down at a long table, he at the head and I was next to him.

"Will you have a Scotch and soda or a cigar?" he asked me.

I declined although, like my publisher-friend, I was anxious to take one of his famous cigars and put it in my pocket as a souvenir, even though I have no grandchildren.

"You know," he said, "I am now going back to my profession which is writing. It was interrupted for a few years by world events." This was certainly a modest understatement.

"That is what I have come to see you about," I replied. "We are prepared to offer you a guarantee of seven hundred fifty thousand dollars against 60 per cent for the American serial rights to your memoirs."

"That is a handsome amount," he said. "I will consider it."

We talked a little more and then shook hands and I left. It turned out the *New York Times* and *Life Magazine* made him a joint offer of $1,000,000 which, of course, topped ours, and he accepted it.

Sir Winston once had a son-in-law named Vic Oliver, an actor, who was married to his daughter Sarah. They have been divorced for several years. According to reliable reports, Sir Winston disliked Oliver for many reasons, but especially be-

cause he insisted on calling the great man "papa." Shortly after
the end of the war, his son-in-law broke in on Churchill one
day.

"Papa," he said, "who do you think was the greatest states-
man of World War II?"

Without a moment's hesitation, Sir Winston replied,
"Mussolini, because he had the guts to shoot his son-in-law."

The great man has now settled down to a philosophical old
age. He has had a reputation as a great drinker and constant
cigar smoker. Actually, I never saw him consume much alco-
hol or be affected by it. Frequently his cigar is not lit. But the
old gentleman has a good memory. On his 82nd birthday, I
sent him the following cable:

"Congratulations on your birthday. Hope you have many
more."

The newspapers reported he received so many letters and
telegrams he would not be able to acknowledge them. There-
fore, I was surprised when I went to the office the next day
and found the following, signed by Winston Churchill:

"Thank you so much for your kind message."

Recently I was in Versailles and visited the ancient shack
which had housed emperors, kings, and their wives and mis-
tresses. The old fellows went in for fancy ceilings which gave
me a stiff neck looking at them. I suppose the regular tenants
viewed these from their beds. That would be more comfortable.

When we came to the Hall of Mirrors where the peace
treaty was signed after the First World War, I thought of
what the Allies had lost at the peace table. It reminded me of
a speech made later by Churchill in discussing the treaty and
its outcome.

"We had the world in our hands," he said as I recall, "and
we, in our folly, threw it all away."

XIV. BILLY ROSE

YEARS AGO, this little giant came to work for us as a steno-
grapher and secretary. He was always diligent and shortly
won the national championship for speed and accuracy. He
then became secretary to Bernard Baruch while Baruch was
chairman of the War Industries Board during the First World
War.

I hadn't seen Billy for several years when, walking up the
aisle after the first act on an opening night, I saw him in front
of me with his wife then—Eleanor Holm.

"Hello, Billy," I said.

He turned and shook hands. Then he said, "Eleanor, I want
you to meet my old boss."

Not too long afterwards, he began to publish a column in
the newspapers, buying the space, to advertise a trap he was
running called "The Diamond Horseshoe"—a night club aiming mostly at out-of-town patrons. The stuff was funny all right.
I called him up and made an appointment to see him. He had
an apartment on top of the Ziegfeld Theater which had been
built by the great showman, Florenz Ziegfeld. My daughter
and her husband went around with me to call on him one
night. Captain Ellison, my son-in-law, had been a dive bomber
pilot in the Marines in the Pacific and had all sorts of decorations, which he never mentioned.

The apartment was a pretty ornate affair with a great window that faced the stage. Billy drew back the drapes and

171

opened it up so the young couple could look across the audience at the performance, which was *Showboat,* while we talked.

"Billy," I began, "you shouldn't give that column away or pay to have it published. I can sell it."

"For how much?" he demanded, getting right down to business.

He was used to big money, so I hesitated a minute.

"We will pay you 60 per cent of the gross and guarantee you a thousand a week," I said.

"It's a deal," he agreed.

As we left I wasn't sure whether I had been smart or not. However, it proved to be one of the most popular newspaper features in the country and soon became the most widely published. There was some suspicion he had a ghost writer which wasn't true.

John Golden summed it up when he said, "If he had a ghost writer who is that good, he would quit after a couple of weeks and start a column of his own."

Billy wrote many fine pieces, but one I regard as a classic. He had run the Aquacade at the New York World's Fair. This was the big show with Eleanor Holm, whom he afterwards married, as the star. Near the main entrance to the Aquacade was a small exhibit with a sign over the door which read: "Billy Rose's Pet Shop."

Every time Billy went to his great spectacle, he passed this place and found the sign staring him in the face. Finally he decided to get Arthur Garfield Hays, his lawyer, and put a stop to the use of his name to peddle bull frogs, etc. Armed with whatever you need to assert your rights under the circumstances, Rose and his lawyer marched belligerently into the offending establishment.

"I'm Billy Rose," he announced, "and this is my lawyer."

"Oh, yes, I was expecting you, Mr. Rosenberg," replied the pet-shop proprietor. Rosenberg is Billy's real moniker.

"Well," went on Billy, "I want you to stop trading on my name to sell your goldfish. Otherwise, we will take action."

The man reached under the counter and opened a drawer. "You see, I brought my birth certificate," he replied. "I thought you might want to see it."

He handed it over. His square name was Billy Rose. The two callers studied it a minute and then turned to him again.

"How much are your canaries?'" asked Billy.

"Five dollars each," he said.

"Let me have two with a cage." He walked out with his new pets.

Now the sequel to this story is that Rose wrote it as one of his columns which shows, according to my book, he is a big man.

When he first started this feature, it was being published in New York in the now defunct *P.M.* We later transferred it to the *Herald Tribune* which paid $160 a week for the New York territory. It went along fine for a couple of years until Billy began to write some pieces telling what he would do if he were running the Metropolitan Opera. These kidded the management in a lighthearted sort of way. Finally he came through with a rather caustic column for release one Monday. It was too strong a dose for the *Herald Tribune* to swallow. The editors decided to kill it. Mrs. Helen Reid of the *Tribune* was active in the Metropolitan. I didn't know about these developments, since I was out on the Pacific Coast at the time.

When Billy heard his essay had been thrown out, he was sore and sent the piece to the *New York Daily News* as a paid advertisement. Out of courtesy, someone in the business department of the *News* called the *Herald Tribune* on Saturday afternoon to ask if there was any objection to running the ad. An old hand on watch answered, and he probably didn't even know his paper was publishing Rose. He agreed it was okay, and the column appeared in Monday's *News* with all its big circulation.

All hell broke loose. Mrs. Reid was in the Adirondacks and heard about the incident after it was too late to stop the ad. Bill Robinson, then executive vice president of the paper and now chairman of Coca Cola, called me up and demanded I come to see him forthwith. Before I had a chance to open my mouth, he told me what he thought of Rose and me. I tried to explain, but that did not appease him.

"We are canceling the column right away," he announced, "and we won't print another piece by him under any circumstances."

There was a silver lining. I caught a taxi and rode over to the *News* office in East Forty-second Street. I went in to see Dick Clarke, the boss and executive editor.

"How would you like to buy the Billy Rose column?" I asked him.

"Yes, we would," he answered. "For how much?"

"On a two-year contract. Four hundred a week the first year and five hundred the second."

"You've made a deal," he answered.

We signed the contract then and there.

The column might be running yet except for a series of events which may be called "the fell clutch of circumstance." Again I was in California when I received word from the office Billy had disappeared into some hospital, the name of which he had kept a secret. When I returned I found him all right. He had had an operation for a relatively minor ailment, and was at home convalescing. He then lived in a sumptuous house in Beekman Place. He asked me to come up to see him.

He was lying in a big bed of ornate design, and, being a little fellow, you had to follow the cigarette smoke in order to find him. He sat up and handed me a column while the nurse lit another cigarette for him.

"Here's my swan song," he said.

"What do you mean?" I asked surprised.

"I'm through. I don't want to write any more. Dr. Evan-Evans has told me I need a rest. My blood pressure is down. All I want to do is go to Florida and lie in the sun on the beach with Eleanor for three months."

This sudden decision irritated me a little, so I decided to diagnose his case.

"I know what is the matter with you," I said. "You have climacterics."

He looked puzzled. "What the hell is that?" he demanded.

I explained, but I couldn't persuade him to continue his column.

Then he ran into some marital complications which attracted a good deal of attention. These resulted in his marrying a very beautiful lady named Joyce Mathews with whom I hope he will live happily ever after. Too late. Since that sentimental line was originally written, they have been divorced.

A year or so later, we revived his column but it never had the verve of the first time around. Editors of papers in the Bible Belt shied away from it because of the unfavorable publicity at the time of Billy's splitup with Eleanor. The feature ran for about a year when he again tired of it.

Today Billy lives in one of the great mansions of New York in the East Nineties. We dined there one night with pleasant companions, including Richard Rodgers, the great composer. Rose showed us through. He has almost as much art as the Metropolitan Museum. He had fitted up an office like a broker's with a ticker and all the paraphernalia. He plays the market successfully, I am sure. He is a very wealthy man. He claims he is happy. When I suggest he might resume writing his column, he throws up his hands in dismay.

"Why should I struggle?" he says. "I don't need the money."

"It might be fun," I suggest.

"No, it would be work for me."

This supports my view that writers always do best when they are hungry.

Rose is one of the most interesting characters I have ever met and one of the smartest. One episode I recall concerned Rose and *The New Yorker*, then edited by Harold Ross. Ross was also an old friend of mine, dating back to when he worked on *The Stars and Stripes* during the First World War. He was brilliant, sardonic, humorous and frank, but no Marilyn Monroe or Clark Gable when it came to looks. He had a big forehead and projecting teeth which were spread far apart. However, he married three beautiful women and wound up with stomach ulcers which soured him a good deal—the ulcers and not the wives.

The New Yorker published a profile of Rose which was far from flattering. It burned Billy up, so he wrote Ross a letter which read somewhat as follows:

"Of course, I could publish a column about you, but I don't wish to waste my big circulation on it. We have probably a hundred times more readers than your magazine. However, I just want to say in closing you are probably the only man in New York who can eat a tomato through a tennis racket."

When Billy Rose took a three-month leave of absence from writing his column to go around the world, I modestly offered to try to fill in. One of the pieces I wrote is a true story about Captain Eddie Rickenbacker. It subsequently appeared in

The Reader's Digest, and I got paid $400 for it. I take the liberty of quoting it as follows:

Circumstantial Evidence

The big Eastern Air Lines plane was making its final approach for a landing at New York's La Guardia Field.

"Wheels down, Jack?" asked the Captain in the routine procedure.

The co-pilot looked at the instrument panel, then as a check he stuck his head out the window to see whether the landing gear was in place. As he did so, his cap blew off. Bareheaded, he replied, "Everything's okay," and the plane made a routine landing. It was 6:30 in the morning.

Joe Higgins was the driver of a milk truck on Long Island and he had a bride and a little house in Queen's Village, near La Guardia. He got this all-night job shortly after his marriage to the girl he had dreamed about while advancing with the Third Army through France.

The early morning hours are lonely and full of shadows, and Joe sometimes used to brood about what his wife was doing. He had just read an article called "Tips on a Happy Marriage" which suggested that husbands should work in the daytime and stay home at night. Joe was turning these matters over in his mind when he arrived home at 7 a.m.

As he reached for his key, an object on the stoop caught his eye and he picked it up. It was a cap with the Eastern Air Lines insignia. He opened the door, stomped in, and roared, "What were you doing last night?" Surprised, Jane answered, "I went to the movies, and then came home to bed."

"You didn't do any flying—high flying?" demanded her husband. He threw the pilot's cap on the bed. "Your friend left his card on the front porch. Even his name is inside it—John Bell."

Jane stared in wonder at the hat as her husband turned toward the front door. "You can keep it as a souvenir!" he shouted. "I'm through!" He slammed the door and was gone.

Jane had heard of Captain Eddie Rickenbacker, then president of Eastern, an old flier himself and a very gallant guy. She wrote a letter explaining what had happened, rushed to the New York offices and handed it to Rick's secretary along with the pilot's cap.

Rick, never a man to let grass grow under his feet, had Jane Higgins whisked to La Guardia, where the head of operations produced the flight log and, shortly afterward, Pilot Bell. They all hustled to the Higginses' home and found Joe packing. Of course he realized he was wrong when he saw the log and heard how the pilot had lost his cap. Bell got his hat back and Joe Higgins his bride, delivered in a fade-out clinch.

"No more sour milk, honey," he said happily. "But anyway, I'm going to apply for a daytime job."

Now when I wrote this originally I put a trick ending on it. The final paragraph divulged that the bride a year later got a divorce from the milkman and married a pilot in United Airlines. The moral was: "Never give your wife an idea." However, the *Digest* editors thought it should have a happy ending, as you can see, and perhaps it should for they are bright young men.

XV. LITERARY GIANTS

BILL SHEPHERD, the *Collier's* correspondent, got around. He made his headquarters near Washington Square when in New York and had his hair cut in the old Brevoort Hotel on lower Fifth Avenue. It turned out his barber used to trim Mark Twain's white locks. One day the barber was telling some of his experiences with the great humorist, and he finally admitted, reluctantly, he had saved some of the writer's hair. Shepherd was impressed.

"You mean you've got it here?" he asked.

The barber produced a small glass from the safe and showed him. There followed some negotiations and a larger tip, and Bill departed the proud possessor of twelve strands in his wallet. Shortly afterwards, he was sent to El Paso, because one of the many revolutions in Mexico of that period was going on. Shepherd was in a grog shop with Chris Hagerty of the A.P. one evening when they began talking about Mark Twain.

It turned out both were great admirers of the author. They had a couple more drinks, and then Shepherd's tongue loosened, and he told his companion about acquiring the hairs.

"You don't mean to say you have got them with you?" demanded Hagerty.

Shepherd drew out his wallet. Carefully he unwrapped the precious trophies and laid them on the table. The official count showed there were still twelve.

"How about giving me six?" said the A.P. man.

Bill resisted this demand, considering it exorbitant. Then Hagerty tried a new tack.

179

"You know my old father back in Chicago worshiped Mark Twain," pleaded Hagerty. "If I could go back home and tell him I met a man with his hair and didn't bring him any, he won't let me in the house. Give me three for him and three for myself."

Just then Bill Willis, correspondent of the old *New York Herald*, came in and saw the hairs on the table. Not realizing or caring about their value or source, he took a deep breath and blew them to hell and gone. Hagerty and Shepherd jumped up and chased him out of the joint and down the street. They came back sadly and had waiters sweeping around in the sawdust trying to recover the missing trophies, but none was found. It took Willis a couple of days to get back to town. The incident broke up a good friendship for at least a week.

This is by way of introduction to some anecdotes about two great writers I have known—Booth Tarkington and Ernest Hemingway. Tark was something of a legend in his own lifetime, just as Hemingway is now.

The great George M. Cohan told me this story:

In his early days, Tarkington was ambidextrous when it came to drinking, but always a gentleman. He would go into a restaurant wearing a pair of white gloves and leave them on the table after the meal. The head waiter would pick them up.

"You've forgotten these, Mr. Tarkington," he would say.

"No, thanks," Tark would answer. "I only wear them once."

It was my good fortune to know Tark and to visit him at his summer place in Kennebunkport, Maine. Among the many stories about him, one concerns the night he was in the Lambs Club with an actor named Roy Atwell. It seems both had been drinking, and the Thespian was in love with a girl playing in a show called *Havana* at the Casino Theater, located at Broad-

way and Thirty-ninth Street, only a stone's throw away. Atwell had had a row with his young lady and wanted to see her
to make it up. In short, he was carrying a well-lit torch for her.
He kept muttering in his cups he wanted to go to "Havana."
Finally Tark got fed up.

"If you want to go to Havana, I'll see what I can do," he
said.

He stepped out, called up the Ward Line, and found there
was a ship sailing early in the morning. He engaged a passage.
He returned to the table to find his friend gloomy and still
muttering about going to "Havana."

"Don't worry a minute," said Tark. "I have everything all
fixed up."

He helped Atwell outside to a taxi and loaded him in. Then
he directed the driver to go to the pier. The actor by this time
didn't know whether he was heading for Havana or Dubuque.
Tark tucked him into his berth and stuck his ticket under the
pillow, feeling like a Boy Scout who has done a good deed.
The next morning surprised the hell out of Atwell. When he
awoke, he looked out the porthole to find he was at sea. He
rang for the steward.

"Where am I?" he demanded.

"On the S.S. *Morro Castle,* bound for Havana," came the
reply.

"Good God," exclaimed the actor, "and I only wanted to
go to Broadway and Thirty-ninth Street."

How he got back and what became of the girl this writer
does not know.

Tark had a man working for him in Maine, a real plain
Yankee named Jed. He was a handy fellow and among other
things drove the car, frequently with Mrs. Tarkington in it.
She thought he ought at least to have a chauffeur's cap in this
stylish community. Tark agreed, so the next time he went to

Boston he bought two, one for himself. After his return, he wore his around for two or three days. Then he produced the one for his man. Jed looked at the cap carefully and tried it on.

"What's that hat?" asked Jed.

"Oh, a cap for fishing, yachting, golf," answered Tark. "I bought one for myself, too."

"Don't think I want it," replied Jed. "Looks like a chauffeur's cap to me."

He continued to wear his old straw when he drove. Tark pointed to two hats, gathering dust in the closet.

"Anyone can have those," he concluded, "who has an automobile and a chauffeur who will wear one."

Julian Street, an intimate friend, related many stories of their stay in Paris. I will try to pick up one little nugget, realizing I won't do it justice. Tark and his friends were gathered in a Montmartre café when an obnoxious American character became annoying with his dull stories and bad behavior. Quietly slipping out, Tark found an understanding and congenial gendarme. By the proper approach, which meant giving him a fistful of francs, the two exchanged costumes in a convenient alley. Returning, with fierce gestures and his baton, Tark quickly cleared the whole place, except for his friends, and paid the proprietor for the privilege.

"I had to do it to get rid of that nuisance," he remarked with great satisfaction as the real gendarme, disguised as an American author, joined them.

It was in later years, when the water wagon was his favorite vehicle, I visited him again in Kennebunkport. He was still just as good a storyteller. He introduced me to a man one day named Cosy Noble, a forlorn figure.

"He used to be a big editor in San Francisco," explained my host, "when Rudyard Kipling came through the town and offered him some stories. He rejected them as no good. After the great author got to be a world figure, Cosy became famous as the man who turned Kipling down. He has been living up here alone and brooding about it ever since."

We certainly did no brooding at the North American Newspaper Alliance when Ernest Hemingway approached us, after the Spanish Civil War had started, and said he wanted to attend in a ringside seat. We made a deal to pay him $500 per story, and he took care of his own expenses. It worked all right for us and for him, too, I guess, for we have been pretty good friends ever since.

As usual, he did an outstanding job. It wasn't very long ago I was looking over some of his stories—20 years after the Spanish Civil War. One of our bright young men thought of putting out two or three again, but I said not without Hemingway's consent. I called him in Havana and explained what I wanted.

"No, don't do that, Jack," he said. "Those are old stories, and I don't wish them published now."

"Sure, that's all right," I answered. "Whatever you say goes. How are you?"

"Fine," he said. "Haven't had a drink in five months."

"Why is that?" I asked.

"So I'll live longer," he replied.

"Why do you want to live longer?"

"To have more fun."

"Are you having more fun?"

"Don't know yet. Haven't had time to find out."

One of my spies, who was in Havana later, reported he had slipped off the water wagon.

Jimmie Lardner, Ring's second son, was working on the Paris edition of the *Herald Tribune*. He was sent to Spain by his boss to cover the war, but when he arrived, he found the New York office had assigned Vincent Sheean to the same job. Young Lardner was so chagrined he cabled his resignation and joined the Lincoln Brigade. He was the last man killed in that outfit, being shot the final night it was in the line.

I was worried about this since Ring Lardner was an old friend of mine and I had known Jimmie from boyhood. When Hemingway returned to the United States, I said to him, "Did you have anything to do with Jimmie Lardner going into the Lincoln Brigade?"

"Hell, no," he replied. "I sat up all one night, trying to talk him out of it."

After he returned from his first trip to the Spanish War, I gave him a lunch in the wine cellar of the St. Regis Hotel in New York—a very nice place with pleasant surroundings. He attracted a crowd of fine guests. After the repast, if that's the right word, Hemingway, Grantland Rice, and I were walking down Fifth Avenue. He had just published a book called *To Have and Have Not,* about Key West fishermen and other tough characters. Rice and I turned literary critics.

"Why do you put all those four-letter words in your book?" one of us asked him.

"Because it's the way they talk," he answered. "I've got to write that way."

We said nothing more about it. He silenced us with his answer.

Hemingway didn't always have a downhill pull. One of his first stories was "Fifty Grand." It was kicked around from one editor to another. Bill Lengel was then working for Ray Long, boss man of the *Cosmopolitan Magazine.* Lengel met Hemingway in Paris and read the manuscript. He sent it along to New York recommending it. Long turned it down because there was "no woman interest." A few years ago I wrote

Ernest, asking him for the details. It was when I was filling in
for Billy Rose on his column. Shortly, I got a reply from which
I will quote in part:

> It made me happy to get your letter and know you were
> fine and being a columnist. [There may be a touch of sarcasm
> in that last crack.—Ed. Note.]
>
> Maybe it was a good idea for Billy Rose to lay off for a while,
> as he will get a lot of stuff moving around. Being a columnist
> is like having to pitch every day. Don't you do too much of it?
>
> On the anecdote for the column thing: Bill Lengel sent
> "Fifty Grand" to Ray Long who turned it down for the reasons
> you stated. He offered to publish it if I would put some woman
> interest in it. I told him I thought the woman interest was
> present but off stage.
>
> Sun also got kicked around. [He refers to his successful book,
> The Sun Also Rises]. But everything beforehand did. Scrib-
> ner's had "Fifty Grand" and offered to publish it for $250 if I
> would cut fifteen hundred words out of it. I said if you cut any
> word, it would not make sense. I had cut it already. They gave
> it to a bright boy named A——— D——— to cut. [Name
> disguised since this gent holds an important editorial job now.
> —Ed. Note.] He was assistant to Bridges, the editor of the
> magazine, and he dutifully cut it. I then showed them how it
> did not make sense. Very bright boy.
>
> Ned Weeks of Atlantic picked it up, and old Ellery Sedgwick
> published in Atlantic Monthly (without cutting or woman
> interest) and paid me $500, I think.
>
> [This is rated as one of the best two fight short stories of re-
> cent years, the other being "Champion" by Ring Lardner.—Ed.
> Note.]
>
> If you go down to Hobe Sound, give my best to Gene and
> Polly Tunney and Phil Barry and his wife. Tell Gene his old
> golf caddy is now champion of Brioni. I won't get back to
> Cuba until second week in May.
>
> What can you cook up as an anecdote? Ask Mike Lerner

about the time I fought a Negro named Willard Saunders at Bimini. Mike was there. You could call him up and get the story. It is sort of a funny story, but rather you got it from Mike than me. If you know Ben Finney, ask him about some of the old Bimini fights. Or call up George Brown, who has a gymnasium at 225 West 57th and is in the phone book. He knows some funny stories. He used to train Greb. You could do a good piece on George. He knows everything about what goes on in town. If you go to see him, give him my best. I'm truly fond of him, and he is one of the truly best people I know in town.

Do you know Hugh Casey, or Kirby Higbe or Larry French, or Augie Galan? If you see any of them, ask them about the old days in Havana. We used to have a lot of fun. [These gents were all Big League ballplayers.]

Anyway good luck, Jack, and, if you are really stuck for anecdotes, will knock off writing novel and bang some out for you. My very best to your wife and lovely daughter.

This is a typical Hemingway letter if he likes you. He was willing to interrupt writing his novel to give me some ammunition. And speaking of my daughter, here is an anecdote I think worth putting in:

When she was fifteen or sixteen, Ernest came to see me one afternoon at our New York apartment to talk about his trip to Spain. My daughter was one of his many admirers. After we had finished our conversation, I opened the door to find her lying flat on her stomach peeking through the crack under the door. I introduced her to Hemingway, and he treated her like a great lady. Later they came to be quite good friends. She is dead now, her end coming tragically and suddenly.

I did go to see George Brown as Hemingway suggested and spent a very entertaining and profitable two hours. He told me many stories, some of which I have forgotten and some I don't feel I should repeat. He admired Ernest very much.

"He was a wonder—great physical stamina," he declared. "You know Shipwreck Kelly, the old football star, who married Brenda Fraser. Well, he boxed with Hemingway one time in Havana and got knocked out for his pains. He wanted revenge so he started training for a return bout. He would come here almost every day and work out with me and others. Finally Ernest arrived in town, not knowing anything about these preparations. Of course, when he hit New York, he touched the high spots.

"Shipwreck invited him to box with him here one afternoon. Hemingway had been up most of the night drinking champagne and anything else which came along. He was like Harry Greb that way. I used to train him, you know. Well, Kelly was ready and in fine shape the next afternoon. The bout started and Ernest took a couple of hard punches before he cooled him again in a couple of rounds. Then he helped himself to a drink, put on his clothes and left, stopping on the way out to shake hands with his opponent who gave up after that."

One of my proudest possessions is a copy of *For Whom the Bell Tolls* which the author sent me. On the fly leaf he wrote:

To Jack Wheeler
    Who gave me the chance to go to that war.
                                 Ernest Hemingway.

XVI. BROADWAY AND OFF

My musical and theatrical career was brief. Although an Epis-
copalean, I became a boy soprano in the Presbyterian church
choir where there was an opening. My salary was $1.25 a
month which seemed to me pretty liberal considering my
performance—probably overpaid.

One summer day the choirmaster took us on a picnic to the
Croton River, and part of the day we spent swimming. Suddenly to my surprise I saw a boy named Richard Gardner
struggling in the water, gasping and sinking. He was near the
side of a rowboat, so I dove in, grabbed him by the hair, and
hauled him to the boat where we shoved him aboard. He
revived, and I turned out to be quite a hero for about half an
hour.

That is the only time I ever actually saved anyone from
drowning. However, I used to have a friend at East Hampton,
Ronnie, who was a lifesaver. One summer he gave me a job
without pay as his assistant. The understanding was I should
rescue all good-looking girls who got into trouble if they were
not in the water above their knees and not over 30.

An unfortunate incident ended my singing engagement. It
was customary to hold our rehearsal once a week, following
which the adult quartet practiced. In this group was a rather
obnoxious tenor with a mustache. He also wore a high hat.
One night after we were dismissed, we waited outside armed
with snowballs. When he appeared, we let him have it and
several shots hit his topper, the target. We all promptly got
fired.

My next public appearance occurred while I was in college and got a job as a super at the Metropolitan Opera. I appeared in several performances but, of course, did no singing. In one opera we carried on the great Caruso in a sedan chair. In another the beautiful Geraldine Farrar appeared. She was the daughter of a Big League first baseman, Sid Farrar, a pretty fair ballplayer.

Robert Mantell was playing Shakespeare in the old Harlem Opera House. He was a well-known ham of those days. The Shakespearian company needed a group of supers, and several of us volunteered, including a tough guy named One Lung Lee and Eddie Collins, who later became a Big League baseman. Now in this particular show, which might have been *Henry, the Eighth,* but I am not sure, there was a battle with old-fashioned weapons. Regular performers made up one army, and we were on the losing side and had to retreat on signal. All went well for the first three evenings. Then I think it was One Lung Lee who said, "Boys, I am tired of being a loser every night. Let's go after them."

We did, and chased the regulars off the stage. Of course, it loused up the plot, and they had to ring down the curtain. We were all run out of the theater, and this was my last stage appearance. Luckily we had gotten paid after each performance.

My next brush with the theater came on the way to the World Series in 1919. To while away the hours on the train, Bud Fisher and I told the story of our Mexican adventures to Porter Emerson Browne, who made a play out of them called *The Bad Man,* a great success in which Holbrook Blinn starred. Browne had never in his life even been to Mexico. And we got none of the royalties.

One of the anecdotes going the rounds in those early days concerned John Barrymore. Jack had the reputation of being a great actor, but irresponsible and unreliable, especially in his younger days. He also had many love affairs in spite of the fact that he was slovenly in his habits. He was playing in San Francisco when the big earthquake rocked and burned the town at about 4 in the morning. Barrymore had just gone to bed, and was thrown by the shock into the bathtub.

According to the story, he got up and dressed and rushed downtown. By this time the soldiers from the Presidio had taken over. One handed Barrymore a shovel and told him to get busy helping to clean up the debris. By way of emphasis, he jabbed a bayonet in his behind, so Jack went to work with the rest. When his uncle, the great actor, John Drew, heard about this he commented: "It takes a convulsion of nature to get Jack to take a bath, and the United States Army to put him to work."

It was my good luck as a young man to meet John Golden, the theatrical producer and song writer. He took me to lunch one day at the Astor Hotel, and after we sat down in the men's grill, he fished some mail out of his pocket and then groped around for his glasses. He couldn't find them, so he beckoned to the head waiter.

"Max," he said, "lend me your glasses so I can read my mail."

The waiter obliged. When Mr. Golden finished reading he turned to me and said, "I'll tell you a story. The first time Charles Frohman went to London years ago, he stopped at the Savoy Hotel. He rang for his breakfast, and a waiter responded, standing stiffly by the door.

" 'Good morning,' said Frohman, 'I'm going to be here for two weeks. I eat my breakfast at the same time every day— 8:30—the same thing, half a grapefruit, two soft-boiled eggs, three minutes, dry toast and coffee. I am not interested in the weather and I hate conversation in the morning.'

" 'Very good, sir,' replied the waiter.

"It proved to be a very delightful stay for the celebrated theatrical producer. Promptly at 8:30 would come a knock on the door. The waiter would walk in and set the breakfast down and leave without opening his trap. He got a big tip when Frohman left.

"However, after his return to New York, Frohman couldn't stop boasting about this perfect servitor he had found in London. He was then living in White Plains with Charlie Dillingham, both bachelors. Frohman never married. Some of his friends got an idea which was to import the Savoy waiter as a surprise birthday present. They sneaked him into the country and at 8:30 on Frohman's birthday morning, there came a knock on his bedroom door.

" 'Come in,' yelled Frohman.

"In walked the waiter with the breakfast tray which he set down and turned on his heel and left without a word. They made him the major domo to run their place, and everything went smoothly until Dillingham decided to get married. When his bride moved in, she found the perfect servant had been cheating them right and left and splitting the take with the grocer, the butcher, and other tradesmen. Reluctantly, they fired the fellow. But Dillingham and Frohman had a closed-door session and got him a job here at the Astor. There he is right now, the man who loaned me his glasses." John handed them back.

"Thank you, Max," he said.

Golden had a quick wit. One of the few lousy shows of his professional career was playing at his theater years ago. A friend came to him for advice.

"John," he said, "I want to take a lady who is not related to me by marriage out for the evening. Where can we go so no one will see us?"

"Here are a couple of tickets for my show," Golden answered, reaching into his pocket. "Take her there. You'll be safe. It's a bust."

For the most part, however, John Golden was one of Broadway's most successful producers. One hot August day, he was starting for a vacation in Nantucket with Charles Dillingham and some other theatrical bigshots. They were leaving the Lambs Club with all the paraphernalia—golf clubs, tennis rackets, etc.—when they passed Jack Hazard, then a down-at-the-heels actor wearing a derby hat and a hangover.

"Where are the millionaires going?" he asked sarcastically.

"To Nantucket," replied Golden.

"Why don't you take me with you?"

"What for?"

"Because I can make you laugh."

"Tell you what I'll do. You get in the taxi and ride as far as Grand Central Station. If you even make me smile, I'll buy you a ticket on the train to Wood's Hole. If you give me a laugh en route, you are on the boat to Nantucket."

Hazard was successful and found himself on the high seas. In the bar of the steamer, he said to Golden, "I have an idea for a show."

He told him the story of *Turn to the Right*. When Hazard got to the part in the second act where the likable crooks give the old lady her mortgage money and then wait outside the house to rob the miser, Golden shook his hand.

"You have sold a show," he said.

It turned out to be a big hit which ran for years on Broadway and later was sold to the movies for $250,000—a huge sum for those days.

Golden always contended that hits had to be built around a single idea. He was talking one day about the importance of titles to shows. Lawrence Perry, the sports writer and theatrical critic, and I were his two auditors.

"I don't think the name makes any difference," insisted John. "When we were producing *Lightnin'* with Frank Bacon, I was scared to death. I was afraid people, especially women, would stay away, because they would think it was about a thunderstorm. It was one of my biggest hits. The two fellers who wrote and produced *Seven Year Itch* worked in my office. I thought it was a lousy title, but look at the crowds trying to buy tickets at the box office. That's what counts."

"The only title I remember which made me go see the show years ago," volunteered Mr. Perry, "was *Getting Gertie's Garter.*"

John Golden used to tell this story:

"When I was a young fellow, I met John L. Sullivan, then the heavyweight champion of the world. I went into a Broadway saloon and someone introduced me. I put out my hand and said, 'Glad to meet you, Mr. Sullivan.'

"I was smoking a big cigar which was in the corner of my mouth. He reached over his big ham of a hand and snatched it from between my teeth. He stuck it in his mouth and took two or three puffs and then handed it back to me.

"'There you are,' he said, 'and remember I wouldn't do that for every sonofabitch.'"

John Golden had a friend who kept a camp in the Adirondacks and frequently went there for a rest. He invited Golden several times, but he declined, not caring much for the rough life.

"How long do you generally stay?" asked the theatrical producer.

"Well," the friend answered, "I have a housekeeper who is

about sixty-five years old. She wears a wig and false teeth and has a harelip. She's no Lillian Russell. When she begins to look good to me, I pack up and come back."

Another bit about John Golden. He pretended to be a great admirer of my wife whom he called "Shiftless." She got the name because she failed to put some stone crabs out to cool which I had collected at great risk to hands and fingers. I told her she was shiftless, and she began to weep, like most women do in a pinch. We met Golden.

"What have you done to Tee?" he demanded, noticing her dabbing her eyes.

"I called her 'Shiftless,' " I explained. He began to laugh, but it stuck.

He would call me. "How is Shiftless this morning?" he would ask.

"In a bad humor up to noon. If you don't believe me, telephone her and pretend you're me."

He was a great imitator. When he got her on the wire, he said in my grave tones, "What do you mean by keeping that number busy all morning?"

For a minute she thought it was her husband and responded accordingly. He called back to report the results and confirm the verdict.

One day Golden turned to me in front of my wife.

"I'll give you fifty thousand dollars and May for Tee," he offered. Needless to explain, May was his wife.

"Leave May out, and you've got a deal," I replied. "I don't want to get married any more." So the transaction never came off, even though my missus liked the idea and often reminds me of the offer.

Percy Hammond was one of the great dramatic critics of

his day. He went to see an opening of a musical comedy years ago. He didn't think much of the show, and his comment was: "The producer should realize that the female knee is a joint and not a source of entertainment."

John Golden and Percy Hammond were warm friends after he came to the *New York Herald Tribune* after several years as drama critic for the *Chicago Tribune*. Golden invited Hammond to spend the week end at his place in Bayside, Long Island, but Golden had a show opening on Friday night. Hammond accepted on the condition John would wait for him three-quarters of an hour while he wrote his review. After the final curtain, the dramatic critic walked up the aisle and found the producer standing in the back of the theater.

"You won't have to wait long, John," he said. "It's such a stinker, I can turn out my story in ten minutes."

"Okay," replied Golden, "but I am going to call a rehearsal right now if it's that bad."

As a result, Hammond had to sit around and wait until 2 in the morning before Golden gave up his rehearsal and was ready to leave for Long Island.

One entertainment spectacle that was even more prolonged than Golden's rehearsal was the six-day bicycle race, which I covered as a cub reporter. The race was held in the old Madison Square Garden, where Stanford White was shot by Harry Thaw. It was a one-man affair, and the contestants kept going for six days each on his own, with little rest, occasionally getting a nap on a cot by the trackside.

The affair was run by Powers and Pollok, a couple of shifty promoters. The race attracted big crowds. Many would come in at 1 or 2 o'clock in the morning. For the price of admission, you could stay as long as you wished, and a lot slept there. The story is that the two promoters sold the pickpocket concession, which proved to be profitable all around, except to the spectators.

A different type of theatrical promotion involved one of the most dignified gentlemen I have ever known—Victor Lawson, owner and publisher of the *Chicago Daily News*. He was old-fashioned and wore a long square-cut morning coat, nearly down to his knees, such as small-town undertakers used to feature as part of their professional uniforms. He didn't drink or smoke and never published a paper on Sunday, although at one time he ran a morning—the *Chicago Record Herald*.

He did a lot of work himself. In his plain office he had a long table and a desk. He tried to read all the serials and other trimmings which went into the paper. The result was that a great collection of books would pile up on his table, as well as all the other debris of the business. When he ran out of space, he bought a new table.

At the beginning of the First World War, a correspondent named E. Alexander Powell, a bit of a faker, came back from France with a collection of films showing some front-line battle scenes. The picture was called *Fighting in France,* and Powell reported the French Government had given it to him as a reward for his excellent reporting. The idea was to get a newspaper in each city to sponsor and promote these films while Morris Gest, the theatrical producer, made the arrangements for theaters and Powell lectured.

The first I heard about the project was when Florence White, then general manager of the old *World,* called me down to his office one day and asked me to try to work out a deal with Gest and Powell. The *World* agreed to sponsor the films in New York. I went to see Gest, who was a great showman. He had an ostentatious and luxurious office. I explained to him what I wanted.

"But we were up at Mr. Hearst's apartment until 3 o'clock this morning, running the films for him. He agreed to make a deal to back them," he said.

"You know he has the reputation of being pro-German," I answered. "You'll make a great hit with the French I guess if *he* is connected with them."

After considerable effort I talked Powell and Gest out of the Hearst deal when I assured them the *World* would go along in New York. I reported my success to Mr. White, who was delighted. The next day I was lunching with Frederick Palmer, the old war-horse correspondent, and told him about the project. He was surprised.

"Why, anyone can get prints of those pictures," he said. "The French give them away for publicity. I have some I am going to use with my lecture."

This disclosure startled the hell out of me. I knew the Hearst people were sore and would do anything to put our show on the bum, so I urged Gest to get going, explaining why. But he was a temperamental artist and held off until he could lease the right theater and steam up the proper publicity. In the meantime, Eddie Hatrick, a smart fellow who ran the Hearst movie business, found out where we were having our prints made and bribed one of the hands to make a duplicate negative.

That set off the fireworks. Before we knew it our competitors had hired a Broadway theater and were advertising *Fighting for France*. Our sluggish impressario finally got under way, and we opened up our rival attraction—*Fighting in France*. Both were the same except for the ads. In the meantime, Mr. Lawson came to town, and Mr. Gest and I took him to dinner and to see the show. Then we went back to Gest's office where the carpet was so thick you would sink in up to your ankles and the lighting so dim you couldn't read the fine print in a contract.

We urged Mr. Lawson to sponsor the film in Chicago, backing it with his powerful *Daily News*. At first he wasn't too much impressed, although he didn't know what had gone on behind the scenes with the Hearst forces. Finally Gest pulled open a desk drawer and produced a photograph of a couple of young fellows in Russian uniforms. He showed it to Mr. Lawson and began to cry.

"It isn't the money I care about, Mr. Lawson," he said. "But God knows where those two boys are tonight. They are my brothers."

I started to weep a little too, and Mr. Lawson's eyes were misty.

"Yes," he agreed. "I'll back it in Chicago."

I went down to the street with him to get him a cab. Then I returned to find Morris Gest sitting with his feet cocked up on his desk smoking a cigarette.

"How did I do, Jack? All right?" he asked.

"Where did you get the picture?" I demanded.

He laughed and put it back in his desk—for future use, I suppose.

The *Chicago News* in its circulation department had fellows just as tough as those on the Hearst papers, and both played plenty rough. Hardly anybody saw either show in Chicago. Each rival would station his roughnecks at the entrance to the theater and bounce out the patrons who tried to buy tickets. The venture was a complete flop all around.

XVII. PRESIDENTS, VICE-PRESIDENTS, AND ALSO-RANS

AFTER Woodrow Wilson died, George Doran, then a prominent book publisher, called me up one day.

"I have two hundred and twenty-four letters Wilson wrote to Mrs. Peck," he announced. "I am going to publish them in a book, but I would like to sell you the serial rights first." I was then the editor of *Liberty Magazine*.

"I doubt it," I answered. "We are a new publication just starting. While I'm no great admirer of Wilson, he died a martyr and people knelt in the snow and prayed in front of his house."

"These are not scandalous," the publisher assured me. "I will send them down and let you look at them."

He did. Most were typewritten, and some were as long as 1500 words. Mrs. Peck was a lady about whom there had been whisperings the first time Wilson ran for President. A few Republicans referred to him as "Peck's bad boy." Anyway, I read these mash notes carefully and they were characteristic of Woodrow—not exactly red hot. Occasionally, he would catch himself and add, "Ellen and I send our warmest regards." Ellen was Wilson's first wife, and the chances are she didn't know anything about sending her regards.

The situation warmed up a little after his wife's death. To me the most interesting letter was the one he wrote her announcing he was going to marry Mrs. Galt, the widow of a rich Washington jeweler. As I recall, it went something like this: "I know you will rejoice with me in my wonderful news and happiness. I am going to marry a beautiful lady, Mrs. Galt."

You could read between the lines and see he was saying to himself, "I hope to God she won't sue me for breach of promise."

As a matter of fact, there was a report that one of Wilson's wealthy friends paid her $200,000 to keep her trap shut.

Anyway, I decided to reject the letters without even asking the price and so informed Doran.

Captain Patterson was then living in Chicago, but spending about a week every month in New York. He popped into the office one day. I couldn't keep my big mouth closed.

"Captain," I began, "I have just turned down two hundred and twenty-four letters Woodrow Wilson wrote to Mrs. Peck."

We went on and talked about something else. Then he came back to it abruptly.

"I think you had better buy those letters," he said. "They ought to get circulation." I insisted it would make a bad impression.

"Go ahead and buy them," he decided.

I called up George Doran. "How much do you want for those Wilson letters?" I asked.

"Fifty thousand dollars," he answered without pausing to catch his breath.

"It's too much. I'll give you twenty-five thousand."

He turned it down. In the meantime, William Fields, a very fine gentleman who was general manager of the *News*, and I worked on Captain Patterson. We finally got him to change his mind about buying the letters. Four or five days later Doran called me.

"I've decided to accept that offer of twenty-five thousand," he said.

"It's too late, George," I replied. "We have gotten the boss to agree with us."

These mash notes were never printed. Mrs. Wilson got a permanent injunction in a Federal Court in Washington preventing their publication on an old principle of English law that letters for publication purposes belong to the author or his heirs, not to the recipient. George Doran had paid $11,000 for the letters and it all went down the drain.

Subsequently, William Allen White wrote a book about Wilson. He devoted a chapter to this alleged romance, saying no biography would be complete without including Mary Allen Peck Hurlburt. He skimmed off the cream. We bought the rights and picked up a lot of sales because circulation manager Annenberg cooked up an ad which said in big type: "Those Whisperings about Woodrow Wilson's Love Affairs."

My friend William Allen White was sore as hell about it, but I passed the buck.

One of my most interesting days was spent with Lloyd George at his country place in Churt outside of London in 1933. He had just written his memoirs, and I wanted to discuss the American serial rights. I spent the morning going through his manuscript which dragged a good deal and didn't give L.G. any the worst of it either—and why should it? Then we had a sumptuous English lunch and talked for two or three hours in the afternoon. I asked him about Woodrow Wilson at the Peace Conference. He was rather scornful.

"You see," he explained, "he didn't know world politics. He was a dreamer ahead of his time."

"Well, Clemenceau and you got him in between you and gave him the squeeze play," I suggested.

He smiled, but had nothing more to say. We did not make a deal on the memoirs.

A canny trader who never got over his Yankee thrift was President Calvin Coolidge. During one summer while he was in the White House, he spent his vacation in the Adirondacks at a place called White Pine Camp.

Bruce Barton had helped Coolidge to the Vice Presidential nomination, and knew him well. He was welcome at the camp, and an exclusive interview was arranged.

The President made his headquarters in a small, bare room over the boathouse, furnished with a roll-top desk and a couple of straight chairs. When he arrived in the morning, he consulted his secretary, Ted Clark, about any urgent business.

"I have a telegram from Charles Evans Hughes, Secretary of State," announced Mr. Clark in the presence of Barton, "saying the Queen of Rumania wishes to pay a visit to the United States, and he wants to know if you approve."

Without any hesitation Coolidge replied, "Tell him it is all right with me so long as there is a thorough understanding she is to pay her own expenses."

He was the kind of a President who would save the taxpayers' money and his own.

Kent Cooper, then general manager of the Associated Press, told me the following tale. It seems Coolidge had a caller who was a little long-winded and was wearing out his welcome. Finally his visitor said, "Mr. President, if I could take home the band of one of your cigars as a souvenir, I would be everlastingly grateful."

Coolidge reached down and pulled open a drawer in his desk, producing a box of cigars. He carefully picked the band off one and put the cigar back.

"There you are," he said as he shook hands.

After he finished his term as Vice President under Coolidge, Charles G. Dawes was named Ambassador to England. He made the mistake of inviting Leon Errol, the comedian with the rubber legs, to visit him at the Embassy. Dawes thought he would be entertaining. He was.

Dawes gave a large dinner party, including among his guests Lady Astor and the British Prime Minister, Ramsay MacDonald. Errol was dressed up as the second man and helped the head butler serve. Of course, Errol put on his act, staggering around the dining room as if drunk, snatching forks, and spilling victuals right and left. In fact, one account had it he dumped some hot soup down Lady Astor's bare back. He would snatch a knife away from a diner just as he was about to attack his squab and say, "Wrong spoon."

When the situation began to look threatening and dangerous, Dawes introduced Errol as the famous American comedian. Still the performance didn't sit well, and there was talk of it for years in British social circles. Besides, Lady Astor had to get her dress cleaned.

After the Prime Minister discovered who Leon Errol was, he began to talk about the theater.

"Sometimes," he remarked, "if I like a show, I go to see it eight or ten times."

"If I don't get it the second time, the hell with it," replied the comedian.

On the whole the dinner party was not a great social success.

One Sunday around this time Bruce Barton, Frank Crowninshield, Grantland Rice, and I were playing golf out at old St. Andrew's. We stopped at the Rice apartment for a refill and got talking politics. We decided Barton was just the man to be the 1932 Republican candidate for President. Grant agreed he could deliver his native Tennessee delegation.

"How about an interview?" I suggested.

"You can quote me as saying anybody can beat Hoover," Barton began as he took another sip.

We had a fine, serious old newspaperman named McCloy, working nights at the North American Newspaper Alliance. I called him and told him Bruce Barton had announced his candidacy. McCloy thought I was serious, and why shouldn't he? He carried a story on the wire that night, and it appeared in several papers the next day, including the *Providence Journal*. Someone sent a clipping to Mr. Hoover with the Barton quote. He called up Bruce and protested. Barton ran for the nearest exit and denied the story. Anyway, he subsequently wrote a piece for *Cosmopolitan* called: "What I Would Do if I Were President."

He admitted he got the idea from our conference and he collected $1500 for it. Rice and I each demanded $500 but never got a cent.

"Well, I mentioned both your names," Barton said. "That ought to pay you off."

We ragged him about this for years.

It wasn't my good luck to meet Herbert Hoover until after he had finished his hitch in the White House. One day he invited Grantland Rice, Deac Aylesworth of NBC, and me to have lunch with him in his apartment at the Waldorf. We met in the lobby.

"Better stop in the men's bar," said Deac. "I'm not sure whether the old man drinks at noon."

We took this precaution and went on upstairs. Larry Richey, Hoover's old secretary, was there too.

"Will you fellows have a drink?" asked Mr. Hoover.

I cleared my throat. "I don't usually drink at lunchtime," I said.

"I don't either," he agreed, "but this looks like an occasion."

We each had a couple, and it turned out to be a delightful
and long lunch. Our host had wit and was informed on sports,
which he discussed with Grantland Rice.

He is a very human man and not the austere figure in a stiff
choker he has been pictured. As a matter of fact he wears soft
collars now. We were all calling him "Chief" before we left.

The Republican Vice-Presidential candidate in 1936 was
Colonel Frank Knox, an old friend of mine from World War I.
In 1931 the Colonel had bought the *Chicago Daily News* and
had moved to Chicago to take charge of his newspaper. Fortunately, Mrs. Knox had asthma and couldn't stand the Mid-
western climate, so she stayed in Manchester, New Hamp-
shire, where there was a gadget on the furnace. She could
breathe okay with its help. My friend got stuck on one of the
girls working on his paper, so he wasn't lonely.

But when the Colonel was nominated for the Vice-Presidency with Alf Landon, he naturally dug Annie, which was
Mrs. Knox's name, out of the mothballs. Photographs were
taken of the Knoxes sitting at home together reading, and
then she would be playing the piano and he would be turning
the music. It was after studying a few of these in the Sunday
rotogravure sections that Alice Roosevelt Longworth remarked, "Politics certainly makes strange bedfellows."

Charley Michelson, a first-class, all-around newspaperman
who worked for F.D.R. and got credit for being the White
House spook, was another old friend of mine.

I put it up to him one day: "Do you write all those speeches
for the President?"

"No, only the good ones," he answered.

He afterwards had a book published called *The Ghost Talks*
which was more or less a confession.

Dr. Frank Lahey, the famous surgeon who ran a clinic in Boston, was spending a winter vacation in Phoenix. One day he confided this story to a friend of mine who swears it is true:

When Franklin Roosevelt was considering running for a fourth term in 1944, Dr. Lahey was called to Washington to examine him. He did this with his usual thoroughness. After the results were known, Dr. Lahey went back to the White House to report. His diagnosis was not good.

"Mr. President," he said, "I want you to know I am a Republican, but my professional reputation is more important to me. I am sorry to tell you, if you run for a fourth term, you will never live to survive it, and may not even be able to start it."

F.D.R. lit a cigarette slowly and looked at him coldly.

"Dr. Lahey," he replied, "I want you to be the first to know, in spite of your findings, I am going to run for a fourth term and expect to survive it."

Of course he didn't, and had hardly started it when he died. According to my friend, Dr. Lahey, who is now dead, made a memorandum of this conversation, but the story has never been published. In spite of our efforts, Dr. Lahey's Boston office insists the memorandum will not be released, but acknowledges it exists.

When Harry Truman was President, he asked James Byrnes whether he would consider being Secretary of State.

"Is that a definite offer?" Byrnes said.

"Yes, it is," answered the President.

"Well, I accept right away," he replied.

"What's your hurry?"

Byrnes answered, "Because I want you to announce it before Bernie Baruch calls up and says he got me the job."

The crack was partly a joke, since Baruch and Byrnes are good friends.

The man Truman replaced in the Number 2 spot under F.D.R., Henry Wallace, is now a neighbor of mine near Ridge-field, Connecticut. After a somewhat checkered career in politics, Wallace today has mellowed and is leading the life of a gentleman farmer. He has made a fortune out of hybrid corn. I see him occasionally, and he is well informed on all subjects. Recently I asked him about an anecdote.

"Henry," I said, "I heard a story about you I don't believe. Do you mind if I tell it?"

"Go ahead," he said.

"When you were campaigning for the Vice-Presidency, you made a speech in Madison Square Garden at Eighth Avenue and Fiftieth Street. The air in the arena was rather close so as you stepped out and smelled the autumn briskness, you passed up your waiting limousine and took off at a jog trot for the Astor Hotel where you were staying. You had a police guard, and the flat-footed cops had to try to keep up. You outdistanced them, and they arrived minutes later panting. The sergeant called up headquarters to report. He said. 'This fellow, Wallace, is a tough one to guard. He ran us from Fiftieth Street to the Astor at Broadway and Forty-fifth. He won. I want to tell you if he speaks in Harlem and tries the same trick, we will be guarding a corpse and not a candidate.'

"Is this story true?"

Much to my surprise Mr. Wallace answered, "It is substantially. As a matter of fact, I was speaking downtown and jogged further than from Madison Square Garden."

It was never my good fortune to know President Eisenhower well, and I didn't expect to, since long ago his coattails were already crowded with riders. But once, shortly after he became president of Columbia University, I went to see him on Morningside Heights to find out if we could make a deal for his memoirs. To impress him, I told him General Pershing had written his reminiscences for us after World War I. This touched off a spark in his memory.

"The Old Man asked me to help him on his memoirs," Eisenhower began. "He gave me a lot of notes, and I went to work, taking great pains to do the best possible job. I turned out three or four chapters and thought the stuff particularly good until I showed it to him. Then he threw my masterpiece away and tackled it himself."

"Do you expect to get any help in writing your story?" I asked him.

"Oh, no," he answered. "I intend to do it all myself."

"Maybe Pershing felt the same way," I concluded.

Then I took advantage of the opportunity to ask a question which long had puzzled me.

"General, why did you let the Russians get into Berlin first? If we had taken the city, the whole postwar situation would have been changed."

"The answer to that one is easy," he said. "It was decided at the Quebec Conference the Soviet troops should be permitted to occupy the German capital. At that time they were only two hundred miles away, and our soldiers were three hundred. We later made better time than we expected. I was following orders."

I thought a minute and then remarked, "It seems to me it was at the battle of Copenhagen, the signal to retreat was run up, and Lord Nelson put his blind eye to the telescope and plunged on to victory. Do you see well out of both eyes?"

He smiled and added he had his orders from higher authority. After all, he came out a winner, so you can't disagree with him too much.

Since that first interview, I have seen him two or three times, and he always remembers my name, which is flattering. One meeting was at a small dinner to announce some aviation awards, and the photographers were making a few pictures. My friend, Amon Carter, invited me to get in one with Ike and a couple of other important guests. The photograph is now framed on the wall of my office.

Around this time—spring of 1952—already there were persistent reports that Eisenhower would be the Republican candidate. The General either sidestepped or denied these.

I met him at a lunch where the annual Father-of-the-Year award was to be handed out. A few days before I had seen Ely Culbertson, the bridge expert.

"I want to get up a game some night with General Eisenhower, Bruce Barton, you, and me," Ely volunteered.

I agreed that would be fine.

Before the lunch, there was a reception for distinguished guests, and I got in on the coattails of Herbert Swope who had brought Eisenhower. Herbert left for a moment, and there the two of us were, alone in a corner each with a Scotch mist in his hand. I floundered around for something to say, and finally remarked, "I understand Ely Culbertson, Bruce Barton, you, and I are going to play bridge some night soon."

Eisenhower seemed a little startled by this announcement and his reply surprised me.

"Oh, I'd love to play bridge with Culbertson," he said.

"What the hell is wrong with Barton and me?" I asked.

"There you go," he answered, and added a phrase later made familiar through countless news conferences: "Someone is always putting words into my mouth."

He was subtly referring then to the talk of his running for the Presidency. The bridge game never took place.

First Mutt and Jeff strip drawn by Bud Fisher in 1907, (see Chapter XI). (Bud Fisher)

XVIII.   LONG SHOTS AND SURE THINGS

GOVERNOR JAMES COX, who ran for the Presidency on the Democratic ticket in 1920, was a friend of mine and an ardent golfer. He took the game seriously. One day several years ago, Kent Cooper, the Governor, and I went to lunch as the guest of Pete Jones, head of Cities Service Company, at the Miami Biltmore. The Governor had brought his golf tools along as a hint. Kent had been sick and didn't want to play, and I was recovering from the flu.

Patty Berg, now the great woman star but then not well known, was practicing on the putting green, so Pete Jones got Ned Sheldon, the local pro, and Patty to make up the foursome. He was apologetic about it.

"I'm sorry, Governor," said our host, "but I've asked a woman to play with us."

Cox scowled but said nothing. It was well known he didn't care for coeducational golf.

"I'll take Ned," he announced, picking the pro for his partner as the bets were being made on the first tee.

"This is Miss Schmalz of Augusta," said Pete, introducing Patty. There was no enthusiasm.

The Governor hit a pretty good shot off the first tee, and Miss "Schmalz" passed him about 30 yards. It was a dog's leg, par five. She pulled out a two wood and knocked her ball up just short of the green. Her chip left her a five-foot putt which

213

she holed for a birdie. Cox who had been struggling along came over to Cooper and me.

"Who is that girl?" he asked.

"Oh, that's Miss Schmalz from Augusta. You have heard of her?"

"Yes, sure," he answered.

As the game progressed, she continued to get pars and birdies. After about five holes, the Governor began to be suspicious. As they went to the tee, he walked over to us again.

"On the level, who is this dame?" he demanded.

Now he was a good customer of mine, and I didn't think I could afford to fool him any longer. So I told him.

"Oh, I knew it all the time," he muttered as he moved off chewing his cigar.

She continued to burn up the course. She had been playing with a collection of old clubs she had picked up here and there. As a reward, Pete Jones bought her a set of matched irons and woods—the first she had ever possessed. Governor Cox paid his bet and congratulated her.

One thing Grantland Rice liked to do was gamble. At the races he would have a pocketful of daily double tickets. One time years ago we were in Palm Beach together, staying at the apartment of a bigshot in Wall Street, Ben Smith. He made a fortune going short of the market in 1929.

Someone gave us a fancy dinner in one of those ornate flea-bags run by winter vacationing members of the Detroit Purple Gang. Along about midnight I missed Grant and went looking for him. I found the establishment had an appendix where patrons could play roulette. Here he was at a table with a couple of house players and two or three more suckers. I quickly took in the situation when I saw he was on the rail for $2500. It was about 2 in the morning. As a friend, the problem was puzzling. If I urged him to pay up and go home, he would always think he could have stayed and gotten even. If he continued, he might go for twice as much. Just then our host, Ben Smith, came along.

"What's going on here?" he demanded, recognizing Grant's plight. "Let's see what we can do. I'll bet a thousand on the red."

The croupier shook his head. "Five hundred is the limit," he insisted.

Well, to make a long story longer, Smith finally won until Rice was only a $67 loser.

"Come on here. Pay up and go home. It's getting late," said Smith.

"Go home, hell," answered Grant. "We've just got the sons-ofbitches on the run."

However, we won the argument, so he got his hat, and we left.

When Harold Ross, brilliant, eccentric editor of *The New Yorker,* married for the third time, he took a couple of gin rummy players along with him on his honeymoon as insurance. Grantland Rice and I met him by chance in Palm Beach, and we more or less took over the management of the beautiful bride with the groom's consent while Ross played cards. One night we went to Bradley's, the famous and stylish gambling joint.

Colonel Bradley had a rule that all his male customers should wear black ties. I was properly attired, but Grant had on a blue coat and white shoes, so they stopped him at the door. Then it was agreed if he put on black shoes, it would be okay. The management had all the croupiers taking off their shoes, trying to find a pair to fit him. No luck! He went to his hotel and changed. If he had gone to bed instead of coming back, he would have been better off. The black shoes cost him $264 he lost at roulette.

Years ago, I joined a somewhat rowdy organization called "The Artists and Writers." I still belong, if I paid my last dues, but it has gotten more respectable with the years and younger members.

Every winter we would head South, picking out the place which gave us the most favorable inducements. Several times we went to Palm Beach, but one winter we selected Havana.

We stayed at the Hotel Nacional, a very stylish joint which had just opened a short time before, and some misguided guy in the management thought we would give it class and publicity. I was occupying a large suite with Deac Aylesworth, then president of NBC, and Kent Cooper, general manager of the Associated Press.

One day Aylesworth, Socker Coe, and I were having what we called lunch at a place named La Floridita, Ernest Hemingway's Havana headquarters, which specialized in fish, crabs, and various kinds of seafood. A word about Coe, a colorful character whose real name was Charles Francis. He was then an outstanding writer of fight and gangster stories for the *Saturday Evening Post*. He was known as "Socker" because he was a husky fellow and during a hitch in the Navy had won the middleweight championship of the Pacific fleet.

Now in the window of this restaurant was a large glass aquarium inhabited by various live species, including an eel about three feet long. Coe turned to me.

"Five dollars if you can catch the eel," he said.

I knew little about eels except they have a reputation for being slippery, but five bucks were five bucks. I went over to the tank and made four or five passes, but each time the victim slipped through my fingers. It caused my companions some amusement and me some chagrin. I sat down.

"Fifty dollars if you can catch the eel," challenged Socker.

"Now you're running into money," I replied.

I stripped off my coat, rolled up my sleeves, stood up on a chair, and chased the eel around through Morro crabs, etc., for fifteen minutes or more. Naturally my antics attracted attention and soon a crowd gathered on the sidewalk, looking through the window, with most of them cheering in Spanish for the eel.

Finally, I returned to the table defeated. Then, after another round of cocktails, Deac Aylesworth came up with an idea.

"Let's buy the eel," he proposed, "and bet suckers they can't catch him. We ought to make a fortune. We'll split him three ways—Coe, Wheeler, and Aylesworth."

The deal was closed. A waiter filled a bucket with water, took a napkin in the palm of his hand, and pulled the fish out of the tank. Why didn't I think of that? Remember it if you ever want to bet against an eel.

We next bought a glass aquarium for $15 which was big enough to furnish living quarters for a small whale. When we arrived at the Hotel Nacional, we gave a stout bellboy a dollar to carry the prize upstairs. Unfortunately he slipped on the tile floor taking a corner too fast and chipped a piece off the glass container. It sprung a bad leak. We put Oscar, the eel, into one of the spare bathtubs and called up some suckers.

John Golden was the first, and we won $25, thus recovering our investment. Then Aylesworth rushed out from the bathroom.

"Don't bet any more," he warned. "Some crook has thrown Daiquiri cocktails in the bathtub, and the eel is sluggish and drunk. Anybody can catch him now."

Our enterprise did not turn out as well as expected, but as

the days went by, we got very fond of the eel which was now pretty tame. Of course, occasionally some of our casual guests got a shock. Early one morning Steve Hannigan showed up with a hangover and asked to use our bathroom to shave or something. No sooner had he entered than he retreated with a yell.

"I saw an eel in there," he cried.

"You must be mistaken, my friend," I answered.

"Well, it could have been a tougher night than I thought," he conceded.

The Cuban newspaper publishers invited us to a big dinner, and I was taking a bath in the tub not occupied by the eel. Suddenly Deac Aylesworth and Kent Cooper appeared with a waste basket. They had already dressed. Cooper dumped Oscar in with me. By now he was tame, so I reached down and grabbed him around the middle and hit Mr. Cooper's dress shirt right in the center stud.

"That ain't funny," he said.

"And it ain't funny to throw a live eel in a bathtub with me, either," I replied.

Well, when it came time to pack, there was the problem of Oscar. We had grown pretty fond of him, but obviously we couldn't take him home with us. It might lead our wives to ask embarrassing questions about our behavior on the trip. Deac Aylesworth came up with a solution.

"We'll put him in the john, flush it, and hope he will get back to his native habitat," he said.

That is just what we did. I trust it turned out for the best.

Ely Culbertson was one of the first great bridge experts. He was a showman besides, married to an attractive lady, Josephine, his first wife, who knew more about bridge than he did. Culbertson began to write a series of articles for our syndicate which was very successful, and I got to know him well. In fact, he tried to teach Bruce Barton, Deac Aylesworth, and me the fine points of the game free with weekly lessons, but never made too much progress.

He organized the Crockford Club, a stylish joint, and to publicize it, announced a match between the Culbertsons and Hal Sims and his wife. The affair was kicked off with a gala dinner and a radio broadcast. This was during Prohibition. Frank Crowninshield, the only non-drinker in our group, was selected to do the announcing. He was getting along pretty good until he stubbed his toe as follows:

"It has certainly been a wonderful occasion, a lovely dinner with expensive wine flowing like water." Fortunately a monitor cut him off the air in time.

Before the big match started, Culbertson and Aylesworth challenged Sims and me to play at a subsequent date for five cents a point. We accepted enthusiastically, because I thought Sims a better player than Culbertson, and I knew damn well I was better than Aylesworth who was no good at all. I invited them for dinner at my apartment the evening of the contest, and Grantland Rice, Pete Jones, and Rex Cole came along as kibitzers. During a lull in the conversation Culbertson said, "My doctor tells me I need more exercise, and I am going to take up golf."

"Did you ever play?" I asked him.

"No," he answered, "but I practiced once for two hours five years ago."

"I'll bet two hundred dollars he can break 180," announced Mr. Jones.

Grantland Rice, Hal Sims, and I snapped up the bet. By this time old Ely must have thought $200 were the usual stakes, so he turned to Deac Aylesworth and said, "If you will give me two strokes a hole, I'll play you for two hundred dollars."

Aylesworth consulted me. "What do you think?" he asked.

"If he ain't lying, you can beat the hell out of him." He took the bet. Actually, Deac was not a very good golfer. I used to be able to give him a stroke a hole and beat him. Then Mr. Jones chimed in.

"I'll bet another two hundred," he said, "that if Deac gives him two strokes a hole, Cully can beat him."

Rice, Sims, and I grabbed that one. Then we adjourned to the bridge table where Sims and I finished winners to the tune of $175 each. The next day we all went out to the Oakland Golf Course on Long Island. Aylesworth and I picked up Culbertson, since we didn't want to risk losing a sucker. He had on plus fours and smooth shoes and carried no golf clubs.

"Tell him," said Deac to me, "it is customary to put your money up in advance." I collected $200 to hold from each of them.

Pete Jones was managing Culbertson and Sims and I Aylesworth. When Jones discovered his man had no clubs, he was a little chagrined but a good sport as always so he bought Cully a matched set for more than $100. Grantland Rice was the referee. Cully got up on the first tee and whiffed five times. Pete claimed they were practice shots, but I insisted no one ever grunted on a practice swing. We agreed to count two and let the other three ride free. Aylesworth hit a low hook off into the rough. He began to improve his lie when Sims rushed over to him with one of the funniest lines I have ever heard, although he was deadly serious.

"Don't do that, you fathead," he said. "You can beat this sonofabitch *without cheating!*"

Our man won the first hole with a 12 against a 17 for his opponent. At the end of the nine, Culbertson was seven down and had had 127 strokes as I recall it. His hands were so sore he couldn't lift a club, and his stockings had slipped down around the tops of his shoes. There wasn't any second nine. Pete Jones disgustedly threw in the sponge, and we all collected our money. It was maybe a month later I ran into Ely.

"It's too bad about that golf match," I said to him. "You'll have better luck next time."

"There ain't going to be any next time," he answered. "I sold those clubs to Hal Sims for fifteen dollars."

Grant used to like to tell about a golfer known as Stealthy Steve, because of his shrewdness and his ability to win bets. He was a good player.

Once Steve had a match with a younger guy for a good bet. He outdrove his rival by about ten yards. Then he turned to his caddy. "Let me have a three wood," he said. The boy handed it to him.

The other fellow had pulled out an iron. He stuck it back and substituted a three wood. He hit a good shot which went about 20 yards over the green. Steve shoved his spoon back in the bag and played a four iron, landing on the green hole high.

"Thought you were going to use a wood," complained his opponent.

"I was," he answered, "until I saw you go over the green." That's called gamesmanship.

Grant used to tell about the different tricks Steve had and propositions he would make. Steve was a rich man and didn't make it all at golf. He was also in the oil business.

He started out with a couple of pros one day. "Tell you what I'll do," he said. "I'll play your worst ball."

It was a new idea. They accepted it and lost their dough.

Just before Christmas, Pete Jones gives a very stylish party, attended by practically all the bigshots in New York. A guest one year brought a pair of dice, and a crap game started which ran along, like most crap games, into early evening. John Golden was the big winner and Deac Aylesworth the leading loser. When the exercises broke up, John stuffed the bills in his pocket without counting them, and headed for Bayside and home. He was greeted a little coolly by his wife, May.

"Have a hard day, John?" she asked.

"Pretty busy rehearsing, and I'm tired out. Why?"

"Didn't you go to any parties?"

Golden pricked up his ears suspiciously. "Yes, I did stop at Pete Jones' annual clambake on my way home for a little while."

"Did you play any games?" she went on. "Didn't you win twenty-six hundred dollars shooting craps?"

"Why, that sonofabitch, Aylesworth," exclaimed her husband.

Aylesworth had called up and told May about John's luck. "And if he says he won a cent less than twenty-six hundred dollars, don't believe him."

"I counted the money," Golden told me later, "and it was exactly twenty-six hundred dollars. How did he know? I had to buy May a new fur coat with it."

After Bob Jones had retired from tournaments, but before he was crippled so he couldn't play, Pete Jones invited Grantland Rice, Bob Jones, and me to fly to Palm Beach to inspect the Palm Beach Country Club course as experts. The course belonged to one of the hotels then owned by Henry L. Dougherty, and the town wanted to condemn part of the property and run a road through it, because some motorists complained the highway along the beach was dangerous and besides, when the tide was high, waves splashed and spotted their cars. These were non-golfers.

We traveled in style in a private plane and played bridge all the way. George MacDonald, the Papal Marquis, who also had an interest in the hotels, was along. Grantland Rice and I were partners and won $18 apiece by the time we reached our destination. Then we played a round at the club. Socker Coe, who was practicing law in Palm Beach at the time, joined up as our attorney.

We later called on the mayor, who was a strange-looking character with the longest sideburns I have ever encountered. Grantland Rice and Bob Jones, as expert witnesses, assured his honor that if a road was cut through, the course would be ruined. This, in turn, would be detrimental to the town, because it would discourage winter visitors. The mayor agreed, and we won our case, although I was only a bystander.

After we left, Socker Coe commented on the mayor's sideburns: "He is the only guy I ever saw in my life in parenthesis."

We played bridge all the way back, and Grant and I won again. It was a good trip.

In my career, I have known several evangelists. The most picturesque of the group was Billy Sunday who had been a Big League ballplayer. The reason he turned preacher, so I have been told, was because he couldn't hit the size of his hat. As I have already reported, he used to write a Monday-morning sermon for the sports pages for us. The ghost was Joe O'Neill, a reporter on the old *Morning World* who probably knew more bartenders than anyone else on Park Row.

Billy had a son named George who, as far as I can find out, never hit the sawdust trail—at least in earnest. He was a sport. One evening during the newspaper publishers' annual meeting in April, 1920, I was entertaining some customers at a restaurant called the Beaux Arts. In the group was George Sunday. He was supporting General Leonard Wood for the

1920 Presidential nomination at the convention to be held in Chicago. One word led to another until he offered to bet me Wood would be nominated.

"How much?" I asked, for I had the field running for me.

"Five hundred dollars even money," he replied. I guess he figured to stop me by the size of the amount.

"You've got a bet," I said. We shook hands on it.

However, to record the wager, the managing editor of the *Portland Journal* wrote out two cards as follows:

"George Sunday bets John Wheeler $500 that General Wood will be nominated at the Republican convention in Chicago."

Sunday signed one and I the other, and each put the evidence in his wallet. After Harding was nominated, I immediately tried and failed to get Sunday on the telephone at the Congress Hotel, Wood's headquarters. I let about a month pass without hearing from him, and then wrote him a polite note. Another month and only silence, so I had a photostat made of the card with his signature and mailed it to him with a stern reminder.

"In case you don't remember our bet," I wrote, "I enclose the record with your signature."

About six months later I was going into lunch in the fancy dining room of the Edgewater Beach Hotel in Chicago when I ran into George with a flashy-looking doll on each arm.

"Hello, Jack," he greeted me, sticking out his hand. I put mine in my pocket.

"How about that bet and the five hundred dollars you owe me?" I demanded in a loud voice.

He tried to hush me.

"I went to Honolulu right after the convention, but don't worry," he whispered. "You'll get it."

"I do worry. The mails were working, and you had a fountain pen," I replied.

I never did get it, although I turned the matter over to my Chicago agent. He was a reporter who worked on the Hearst papers. I offered him $250 if he could collect, figuring he would make Sunday's life miserable. He did, but no soap. I think George Sunday is dead now, and I don't blame his father. Life was made too easy for him.

Once when Bud Fisher was spending a month in Saratoga, he telephoned me he had a horse, Hyperion, which he was putting in a $5000 claiming race. He had hired Earl Sande, the outstanding jockey, to ride him. He couldn't lose and the price would be about 8 to 5. Bud urged me to hustle to Saratoga to witness this triumph. I passed the good news along to Ring Lardner who was looking for some easy money at the time, too. We got on the Hudson River night boat with our wives and an automobile and sailed for the Spa.

The next afternoon, I didn't do so good betting on the early races, but I wasn't worried with this ace in the hole.

Before the sixth event, Bud said to me, "Are you behind?" I nodded.

"Well, bet enough to get even and then some," he advised.

In those days there were oral bookmakers and all you had to do was to write the amount of your wager on a card if the man trusted you. I went to Johnny Walters and bet $500, the most I have ever risked on a horse race. Then I walked to the end of the clubhouse porch to get a view of this spectacle, something I had been waiting for all my life. Fisher bet $10,000. I lit a cigar. The horses were starting up the chute, and the old-fashioned web barrier was used instead of the modern gate.

Like a race-track pro, I put up my glasses to watch things carefully. Sande was on our nag all right. Then the starter sprang the barrier, and Hyperion reared, dumping his star jockey in the middle of the track. The horse ran around without a rider and won easily, but it didn't count. Somebody claimed him, and we all lost our money. The moral is there is no sure thing at the race track.

Fisher had a companion named Harry Friend, who when not "Yessing" Bud was a reporter on the *Morning World*. He adhered to the old style. He would rather crawl over a transom to get a story than go through the door, even if unlocked. One August the cartoonist invited Friend to spend his vacation with him at Saratoga. They went to the track every day, and soon the guest was well ahead of the bookies. By the final afternoon, he was a $2400 winner, and began to think he was John W. "Bet-a-Million" Gates.

His luck turned bad in the early races, and then an odds-on favorite came along at something like 2 to 5. Friend wrote out a ticket for $5000 and you've guessed it. The horse was beaten. At the end of the day, his winnings were all gone, and he owed $7500 which he didn't have. After the last event, someone found him out in the infield eating grass. Johnny Walters, the bookmaker, tried to claim he thought Friend was betting for Fisher, but he didn't get far with that. Harry became a retired race goer from then on.

Herbert Swope was always a big better—poker, racing, politics. Around about February, 1936, a group of us was sitting around a table in the dining department of Colonel Bradley's gambling emporium in Palm Beach. In our cast of characters were Grantland Rice, Gene Tunney, Bruce Barton, and Ben Smith. Herbert came in with his wife and several other companions. He stopped at our table to greet Grant and me cordially and Smith coolly. The talk turned to politics and the coming Presidential election. Tunney asked for Swope's opinion.

"Oh, I think F.D.R. will win again," he said with conviction.

After some more chit-chat, he moved on to an adjoining table. Now Smith didn't like Swope. He was jealous of him and resented his assurance and prominence. He turned to me.

"Go over and offer to bet him ten thousand dollars that Roosevelt will be licked," he said.

I shook my head. "I'm not your messenger boy," I replied. "If you want to bet him, go over yourself. I don't want to bet against Roosevelt."

"I don't want him to know who is putting up the money," explained Smith.

Then he turned to Grantland Rice who was much more obliging and had a better disposition than I have. (If there is any doubt on that score, ask my wife.)

"Granny," he said, "go and offer to bet him ten thousand dollars, but don't tell him who is putting up the money."

Rice approached Swope and announced his purpose.

"Who's putting up the dough?" Swope demanded. "Surely you're not, Granny."

"Oh, that's all right," Grant answered. "The money is good."

Herbert suspected it was Smith. "Sure. Go back and tell Ben he's got a bet."

After Rice had made his report, Tunney announced he would like to take half the wager. Smith agreed to this. Of course, Swope was no dope, and the next morning he sent a memorandum around to Grant Rice signed. This registered the bet. He asked for and got confirmation. Of course, he won in a walk, since Alf Landon carried only two states.

But there is a sequel worth telling. Starting in the early fall of 1936, the former heavyweight champion and his bride took a leisurely trip around the world with John Oliver La Gorce and his wife. According to Gene, before he took off, he asked Ben Smith to declare him in for 50 per cent on any election bets he made while Gene was away. As it turned out, when Ben saw which way the wind was blowing, the broker switched and finally finished winning $25,000 on F.D.R. But he forgot about Tunney's interest, so Gene, when he returned, was stuck for $5000. In conclusion, these two have not been warm friends since.

Ben Smith and Tom Bragg, another big operator who went short of the stock market in 1929 and made a fortune, were good friends. They loved to rib back and forth and play jokes which were rather crude. One time Bragg was in London and attended a fight between an Irishman and a Swede. Afterwards he went to the Savoy Hotel where several guests ate expensive food and drank champagne. Someone raised the question of the check.

"Don't worry," said Bragg. "I'll promote a sucker into paying it."

Then he went outside and called Ben Smith at his home in Bedford Village, New York. Smith had some dinner guests and was in a hurry.

"There's a prizefight here in London tonight," Bragg said. "Do you want me to place a bet for you?"

"Sure. Two hundred pounds," answered Smith.

"Which one?" asked Bragg, knowing Ben would pick out the Irishman. He did and hung up the phone.

Of course what Smith had not figured out in his haste was the difference in time. The fight was already over, and the Swede had won. Bragg went back to his table satisfied.

"It's all right. I have taken care of it," he reported.

The next morning when he got down to his office, Smith found this cable: "Too bad. The Swede won. Is it convenient to send money?"

I heard Ben Smith tell this story on himself.

Years ago, I went to a championship fight between Primo
Carnera and Max Baer with Grantland Rice and Bob Jones.
Luckily I found myself sitting next to Clare Boothe Luce,
before she was Mrs. Luce.

"Do you want to bet on the fight?" she asked me.

I nodded. "Which one do you take?" I asked.

"Carnera," she answered. He was then champion.

"How much?"

"Twenty-five dollars."

"Okay," I replied. "I will give you even money, although,
so you won't think I'm a sucker, I know the official odds are
7 to 5 on Carnera. Also I have bet with women before, so how
about putting up the cash?"

She dug down in her purse and produced $25. I pulled the
same amount out of my pocket, and we handed the $50 to Bob
Jones as stakeholder. In the eleventh round Baer knocked
Carnera kicking, and I collected the dough. This must have
made some impression on Mrs. L. for I heard afterwards that
she had told Bernard Baruch about it.

"Always let the other fellow make the proposition," replied
wise Mr. Baruch.

There is sound philosophy in that remark.

Which reminds me of Damon Runyon's account of the advice the old-time faro dealer gave to his boy, when he was
starting out in life.

"Son," he said, "if you meet a gambler who wants to bet
you he can make the one-eyed jack jump out of the deck and
squirt cider in your ear, don't take it. If you do, you are liable
to wind up with an ear full of cider."

In concluding this chapter, I want to put in an anecdote
about my mother. She was never a gambler, but she worked
out a system to beat the races. Once she was visiting us in

Florida, and we went to Hialeah. Before the second race, I asked her if she wanted to bet. She handed me a five-dollar bill.

"You decide," she said.

I put it on a long shot picked by Maryland George who ran a tip sheet. The horse came in and she won $85. She put the bills in her pocketbook.

"What do you want to bet on in the next race?" I asked her. She shook her head.

"I'm not betting any more," she said. And she didn't, not that day nor the next nor while she was in Florida, nor ever.

After she died, I found an envelope in her safe-deposit box. On it was marked the date and this note:

"Eighty-five dollars won at the race track."

She had never spent it. Maybe she thought it was dishonest to beat the mutuels.

XIX. SECRETS OF HIGH FINANCE

WHEN I was a boy in Yonkers, we were taught that thrift was a great thing. This was before F.D.R., Harry Hopkins, and the New Deal. Hopkins' slogan was "tax and tax and tax and spend, and spend, and spend and elect, and elect, and elect." There were a lot of sayings my wise old grandmother used to quote to me like "Save the pennies and the dollars will take care of themselves."

John E. Andrus, one of the foremost residents of Yonkers if not the foremost, was a good example. He was rated among the ten richest men in the United States and owned a medicine factory, about half of Minneapolis, and many other assets. He was no dude and for years wore an overcoat which was so shiny in the back, if he slipped and fell down, he would have slid for half a block.

Now Mr. Andrus lived in a handsome house in north Yonkers and did not bother to keep an automobile, an uncertain novelty in those days. He traveled on the Park Avenue trolley car line to his office near Getty Square. He had a friend who lived in south Yonkers and journeyed north daily by trolley. The fare was five cents, and it was possible to get a transfer to change in Getty Square. Mr. Andrus and his friend each got one transfer daily and traded them, thus making the round trip for a nickel. This was considered a fine example of how to lay up something for a rainy day, although perhaps a little crooked. Mr. Andrus was also a devout Methodist and a liberal contributor to the church.

One day at the Coffee House Club George Abbott and some others were talking about the old idea that there is a little bit of larceny in all of us, especially when we were kids. It reminded me of a boyhood experience of which I am a little ashamed now.

The Yonkers track then was called Empire City, and they used to have automobile races there which were pretty exciting. One Saturday four or five of us wanted to attend, but were short the price of admission.

We trudged a couple of miles out to the track, and, by boosting and pulling, we managed to climb the back fence—a tough one to get over. Two of us tore holes in our trousers. We worked our way around to the grandstand and joined the crowd. Then up came a hard shower, and the races were postponed until Monday. It was announced the spectators could either get rain checks or their money back by going to the ticket windows. We fell into line. I was the head of our contingent. I heard the exchange between the man two slots ahead of me at the box office.

"What color was your ticket?" demanded the fellow behind the cage.

"White," he replied.

"No good. That's complimentary. Next."

The next man said green and a dollar bill was passed out.

"Green," I whispered to my friend behind me. Each of us collected a dollar, although we had come in over the fence. Then we went back to Getty Square and gorged ourselves on ice cream sodas at Wray's drug store. We were that age. Now I suppose I should send the dollar back with interest, but I don't know where to mail it.

W. C. Fields used to say, "You can't cheat an honest man," but many an otherwise honest man seems to like to cheat a little—for instance, Otto Kahn, the banker. He had an enormous estate at Huntington on Long Island with a private 18-hole golf course. With Bob Davis, the old editor, and Kent Cooper I was invited there two or three times. Playing for small stakes—a dollar Nassau—the banker would cheat your eyes out. I have never had an opponent who could hit so many full brassy shots out of the woods if you didn't follow him. Yet he would turn around and give $25,000 to the Metropolitan Opera and think nothing of it.

Albert Lasker was another rich man it was my good luck to know. I have heard his income was $10,000 a day. Toward the end of his life he gave up wearing a hat.

"Aren't you afraid of catching cold?" I asked him.

"Not at all," he answered. "It is good for me and the fresh air makes my hair grow. Besides, I save a quarter every time I go into a restaurant and don't have to check my hat."

Mr. Lasker could probably have bought the restaurant without noticing it. But he figured the upkeep on a hat was too much.

John Golden also had a thrifty habit. He and I would ride over to the Dutch Treat lunch on Tuesday. Even on the coldest days, he would shed his coat in his car and leave it there. So would I.

"It saves time and a quarter," he explained to any new acquaintances.

Ed Hill was a colorful, old-time New York reporter. He was a first-class man and a fine writer, but true to the traditions of those days, he hated to pass a saloon without making a purchase. He had a curious way of trying to save money when he imbibed a few. It also proved to be expensive. He would rent a Carey car at $10 an hour, or whatever it cost in those days. Whenever he would stop, he would take off his hat and coat and leave them in the vehicle to save the quarter tip to the hat-check girl.

Tad, the great cartoonist, had a faculty for hanging nicknames on prominent persons which stuck. Arthur Brisbane, the famous editor, he dubbed "Double Dome." You could almost hear the great man think out loud when his brows wrinkled.

Now even though Brisbane received a big salary, he had a reputation for being a penny pincher, so Tad said, "If you want to get in to see Double Dome, all you have to do is to throw a nickel over the transom."

Then Tad drew a cartoon of a guy painting a ceiling. The caption read, "If Michael Angelo worked on this paper . . ."

One typical anecdote about Harry Stevens, the race-track caterer. He was a hustling, thrifty man when he started and in later life very generous. His office was on Fifth Avenue. One day he rushed into Child's Restaurant to get a quick bite of lunch. He ordered a sandwich and found a piece of ham in it about as big as a hangnail. He didn't complain to the manager—not at all. Instead he asked the manager where the ham cutter was. Stevens went back to the kitchen and looked him up.

"I don't know what you are getting here," he said, "but you are worth more to me." So he hired him on the spot.

Stevens told me this story one day at the Polo Grounds. Then he pointed to his commissary department.

"He is back there now," he boasted proudly. "He is a wonder. He can take one ham and feed the U.S. Army with it."

Our Army was slightly smaller in those days.

It has been my good fortune to know many prominent

publishers. In making my early rounds as a syndicate sales-
man, I met Joseph Medill Patterson of the *Chicago Tribune,*
who was always very nice to me and occasionally bought a
feature. He then lived in Chicago, but came to New York
regularly after the *New York Daily News* was started. We
became friends and used to go to the races together and in-
dulged in other companionable activities. He walked into our
office in the old *World* Building unannounced one day in 1923.

"I want to offer you a job," he began, "and, if you are not
interested, I won't go into details."

"That depends," I answered, "where I would have to live
and whether I would have to give up this business."

"You can stay in New York and continue your interest in
the Bell Syndicate. We will make a three-year contract and
pay you twenty-five thousand dollars a year."

"Sure I'm interested," I responded promptly before he could
change his mind.

He went on to explain they planned to start a weekly magazine to be printed on some presses Colonel McCormick had
bought in Germany right after the war. It was to be called
"The Coloroto Weekly."

"Tell you what I'll do," I said. "If you will give me a quarter
interest in it, I will work for you for nothing."

He shook his head.

"No," he answered, "our corporate setup would not permit
it."

We made a deal on his terms, which turned out to be fortu-
nate for me later, since at one time the magazine was losing
$75,000 weekly until I got it up to $80,000 for a couple of
weeks, so with my 25-per-cent share I wouldn't have lasted
very long.

I protested that the name didn't mean anything, that "Coloroto" sounded like a cheap cigar or a bum soprano. I believe

maybe Colonel McCormick thought up that name because the presses he bought in Germany were supposed to be hot stuff and print in color. Anyway, I ran into strong resistance which was finally overcome when Irvin Cobb went to lunch with the boss and me one day and laughed him out of it.

Around this time the *Chicago Tribune* was run jointly by both Colonel McCormick and Captain Patterson. One would have charge of the editorial page for a month and then the other would succeed him. This explained the frequently contrasting policy. On becoming editor of the new magazine, one of the first admonitions I received from William Fields, the *Tribune's* general manager and an old friend, was never to say anything which would cause friction between the two bosses. Actually, there was enough rivalry already.

Arthur Brisbane, being a Hearst editor, wasn't bound by any *Tribune* rules. The story is he used to go to Chicago, seek out McCormick, and throw in some such remark as, "Too bad you have Joe Patterson hanging around your neck. With your brains, you should be the sole boss."

Then he would meet the Captain at lunch and stir things up by saying, "You are the genius behind the paper. I don't see how you get along with McCormick."

Of course Brisbane did everything he could to upset the *Tribune* because Hearst owned the *Chicago Examiner*, which continued to run in second place.

But to get back to my experiences as a magazine editor.

There was a gent named Max Annenberg who was circulation manager of the *Tribune* and apparently knew where the bodies were buried for he had a lot of influence in the whole organization. I had been cautioned not to put my finger in his mouth, and it was about him Walter Davenport remarked, "He double-crosses himself to keep in practice."

Anyway, Mr. Annenberg was a genius at thinking up contests, and he decided the thing to do was to offer $25,000 as a prize to the man, woman, or child who submitted the winning name for the new magazine, along with a 50-word letter telling why, to get around the lottery laws. Boy, did we get answers! The Christmas-card business the U.S. Post Office handles was small compared to what they had to carry for us. We did our best to sort them out and finally the judges picked "Liberty," as submitted by some fellow in Gallipolis, Ohio.

As it turned out, the winner had always lived a respectable life, going home at night regularly and keeping his eyes in the boat as far as anyone knew. But no sooner did he collect the $25,000 than he lammed out of town with the village blonde, or she might have been a brunette, deserting his family for the primrose path. How long the dough lasted I don't know or what became of him.

We started *Liberty* off with a bang, since the advertisers were eager to get aboard because of the reputation of the *Chicago Tribune*. However, no one had ever thought of trying a dry run on those presses to see if they worked. The printing was atrocious, and we threw away 200,000 copies of the first issue as spoils, and we might as well have done the same thing with the rest. We had planned to begin with 500,000 circulation for the first six months. After the initial issue, advertisers canceled right and left, because you could barely read the copy or make out the pictures. We changed over to the Cuneo Press as soon as possible, but the damage had been done. The switch took several weeks.

To recoup, I was instructed to get all the circulation we could, which was not tough, as we were spending money like water and producing a good magazine with the best authors. Soon the circulation went to a million, but the more we sold at five cents each, the more money we lost without advertising to sustain the publication. We never did get the advertisers back. Here is a sidelight:

We had one loyal advertiser who stuck with us on the expensive back cover—the Hickok Belt Company. Now as editor I was trying to put out a magazine which appealed to mass readers. Somebody told me one day that Karl Bickell, who was then president of the United Press, had some sort of stomach trouble and had visited a specialist named Dr. Einhorn. The doctor looked the patient over carefully and then asked a question.

"Do you wear a belt?"

Mr. Bickell admitted he did.

"Throw it away and put on suspenders," the doctor advised, "and your stomach will be all right."

The cure was reported to have worked. Now I thought this is an interesting subject since all men have stomachs, many worry about them, and each one has to hold up his pants. Hugh Fullerton, a veteran, was then on the staff, so I sent him up to get an interview with the eminent M.D. He came back and wrote out the interview, supporting the theory that suspenders agreed better with masculine stomachs than belts. We published it prominently.

No sooner had the magazine hit the street than the advertising manager, a fellow named Perry, came in to see me, pale and trembling. He got right to the point.

"What the hell did you print that piece about suspenders for?" he demanded. "Mr. Hickok is on the telephone raising the devil and says he is going to cancel all his advertising."

It was no time for panic, so I replied, "Don't get excited. Let me speak to him."

"With pleasure," he answered.

I took up the receiver. There was a spluttering sound. It was Hickok.

"Mr. Hickok," I began, "I understand you are upset about our suspender story." (That was the prize understatement of the year.) There was still a hissing sound.

"Of course," I went on, "this is a controversial subject, and we want to be fair to all concerned, so if you will be patient, I think you will be satisfied."

He stopped sputtering and finally agreed to hold off his cancellation. I had no idea what I was going to do, but while shaving the next morning, an inspiration came to me. There was in New York in those days a beautiful and socially prominent lady named Julia Hoyt. I knew her. I called her up and made her a handsome offer if she would write us a story about belts, pointing out that no man in Newport, Bar Harbor, Southampton, Palm Beach, or other social centers, or in his right senses, would be considered worth inviting to a dog fight if he wore suspenders. He had to have on a belt. In fact, she gave the impression all the fashionable hostesses inspected their male guests for Hickok belts before letting them in.

Anyway, we published this story prominently with photographs of the beautiful Miss Hoyt chatting with men, all of them with their belts prominently exposed. We had males of all sizes—fat, thin, and medium. We kept the Hickock advertising as long as I stayed with the magazine.

By this time Ring Lardner was writing regularly for *Liberty*. He did a short story called "Haircut" about a practical joker. It was a beautiful job and has been recognized as a classic ever since.

Max Annenberg came into my office one day. "Jack," he said, "I wish you wouldn't publish any more barbershop stories by Lardner. I didn't know what that last one was about."

To build circulation, Annenberg was forever thinking up contests and dropping them in my lap. We ran one about dogs. It was simple enough. We would publish the tail end of a St.

Bernard, the middle of a Dachshund or Pekinese, and the head of a poodle. These various anatomical animal parts would be all jumbled on a page. The reader was supposed to match them up and paste them together. The prizes were about 50 dogs—each the favorite breed of the winners. Of course, we got a lot of answers and some circulation which we did not need at that time.

Anyway, the dogs were purchased at a kennel and duly shipped to their various destinations. Unfortunately it was in the summer, and a very hot spell hit the country. Many of the poor pups arrived dead. We began to get indignant letters from faithful readers.

"I expected a live dog," several began. "The one that came was dead."

This situation was somewhat embarrassing. We waited for a cool wave and sent out duplicates.

All of which would seem to indicate that at that time I had a lot of nerve. Actually, though, when I first started in the news syndicate business I was plagued by timidity caused, I would guess, by fear of failure.

Bradford Merrill was then general manager of the Hearst paper, and I would go to see him about buying features. On the way over to his office in William Street, I would talk to myself.

"Suppose the old guy does turn you down, what the hell of it? It ain't going to kill you."

He was a fine old gentleman, and he became a helpful, good customer and friend.

There was a preacher of a big church in Brooklyn whom I knew. He had a whimsical humor. I met him on the train one day when I was scheduled to make a speech that evening, my first.

"Are you nervous?" he asked me.

"Sure I am," I replied.

"Well, I'll tell you how I overcame it when I first started to preach," he said with a smile. "When I got up in the pulpit, I would look to the left and then to the right and say to myself, 'You can all go to hell.'

"After that I pitched in and tried to save them, and I wasn't timid any more either."

Hugh Fullerton used to tell about a big executive who had to make frequent after-dinner speeches. He would fret and worry about these.

"Forget the crowd," Fullerton advised. "You know that office boy you bawl out every day. Get him a seat and put him right up in the front. Then make your speech to him, and you'll be all right."

It worked, and the office boy received a raise. He never knew why, because he got bawled out just as much as ever in the daytime.

Another story based on human psychology concerns a fabulous character named Charles R. Flint, who operated very successfully in Wall Street about the turn of the century. At one spot in his career, he ran short of money and, knowing J. P. Morgan, the elder, slightly, he approached him about a loan.

"Meet me at my office at 12 o'clock," said Mr. M.

The two men strolled around the financial district for half an hour. It was a nice day. The banker talked about the weather and yachting, but didn't mention money. Mr. Flint was getting nervous when they headed back toward 23 Wall Street. As both approached the entrance, he asked, "But, Mr. Morgan, how about that million dollars I want to borrow?"

Morgan stuck out his hand to say good-by, and answered, "Oh, you won't have any trouble getting it now that we have been seen together."

One association that ended up profitably all around began in Stillson's, the hangout for *Chicago Tribune* staffers opposite the old *Tribune* building in the Chicago Loop. Sol Hess was a Chicago jeweler who liked to associate with newspapermen and pay the tabs, so he was welcome. Among those he met in this rendezvous were Ring Lardner, Clare Briggs, John Mc-Cutcheon, and a struggling cartoonist, Sid Smith. Sid was then drawing a strip called "Doc Yak" which was pretty lousy. He didn't care for work and liked to drink and drive his automobile at speeds up to 100 miles an hour. Later there was a club organized with some such title as "I Rode with Sid Smith Once." It had a large membership. Smith finally killed himself in an automobile accident.

When he met Hess, he met a fortune, for Hess had a new idea for a strip which combined continuity and humor. It was called "The Gumps" and almost immediately was a great success. Sol wrote the balloons as a labor of love and for the privilege of hanging around with the newspaper crowd. Smith, however, made one big mistake. When his contract ran out with the *Tribune*, he held out for big figures and got them, as well as a Rolls Royce for a bonus. Then he offered Hess $200 a week to continue to write the comic. Knowing the facts, Hess was insulted and told Smith he was going to quit.

I heard of this situation by the grapevine, and rushed to Chicago to talk to the erstwhile ghost writer. We made a deal with Hess which was the beginning of a long and friendly association that lasted until the day of his death. He had in mind a strip, "The Nebbs," which had the same pattern and his sparkling humor. We hired a young artist named Wally Carlson to do the drawing. I guaranteed Hess 60 per cent against a guarantee of $800 a week. After we had signed the contract, I didn't know whether I had made a bad deal or not, but we had to gamble in those days.

First I went to see Bradford Merrill, then general manager of the Hearst papers, and he asked me to show the samples to the boss himself, William Randolph Hearst. He okayed it for his whole string at a price which got us off the nut. From then on it grew, and we all prospered. Hess was a fine, generous associate. The "Gumps" continued on its momentum, but it was never the same as it had been when Hess was doing the job.

The only contract we ever had actually signed by William Randolph Hearst was for a strip George Ade was writing for us. One of our salesmen had been on the Coast, and I gave him a letter to Mr. Hearst, on the off chance it would do some good. It did. Hearst bought the feature for all his papers.

At that time Victor Polachek was general manager, having found the key to the office ahead of Victor Watson who was also scrambling for the job after Bradford Merrill died. Polachek called me up and insisted I go to see him at once.

"What do you mean by making a contract with W.R.?" he demanded as soon as I got inside the door. "Don't you know I buy features around here now?"

"Well, of course, we are in the business of selling," I replied. "One of our salesmen saw Mr. Hearst, and he bought the strip. But I brought the contract with me," I added, pulling it out of my pocket. "I'll tell you what I will do if you are unhappy about it—I'll tear it up right here."

He seemed surprised. "Oh, no, don't do that," he answered.

It was just a bluff. I knew he wouldn't let me tear up a contract signed by Mr. Hearst.

Naturally, in the course of my career I've been on the receiving end of some pretty fast talk myself. For instance in 1941 Bruce Barton, Clarence Budington Kelland, and I bought a ranch in Arizona about 120 miles from Phoenix. Why the hell we went into it I don't know except there was talk of inflation, the threat of war, and one of the partners was a little sweet on the previous owner—Viola McNeil. She was a pretty good-looking girl with breezy Western manners and an eye for city slickers. She found three in us.

The layout consisted of 50,000 acres, mostly leased, an old house, and a river which ran through the land. After we took off from Congress Junction, we went about 30 miles over rough roads. If you got into the place and it rained you couldn't get out because the creeks overflowed, but it practically never rained so that was not much of a problem.

Viola nominated her brother, Arch, as the manager and a man of experience in such matters. We bought a lot of her cattle and put our brand on them. Things looked rosy at the start. We even borrowed $36,000 at the bank to increase our herd.

Then our troubles began. Arch was married to a trained nurse, and he had stomach ulcers, so she said he mustn't ride a horse. We had a couple of cowboys, one a Mexican who we found later was robbing us blind. There was no water in the river, and we couldn't find our cattle. The bulls were sluggish with the expected results.

Bud Kelland was the one optimist. He would figure out the calf crop to a fraction, notwithstanding we could seldom find the calves. He could forecast the profits, and the worst year we ever had on paper with Bud doing the calculating was a net of $36,000. The fact we faced after three years was we never made a dime but lost plenty, and Barton and I were ready to retire as ranchers. We put away our Western clothes and visited a local real estate man. It was a shame because each of us had built a comfortable house on the property at considerable expense.

A fellow named Dan Gainey from Minnesota came along

and bought it at a bargain price. We thought we had found a sucker and were relieved to get out, even though the venture cost us each $35,000. However, a year or so after it was sold, a state highway was run through the property, and the demand for Arizona land increased, so we should have held on. I don't know whether the bulls are working and whether there is any water in the river yet.

Damon Runyon once said, "The toughest thing in the world is to be rich when you're broke."

I had a friend named Gerhard Dahl who had been a big wheel in the financial world and then went broke after 1929. He still tried to live up to his past habits, which were not exemplary. One night when he was in the chips I saw him lose $80,000 in a chemin-de-fer game at Bradley's in Palm Beach.

He also had an unfortunate experience. A lady named Louise Lawson was found murdered in her apartment one morning and Gerry Dahl's framed photo was on the piano with a loving inscription which gave him considerable publicity. The crime was never solved, and of course my friend had nothing to do with it or he would not have left his picture. He explained to the press he was interested in her musical career and helping her out financially.

He wound up so broke he called at about 6:30 one night and asked me to stop by the second-rate hotel where he was living and lend him $10 because his credit had been cut off. I had previously let him have a little money to tide him over since, when he thought he had $10,000,000, we had visited him at his homes in Palm Beach and Smithtown. I telephoned the hotel manager and told him who I was and assured him, if he would restore Dahl's credit, I would send him a check in the morning.

"We are not that hardhearted," he replied. "We have only cut it off for liquor, not for food and lodging."

I agreed that was okay.

Walter Howey, the colorful Hearst editor who had been the prototype for the rough managing editor in *Front Page* written by Charley MacArthur and Ben Hecht, was then the boss of the *American Weekly*, the Sunday supplement. He was an old friend so I went to him and told him about Dahl.

"Why don't you run a success story in reverse?" I asked him. "Tell about the guy who was at the top and wound up in the gutter."

He agreed to pay $3000 for the series and assigned a ghost writer, who was not too careful about the facts, to turn out the articles. This frank confession about Dahl's downfall attracted a lot of attention, especially among his old, rich friends. Dahl collected his money in cash.

"Gerry," I said to him, "you know two things—banking and law. Why don't you go to some town, get a modest job, and settle down?"

He listened, but paid no attention. It didn't take him long to burn up this bankroll, and he died broke with no friends. One man who had helped him out, Harvey Gibson, the banker, was cut down by the grim reaper ahead of him.

Yes, "the toughest thing in the world is to be rich when you're broke."

XX. LADIES OF NOTE

ALTHOUGH this is not a romantic reminiscence, it is my belief the female sex deserves (if that is the right word?) a place in it. Maybe I have been lucky, but I have always proceeded on the theory a woman would never hurt you much if you treated her half-way decently. On the other hand, if one of them starts anything, battle her; don't settle. Damon Runyon used to say the only way to fight a woman is with your hat. When the row begins, put it on and walk out.

There was a firm of lawyers in Rockville Center, Long Island, named Graham and Utterhart. They were specialists in defending ladies who shot their husbands or sweethearts in a fit of temper, especially if the cad were going to walk out on her. One story had it that a prospective client went to them in the rush season and tried to retain them to defend her.

"I am going to shoot my husband this week the first chance I get," she announced.

"Put it off until next month," one of the partners advised. "We are now too busy to handle any more cases."

There was a dashing, handsome young fellow named Jack de Saulles, circulating around just after the turn of the century. He had been the All-American quarterback on a star-studded Yale team. Business took him to Chile where he met a beautiful young lady—Bianca. As might be expected, they were married and came to live in New York. In due course, they had a son.

Joan Sawyer was a red-headed dame making a hit as a society dancer at the New York Theater roof. Her partner was a swarthy South American. She had many admirers who liked her for other qualities besides her dancing. By now Mr. De Saulles' marriage had begun to wear thin, and he became fascinated by the dancer. Soon word leaked back to his missus that Jack was more interested in the Terpsichorean art than Arthur Murray is today. One thing led to another, and they were divorced.

Under the court ruling, each was to have custody of the young son for a specified period. One night De Saulles returned the boy to his mother, in accordance with the legal requirements. She greeted him by pulling out a six-shooter and killing him deader than a mackerel. She was a quick-tempered, hot-blooded dame. Also he had made the mistake of teaching her to shoot.

Of course, she hired Graham and Utterhart to defend her. It was a sensational case, attended by a large group of reporters, including this one. She was good-looking with a nice pair of gams which she didn't try to conceal from the judge or jury or the newspapermen. As expected, after a good deal of testimony which tried to prove the dead football player was a heel and deserved to be shot, she was acquitted amid cheers.

That night she gave a hell of a party at the old Brevoort Hotel on Fifth Avenue for her mouthpieces, the newspapermen, the district attorney, and I think maybe the judge. It lasted late. However, if any of my female readers are thinking of committing murder, I think Graham and Utterhart have gone out of business—both dead. I don't know what became of her.

There was a saloon run by a genial Irishman named Tim Shine catter-cornered across from the old *Herald* building at

the corner of what was then Thirty-sixth Street and Sixth
Avenue. It was an old-fashioned institution conducted pri-
marily for men although there was a side door and a dingy
back room where lady patrons could sit in uncomfortable
chairs and have a drink.

The gin mill was a gathering place for *Herald* employees,
particularly in the early-morning hours. Tom Geraghty from
Rushville, Indiana, was on the *Herald* staff. He was an eager,
handsome young fellow who carried a cane and wanted to find
out what made the big city tick. In his travels he met a rather
good-looking athletic lady who was the champion woman bag
puncher of the world. She was displaying her talents by appearing at Hammerstein's Victoria vaudeville theater.

One night after hours Tom and I met a talkative gent in
Shine's who began to expound his theories on how to treat the
other sex. He was a disciple of the rough school.

"The thing to do if you get into an argument is to punch her
right in the nose," he said. "None of this Harry Thaw stuff like
slapping. Now last night I hit my girl on the chin, and when
she came to, she was just as sweet and nice and everything was
fine. I am going to try it out whenever I get a chance."

Well Geraghty made a date for this Lothario to meet us the
next night, using as bait a promise he would introduce him to
a beautiful girl. Then he arranged for the champion woman
bag puncher to join us after her show. To make a long story
longer, we got the gent to discuss his romantic theories and
led him on until he finally decided to try his theories out on
our companion. He made one pass at her which she ducked,
and then she proceeded to let him have it as if he were the
heavy bag. She knocked him off his chair, and when he got up
spitting sawdust, she cracked him again. The second time he
went down for keeps, and we left before it became a general

row. What became of him and his theories this reporter does not know.

One of the great New York beauties after the turn of the century was Lillian Lorraine of the Follies. Flo Ziegfeld, the proprietor, was in love with her, although he was married to the stage star Billie Burke at the time. This young lady was temperamental and unpredictable, which qualities perhaps made her attractive to men.

I first met her at Bud Fisher's apartment one night when the cartoonist was giving a gay party. She was wearing a diamond necklace and boasting about its donor. Suddenly she decided she didn't like her benefactor any more and to back up her opinion put her fingers inside the bauble, broke the string, and diamonds spilled all over the floor. Fisher and I scrambled around picking up the jewels and returning them. I guess she got them all back, although Bud showed up a week or so later with a new diamond ring.

In those days roof gardens were the fashionable rendez-vous of New York sports, and Ziegfeld made Lillian Lorraine the lead in a summer show on the New Amsterdam roof. I happened to be among those present the opening night, and Flo was foolishly sitting in the first row. It seems his star and he had had some kind of an argument before the curtain went up, and she was still boiling. She had a scene with a champagne bottle in it. She spotted Ziegfeld and walked to the front of the stage and flung the bottle at his noggin. If he hadn't ducked, she might have hit the target.

The poor girl has been dead these many years, deserted, broke, and lonely during her last days.

When Sir Winston Churchill was a young man, Richard Harding Davis was a friend of his. Davis spent much time in

London, and on one of his visits Ethel Barrymore was playing there. He introduced her to Churchill, who immediately recognized her charm, beauty, and other qualities. When Davis was not escorting her, Sir Winston took charge.

The sequel to this anecdote was told me years later by Hope Harding Davis, the war correspondent's daughter. It seems that her father was calling on Miss Barrymore in her New York apartment one day when he noticed a stack of unopened letters. He recognized the familiar handwriting on the envelopes as Churchill's. The actress apparently had lost interest and had not taken the time to read the missives. Of course, Churchill was not then the important man he was later. And this great beauty had many admirers who wrote her letters. When it came to reading them, evidently she was no bookworm.

Along about 1932, a very pretty young lady came into my office with a letter from the book editor of the old *New York Sun.* Her name was Sheilah Graham, an English girl who had been on the London stage as one of "C. B. Cochran's young ladies" and had been doing some literary exercises on the side. She showed me a few clippings, one from the *Sunday Express* about stage-door johnnies and their tricks. Like many of my callers, she wanted to write a newspaper column, only she was better looking. I kept the clips and, after she returned to England, sent them back to her, with a polite letter. But I found out later she is a girl who will not take no for an answer.

It was in the winter of 1933 that Lou Maxon, the advertising man, and I went abroad on a jaunt, mostly business but partly pleasure. One Saturday night we were sitting around our suite in the Savoy Hotel, and I was looking over some notes my secretary had given me. One said: "Call Sheilah Graham." It gave her address and telephone number.

"Lou," I said, "there was a hell of a pretty girl who came into the office to see me. What do you say I telephone and ask her to have dinner with us?"

"Anything is better than eating with you alone," Lou answered.

She was home, and accepted quickly. She explained her husband was in the hospital recovering from an operation.

"That's too bad. Is it serious?" I asked.

"I don't think so," she answered. "The doctor only charged five pounds."

She showed up promptly and was no disappointment. We had a pleasant evening together, and she was amusing. Maxon and I matched to see who would have the honor of escorting her home, and I won—or lost, for I paid the taxi fare. Lou went on to Paris, and Miss G. and I spent some time together, going about London to shows, dinner, and shops. Her husband, whom she later divorced, was still convalescing. She kept insisting she wanted to come to America, and I kept discouraging her. Finally I sailed on the old *Bremen,* and by this time we were good friends. Her parting words were a little startling.

"I'll see you in New York soon," she said.

The next June I received a cable announcing her departure and the name of the ship on which she was arriving. I met her. What else could a gentleman do? She reached the U.S.A. with $100 and plenty of ambition. I managed to find her a job on the *New York Mirror* where she made good as a hard-working reporter. Then she moved to the *New York Evening Journal* and got a by-line.

"What can I write to attract mail?" she asked me one day.

"Write a piece," I suggested, "saying it is outrageous to keep a dog in New York, especially in an apartment. It isn't fair either to the dog or his owners."

She took my advice, and it got mail all right. Not only were there indignant letters addressed to her, reminding her that a dog is man's best friend, but some subscribers wrote to the editor demanding she be fired. She wasn't, but she didn't ask me for ideas after that.

She kept insisting she wanted to do a column of her own. The North American Newspaper Alliance had a young lady, named Mollie Merrick, who was writing a daily piece from Hollywood about the goings-on there and the hams who inhabit that burg. Her contract was running out, and she had some shrewd adviser who insisted she demand more money. This fitted into my plans.

"Sheilah," I asked her, "how would you like to go to Hollywood and turn out a daily column on the movies?"

She jumped at the chance and has been there ever since. That was 23 years ago. She is now the top columnist. She has written a book, *Beloved Infidel,* which has been made into a successful movie. It seems to me I should get credit for at least an assist in the box score of her career.

Fannie Hurst and Edna Ferber were both practicing writers and very successful in the Twenties. *Liberty Magazine* ran a contest offering a prize of $25,000 for a moving-picture scenario, and an additional $25,000 if the author also wrote the serial which was to be published in the weekly. Of course, we were swamped with answers from amateurs and pros, too. Famous Players-Lasky was a partner in the enterprise.

We finally selected a story by Fannie Hurst called "Mannequin," about a beautiful Russian girl, separated from her parents, who survived the pogrom and eventually landed in America. She was later identified by a shawl she had brought from her homeland. It was a fast-moving tale with love and color.

After meeting in Jesse Lasky's office with Walter Wanger,

we called Miss Hurst and told her she was the winner. Naturally she was pleased. Who wouldn't be? Then after I got back to my office I found Bill Lebaron, one of the editors of *Cosmopolitan Magazine*, had telephoned me. When I got him, he said he had heard about our selection and did I know she had written a similar short serial for them five or six years ago, called "*Rouge et Noir*," along the same lines? He sent me a copy, and he was right.

This complication called for another meeting, and we decided on a scenario called "White Pants Willie," by Elmer Davis, later a top news broadcaster. It was a good story, too. We tried to get Davis on the telephone, but he was out at the ball park. We left word for him to show up the next morning at 11. In the meantime Miss Hurst called me to explain how she could overcome the objection to the similarity, and I put it up to the brain trust. We agreed to go back to "Mannequin."

The next morning when Davis, a very nice guy, showed up, there was an embarrassing silence. Finally I broke it.

"Elmer," I said, "at 3 o'clock yesterday afternoon, we were trying to reach you to say you had won fifty thousand dollars, but you were out at the ball game. Now the situation has changed." I reported what had developed in the meantime.

"It looks like an expensive ball game," he remarked ruefully.

"Well, you can't hang around the house all day waiting for someone to call you up and pay you fifty thousand dollars."

As a matter of fact, he came out of it pretty well. I bought a serial from him, and later it was made into a movie.

Edna Ferber has always been one of the best writers of either sex in my book, and her success confirms my rating. When Bruno Richard Hauptmann was tried for the kidnaping and murder of the Lindbergh baby, the North American

Newspaper Alliance made a deal with her to cover this sensational trial. The Jersey court of justice was turned into a Roman holiday with social ladies and stage celebrities, dripping with mink, attending. One of the first stories Miss Ferber wrote for us took up this angle in a very sardonic vein. It was published widely and appeared in the *New York Times*.

Adela Rogers St. John, who was covering the same show for the Hearst papers, invited my wife to go with her for the next day's session. My wife had read the caustic Ferber story on fur coats, so she put on a thin cloth one, leaving her mink in the mothballs. She caught a cold which developed into pneumonia, and she was laid up three weeks. Such is the power of a good pen, and Miss Ferber still has a strong one.

When Captain Eddie Rickenbacker was 50 years old, a group of his friends organized a birthday party for him at "21," the stylish restaurant. It turned out to be a success, for it cost each host $20.

"I didn't know we got that drunk," remarked Bugs Baer, as he kicked in his share.

Bugs and I then went across the street to Club 18, a high-class fleabag run by Jack White. A lady patron couldn't go to the powder room without being insulted publicly by the master of ceremonies. There we met Peggy Hopkins Joyce and some casual escort who couldn't have been so hot, since she invited Bugs and me to sit down at the table. Peggy was beautiful and could charm the hell out of you, making you think you were the only one she was interested in.

"I would like to go into the newspaper business," she announced suddenly.

"What can you do?" I asked her.

"Write a column."

"So can everybody else. But if you will turn out a lovelorn

column of the right sort, it should sell. You have been married five times, always to rich husbands. Tell the girls how to pick out a wealthy mate and how to be a good wing shot. None of this advice about marrying the poor guy for love alone and forget about money."

She agreed it was a good idea and promised to deliver some samples the next day. It was the last I ever heard of the idea, which is what frequently happens to brilliant notions thought up in a blind pig about 2 in the morning.

Phil Payne was managing editor of the *New York Daily News* shortly after it started publication. Like many another, he got stuck on Miss Joyce. As evidence of his ardor, he began to run photographs of her all over the paper. Captain Patterson, the publisher and his boss, caught on to it after a while and issued a warning.

"If you publish one more picture of Peggy Joyce," he said, "You are fired."

Payne put one on the front page, and the Captain made good. So did Phil. He got a job as managing editor of the *New York Mirror*. One night I arrived late at a fight between Gene Tunney and Georges Carpentier and sat down in a press seat next to a pretty lady and Payne.

"I want you to meet the Countess Morner," Payne said.

It was dark, and I didn't recognize her as Peggy Joyce. The Count was her current husband. She charmed me, and I began to feel I was pretty good. She seemed to be interested only in me, I thought. Then suddenly I realized who she was.

Phil Payne had a sad ending. Just as the "Old Glory" airplane was to take off for Rome on one of the first transatlantic flights, Payne hopped in. All three aboard were lost somewhere over the Atlantic.

Sally Rand got credit for saving the Chicago World's Fair

financially in 1933. She danced with the help of a couple of fans that were used to conceal vital spots in her anatomy. She drew crowds several times a day. It wasn't an immodest performance because of her adroit use of the props. Compared to modern-day strip teasers, she might be playing church festivals now.

She was appearing at a Miami night club several years ago. Grantland Rice, Francis Ouimet, Bill Danforth, and I went to take in the show. After she had dressed, she joined us at our table and told us about her ambition to be a writer. In fact she had already turned out several verses which she gave me to take home to read. Some of these seemed to smack of Edna St. Vincent Millay. For example one started:

"Take back this stinking gift of life."

One afternoon, I stopped about 4 o'clock to return her manuscript, and she invited me in for a drink. I always thought she was a smart girl until later she married a cowboy who appeared in rodeos and risked his neck daily. However, she soon corrected this by divorcing him. During my visit she was very frank and told me about her weaknesses.

"Since you have no romantic interest in me," she began, "I will admit my thighs are too thick, and I have other defects which I can hide with the fans."

"How do you know I won't arch my neck at you?" I asked.

"Because I don't want you to, and I am the one who decides," she aswered with finality.

As I got in my car to depart, she said, "Where are you going now?"

"Over to see George Ade."

"Take me with you."

"Jump in."

She did, and we arrived at the home of the Hoosier humorist, where he lived quietly with his housekeeper. He was also hard of hearing.

"George," I said, "this is Sally Rand."

He missed it the first time. I shouted louder. Then he smiled.

"Not Sally Rand, the fan dancer?"

I nodded.

"Well, sit down," he invited.

They spent an hour reminiscing about Chicago before the housekeeper called him for his supper. It was the last time I ever saw George Ade.

Clare Boothe Luce has been a friend of mine for many years. Back in the 1930's while my wife was in East Hampton for the summer, I gave a dinner party at my New York apartment one night. (I found keeping house during the summer very simple. To avoid thinking daily, I had the same things for dinner every night—steak, hashed brown potatoes, succotash or asparagus. Then I would only have to tell Lee Estrella, our cook who is still with us, how many would put on the feed bags.)

On this particular occasion, as I recall, there were three of each sex—Mrs. Luce, who was not yet Mrs. Luce, Sheilah Graham, another young lady whose name I have forgotten, Grantland Rice, George Buckley, and yours truly. Mrs. Luce had spent the previous week end with the Herbert Bayard Swopes, and the cast there included several intellectuals. It seemed they played games. Mrs. Luce introduced one of the games to us.

"If the Pope, the Prince of Wales, the President of the United States, and Charlie Chaplin all died on the same day, which would get the biggest obituary?"

I supported the President for American newspapers and the

Pope on a world-wide basis. She insisted it would be Chaplin, who was then at the peak of his career, before he had publicly begun to veer to the left.

"You're crazy," I said bluntly. "You shouldn't hang around with those big brains."

Of course, there was very little chance of ever proving which was right by events themselves. If Chaplin were to die today, I doubt if he would even get a top head on the obit page.

Then Grantland Rice introduced one of his favorite indoor pastimes, picking the all-heel, all-American team. This was started years ago out on the Pacific Coast when Gene Fowler, Bill Fields, the actor and comedian Mark Kelly, and Grant would get together. It was like selecting the passengers you would put on the *Lusitania* if you could make up the list and knew she was going to be sunk. This quartet would argue for hours about one candidate.

"No," Fowler would say, "he is not enough of a sonofobitch to make the all-American. He might get on the all-western, but I am not sure he is good enough for that even."

"But he let his mother go hungry when he was making twenty-five hundred a week as an actor," argued Bill Fields.

"Do you think that one play qualifies him?" asked Mark Kelly. "I don't. He has to be more versatile."

This evening at my apartment Clare Luce and the men had many candidates. She started out by nominating a newspaper publisher who will be nameless, because he is now dead. He had no trouble getting on. We made him captain and quarter-back right away without a dissenting vote. Then someone put up a well-known movie star and his son. We put one at left end and the other as a running halfback. As far as I know, no woman ever made it. We were too gallant.

When this reporter first knew Clare Boothe Luce, she was

young, beautiful, and always gay. Women in small groups did not like her usually, because she was prettier than most and smarter, a tough combination to beat. Then, too, she wrote that rather bitter play *The Women*, which turned the fluoroscope ruthlessly on females. But on her feet, talking to large crowds, the girls were for her as well as the boys.

When she was running for Congress from Connecticut, she was making a speech in Danbury, which in those days thrived on the hat business. She had failed to wear a hat, and someone must have reminded her of the slip, for she opened her remarks by referring to it.

"You see I forgot to put on a hat to come to this town of all places," she said. "Well, I want you to know that I own about twenty. Whenever I am in the dumps, I buy a new one. I told this to my husband, and he cracked sarcastically, 'I have been wondering where you bought those atrocities you wear.'"

From then on she had the crowd with her.

In the delightful period between the World Wars, there were two softball teams whose line-ups were more impressive than their performances. One was captained by Teddy Roosevelt, Jr., called the "Nine Old Men" after the U.S. Supreme Court of that time, and the other was run by Lowell Thomas. The games usually took place either in Quaker Hill, where Thomas lived, or at Oyster Bay, where the Roosevelt homestead was.

Among the players, besides the captain, were Gene Sarazen, Grantland Rice, Heywood Broun, John Golden, Bill Carey, and a string of other celebrities. The games themselves were something of a joke. Whenever Broun, who then weighed in at about 265 pounds, was lucky enough to get on base, which was seldom, his wife, Connie, ran for him. She was a sensation in her shorts.

One Sunday, Grantland Rice, Gene Sarazen, and I went to Westbrook Pegler's house in Pound Ridge after the game. One of his guests was Anita Colby, a very beautiful lady then, and she is still no slouch. She was wearing tight slacks and platform shoes with elevated soles.

Grant was always looking for something to gamble on, so he said to Sarazen, "Come on, Gene. Jack and I will play Anita and you, pitching for that tree for a dollar a shot. The two closest win."

We started the match. Miss Colby took an iron and made a swipe at the ball, going over it by about a foot. She missed again on her second and third tries. Gene looked on with concern. Then he got an idea.

"I think, if you took your shoes off, you would do better," he suggested, looking at the thick soles. She followed his instructions and tried again. No luck. She missed two more by as big margins.

Pegler considered the situation thoughtfully and then said, "Maybe you'll do better if you take your pants off."

Miss Colby promptly turned the idea down, withdrew from the competition, and the match was called off.

May Wilson Preston was a top illustrator and one of the gayest and most charming ladies I have ever met. The world and her many friends are poorer because she is gone. Frank Crowninshield, then editor of *Vanity Fair,* knew her well, and he first told me the following story of her younger and poorer days when she was struggling to build a reputation.

May lived with her father who was aging. One night when she came home he looked worried.

"What's the matter, Dad?" she asked him.

"I have been having some pain lately," he explained, "and

went to see Dr. Bentley Squires. He told me I should have an operation on my prostate gland."

Dr. Squires was a famous New York surgeon of that period. "Did you ask him about his fee?" inquired his daughter, anxiously.

"Yes," he answered. "The doctor said it would be five thousand dollars."

May raised her eyebrows, since the amount was out of reach at that time.

"I think I had better go talk to him," she said.

The next day she called on the eminent surgeon. "I understand you want to take out my father's prostate gland for five thousand dollars," she began.

The doctor nodded agreement. Then he went over to the wall of his office where there was a large chart, showing the human anatomy. He carefully explained the intricacies of the operation.

"You see I make an incision here," he said, pointing to the torso. "Then I have to cut through this tissue. It is a very delicate job."

May Preston followed the description carefully, as he pointed with his finger at the chart. When he was through, she startled him by saying, "Thank you, Doctor. Don't give it another thought. I understand the operation perfectly and will do it myself."

He was so amused by this remark he finally took the old man's prostate out for $250, and she paid him $50 a month.

No chapter on women would be complete without including Marilyn Monroe. The first time I ever saw her was a good many years ago in the Beverly Hills Hotel at a cocktail party, given by Mike Cowles, editor and publisher of *Look Magazine*. I happened to be in Hollywood at the time, and he very nicely invited me to the gathering which was studded with current movie stars of both sexes. Someone introduced me to Miss Monroe, who was then practically unknown, so there wasn't too much competition, and we had a chance to engage in conversation.

"Someday you are going to be a great star," I began, which seemed to be a good opening. Anyway it pleased her.

The years went by and again I was in the film capital. By this time my prediction had come true. Sheilah Graham, our columnist, met me at the airport and invited me for dinner the next night.

"Who else would you like me to have?" she asked.

"Marilyn Monroe," I answered without hesitation. This was before she had married Joe DiMaggio. She showed up a little late, but she remembered what I had said about her becoming a great star.

Someone told her I had once been a baseball writer. "What do old ballplayers do after they get through?" she asked me.

"Oh, they either become managers or radio announcers or marry good-looking moving-picture actresses," I answered.

We became friends, and we would meet occasionally. One evening my wife and I went to a first-night performance which was also attended by Miss Monroe. Of course, she attracted a crowd.

Between the acts I said to my missus, "Would you like to meet Marilyn Monroe?"

She accepted eagerly.

We went around to where Miss Monroe was sitting, surrounded by admirers and autograph hunters. I pushed through the crowd, and when she saw me, she greeted me cordially. She had that charm which, like Peggy Joyce's, makes you think she is more interested in you than anybody else at that moment.

"Oh, Mr. Wheeler," she said.

I introduced my wife, and she was effusive.

"Did you notice," I asked on the way back to our seats, "she seemed a little surprised?"

My wife agreed.

"That's because I have been telling her I am not married," I explained. Much to my consternation my wife believed me.

In April each year newspaper publishers from all over the country gather in New York for their annual A.N.P.A. convention. There are more cocktail parties than meetings. We would give one annually for the benefit of our customers, presumably. Miss Monroe was good enough to attend two or three and, of course, became quite an attraction when the word spread. We might as well have put her name up in lights. Not only did we have publishers and editors, but half again as many gate crashers. Most of them tried to surround the movie star.

Three years ago one of the unwelcome guests who was well oiled tried to unzip Miss Monroe's dress. We threw the bum out and quit giving the cocktail party, which meant quite an overall saving. In my book, she is a girl who deserves a lot of credit.

One of the great ladies I met in the course of my career was Emily Post. Frank Crowninshield got her started writing on etiquette a good many years ago. She turned out a daily column for the Bell Syndicate on the subject for a long time.

One day Henry Snevily, an associate of mine, and I were lunching in her apartment. The main course was lamb chops, and my friend was naturally trying to make a good impression with his manners, holding his little finger out and everything. He was cutting his chop when it suddenly skidded and landed on the dining room rug. Our hostess never interrupted her conversation. She rang for the maid and pointed to the floor. Shortly the waitress reappeared with a dustpan, swept up the chop, and disappeared. Soon she returned with a substitute. It was a perfect performance, although I never knew whether the chop was a fresh one or the first one taken out into the kitchen and dusted off.

My sister-in-law, Lady Thompson, is not very good at telling jokes. Neither am I. Anyway, I told her one about the fellow who took the beautiful girl out to dinner. He was fascinated by her, but the conversation lagged. He tried all sorts of subjects—sports, politics, gossip, scandal, etc.—but got no response. Finally, exasperated, he turned to his companion and said: "The trouble with you is that you're stupid."

"You ought to have seen my grandfather. He was away over like this." She hunched her shoulders forward and bent down.

I overheard Miss Thompson repeating it, but the trouble was when she came to the snapper, she said; "The trouble with you is that you're dumb."

And then she ran into a dead end.

One of the brighter chapters in my past has to do with Mary Martin and Dick Halliday, her husband. It is my belief these two would not be married now except for me, and they will acknowledge that I played at least a small part.

I knew Dick's father, a colorful fellow who was a newspaperman in Chicago, Denver, and New York. There is a story that when he was a cub reporter on one of the Chicago dailies, during the rough and ready days, the city editor told him to go to the Great Northern Hotel and get the register. Of course, what the editor meant was to get a list of the names of the guests. In those days most of these hostelries had the register on a pivot which the clerk would swing around toward the client. Finally, energetic reporter Halliday showed up back at the office, breathless, carrying the whole book—pulled out by its roots from the socket. He explained, "I had a hell of a time getting it loose, but here it is."

When his son finished college, I was the editor of *Liberty Magazine,* and Dick came into the office to see me and to ask for a job.

"But I haven't any job," I explained to him. "We have a bigger staff now than we can afford."

He seemed crestfallen. "If you don't give me a job," he said, "I am going to get to be an actor."

"My God, that can't happen," I replied.

He was and is a handsome, personable fellow, so I assigned him to the task of visiting well-known authors, especially ladies, to see what they were writing and to try to pick up first-class stories. He made a hit, particularly with prima donnas like Edna Ferber and Fannie Hurst. When I retired as editor at the end of my contract, Captain Patterson took over and promoted my young protégé to be motion-picture critic. As a result of these activities, Dick later became story editor of Paramount. He met Mary Martin in Hollywood, and they were married.

Now I insist I started the sequence of events which led to matrimony and am proud the union has turned out so well over a period of a great many years. Both are always very nice to me. It wasn't so long ago Dick Halliday sent me seats for the opening of *The Sound of Music,* Mary's latest musical. After the applause stopped and the curtain had gone down for the last time, I went to the stage door to thank Dick.

"Mary would like to see you," he said.

"Oh, I don't want to bother her."

He took me by the arm and led me upstairs to her dressing

room which was filled with flowers and admirers. She came over and grabbed my hand and kissed me as ardently as if I had been the leading man instead of the harmless old fellow I am. I didn't wash my face for a couple of days. I was proud of the lip rouge, like the guy who shook the hand of John L. Sullivan when he was heavyweight champion.

As a sidelight on Mary Martin and Dick Halliday, they took us to dinner one night at the Stork Club. As we were entering, my wife and Dick preceded us, and Mary waited for me in the foyer while I checked my hat. A drunken female patron on her way out, feeling in a sarcastic mood, looked at my companion and said, "Well, now I see you have your hair red. The last time it was dark."

Mary accepted the sally and replied, "Oh, I like to change its color occasionally. It makes me feel good."

There was a further exchange, and then the sarcastic female looked at me and my gray hair.

"Is that *daddy*?" she demanded as she stepped through the revolving door.

I didn't have a chance to reply, but I wished I could have had her alone in a soundproof room for about five minutes.

Frank Crowninshield was one of the greatest gentlemen, in the true sense of the word, and kindest I have ever known. Although he had many friends in the literary and social sets, he seemed to prefer to hang around with such doubtful characters as Deac Aylesworth, Bruce Barton, Grantland Rice, Pete Jones, and me. He neither drank nor smoked and, in fact, never married, but he was a wonderful and agreeable companion.

He was a master at writing letters, especially in longhand. After spending a week end with us at our farm in Ridgefield, Connecticut, where he was a frequent visitor, he wrote a thank-you note to my wife. At that time we had a cat named

Marie, who, during the course of her life, had produced 100 kittens before she died of old age. The following is one of the delightful letters received:

Dear Tee:

I shall never stop being grateful to you for that heavenly interlude in a life of agony and woe. You are *so* good to me and I loved it *all*, particularly the thrilling and even disquieting knowledge that I was near you. It is no wonder that Marie and I love you so devotedly. If you will send me a bell, like Marie's, I shall be happy to put it around my neck.

Fondly,

Crown

P.S. Please put your name on it—as, if I were ever lost, I should want to be returned to you.

And here is the mash note he addressed to our cat:

Mrs. Marie Wheeler,
C/o Mrs. John N. Wheeler,
Catnip Grange, Ridgefield,
Connecticut.

Dear Marie:

Only a line to express the hope that your "quints" are still thriving and that they are no longer incarcerated in that dark and smelly old barn.

I thought that all of your four daughters were modest and unassuming, but I must say, candidly, that your little boy, (the one with the striped suit—like Ben Smith's) seemed brusque and, shall we say? a trifle grasping.

I saw by the papers today that the price of milk has gone up again but I hope that you will still continue to give the children nothing but your Grade A quality.

Isn't it saddening, dear Marie, to think that there should still be, in the world, demons in human form who not only

despise cats but would like to see them all exterminated? I
allude, of course, to that hyena called Barton* and his preda-
tory friend, Jack,** the old gray werewolf. I hope, dear Marie,
that you will always try to keep near you that beautiful lady
angel whom we both so greatly love and revere. She is the only
lady I know who possesses the heart and compassionate nature
of your friend, and everybody's friend, Alice—a young lady
who not only liked cats and kittens but took them with her in
her travels. I hope you will be very nice to the angel, dear
Marie, as you will never again meet a lady so beautiful and so
tenderhearted. Please tell her that I enjoyed my week-end
party with her as much as you enjoyed your basket party. I
am grateful to her for having taken me on so pleasant a journey
and for letting me explore, with your friendly aid, the country
that lies beyond her Looking Glass and that borders so miracu-
lously the frontiers of Wonderland.

Your loving friend, The White Rabbit.

That beautiful and tenderhearted lady, a Southern girl, is
one of the most fascinating I have ever known, and her accomplishments are many. She has been handicapped by a
dumb husband and too much modesty. She has taught me
many things and given me companionship and happiness. Of
course, she shall be nameless, but this paragraph is a tribute
to her.

When Frank Crowninshield was an editor with Condé Nast
in the early part of the century, he discovered many famous
writers, including Dorothy Parker, Robert Benchley, and several others. Recently a book by Cleveland Amory and Frank's
great-nephew, Frederic Bradlee, called *Vanity Fair*, has been

* Bruce Barton.
** John Wheeler.

published, made up of selected stories and art work from the magazine which he created.

In addition to his literary accomplishments, Mr. Crowninshield was an art connoisseur and bon vivant. He was also much sought after by the top-drawer New York society leaders of both sexes and was a witty asset to any gathering.

He was one of the first, if not the first, to introduce French art into this country, and I must say some of the objects were a little puzzling to me. In fact one night when we were at his apartment Bruce Barton said, "Crown, you ought to put labels on these pictures showing which is the top."

I come to relate a "now-it-can-be-told" anecdote. Frank invited the Bartons, the Grantland Rices, and us to dinner one New Year's Eve. It turned out to be a pretty gay party, for we were all much younger in those days. Kate Rice was full of the spirit of the occasion. She picked up a small figure off the mantel, which she evidently thought was made of a soft substance, and cracked Frank's dignified brother Edward on the head with it, cutting a big gash in his forehead. This came as such a surprise to Mrs. Rice she hit herself with the same result.

As amateur physicians, we patched up the two victims as best we could. We took a big wad of cotton and put it on Edward Crowninshield's head and found a derby hat to hold the bandage in place. Soon the blood began to leak around the fringes which was a kind of startling sight. The ladies doctored up Mrs. Rice. Just before midnight dignified Condé Nast and his recent bride dropped in to wish the gathering a happy New Year and were shocked to see what looked like a hospital ward. We offered some fake explanation.

Grantland Rice was a gentle soul who could take all sorts of things in his stride. The next morning we began to worry. The lady to whom I am related by marriage could not restrain her curiosity, so she called her friend. Without any preliminaries, she said, "What did Granny say to you last night when you got home, Kate? Did he bawl you out?"

"I'll say he did—the worst I've ever had."

"Did he!" she exclaimed. "What did he say?"

"He said, 'Kitty, how could you?' "

Once when my daughter was about fourteen, Mr. Crowinshield made an address at Brearley School, where she was a pupil. As he finished his talk, he said, "And now I will escort my fiancée, Miss Elizabeth Wheeler, from the hall."

He walked to her seat and held out his arm. Blushing, she departed with him, actually a little proud of this attention.

He was a surprising man and always gallant. Several years ago my wife was riding on a Lexington Avenue bus during the summer when the windows were open. The vehicle stopped for a red light, and she saw Mr. Crowninshield strolling down the street.

"Oh, Frank," she called.

He looked around and doffed his Homburg with a great sweep, walked over, reached in through the window, and pulled her hand out. He kissed it gallantly, much to the surprise of the passengers and the conductor. Then the bus started up, and he went on his way.

He could revive entertaining tales about the sports at the turn of the century and knew Stanford White, the architect who was shot by Harry Thaw, Evelyn Nesbit Thaw, the cause, Berry Wall, and others. He used to tell about a friend whose main accomplishment was his ability to spit over a hansom cab without hitting the driver, even in a stiff breeze. This vehicle rose perpendicularly about ten feet above the asphalt.

"Did you know the Grand Central Station was planned on the back of an ordinary envelope?" he asked me one day.

Of course I didn't. I thought it had required several large drafting boards.

"Just an envelope like this," he said, picking up a medium-sized one. "Warren and Wetmore, architects, were engaged to design the façade, exterior details, and decoration of the main structure. Lying in bed one day, Mr. Wetmore got an idea as many do and called his valet, Charles Bollard, telling him to pack a bag, adding they were going on an imaginary journey to Boston. Then he picked up a letter received in the mail a few hours before and stuffed it in his pocket.

"En route to the station, which had not yet been built on the back of the envelope, he drew the start of a plan which was nothing more than a long arrow, pointing to the area where the trains would stand. He told the driver to go to Forty-second Street and Vanderbilt Avenue. He turned to his man and said, 'Now, Bollard, you will watch me design an ideal railroad depot, and here is where we begin.'

"Then he proceeded to lay out the floor plan. He decided a traveler would want to buy papers and magazines to read on the journey so he marked a place for the newsstand twenty paces from the entrance on the way to the waiting room. Twenty paces further he located the ticket offices. Then he put the Bureau of Information in the center where it would be handy. He finally filled up the envelope, and they went home and unpacked the bag. That's how Charley Wetmore laid out his initial plan years ago, and it has been working ever since.

"Come," my friend suggested, rising from his desk and leading the way from his building through an entrance into the station. "Let us see how the figures I have cited compare." Thereupon, beginning at Forty-second Street, plowing straight ahead like a Sherman tank through milling passengers, he paced off the distances and found them to be correct.

"Twenty paces is right," he said.

"Well, as to that envelope: the railroad authorities looked over the scrawl, approved it, and asked for a finished and measured plan of the drawings."

It's too bad Mr. Crowninshield did not live to finish his memoirs. He could have told many interesting stories and some he could never have told.

He died of cancer at 76. I was a pallbearer at his funeral. Knowing he was approaching the final exit, he made all the arrangements. The church was crowded. I don't remember ever seeing so many women weeping.

XXI. SOCIAL ACTIVITIES

A REPORTER on a morning newspaper had very little time for social activities since he worked at night and slept in the daytime. Someone once asked Franklin P. Adams what became of all the pretty girls you see at football games between the contests.

"They don't hang around all-night gin mills like you newspaper guys do," he replied.

One evening on my day off Herbert Swope asked me to have dinner at his apartment on Riverside Drive. When we arrived, he began to change into a dinner coat which puzzled me.

"What are you putting on a Tuxedo for?" I asked him.

"Well, I had to freshen up so I thought I might as well. We are going over to Grantland Rice's later."

"Not we," I said. "First I haven't been invited and second I haven't any black tie."

"Oh, that doesn't make any difference," Swope assured me. "I told him you were coming and half the guests won't be dressed anyway."

He finally persuaded me, although I still had my doubts. When we arrived, the door was opened by a pinch-hitting butler in tails, so I knew it was a big affair. Everybody was dressed except Wheeler. Grantland greeted me with his usual hospitality and, to make me feel at home, invited me to partake of some of the strongest grog I have ever swallowed, disguised under the name of punch. It worked. I began to think I was Vernon Castle or somebody and was dancing gaily with all the girls. Along about 2 in the morning, I had a particularly

275

attractive companion, and it looked as if the party was breaking up.

"How would you like to go down to Jack's for some bacon
and scrambled eggs?" I said.

She agreed it was an excellent idea. I had my old Chalmers
car outside which looked pretty good and affluent at 2:30 in
the morning. We started downtown. Then she said, "How
would you like to come to my apartment, and I'll cook you
some scrambled eggs and bacon?"

I accepted promptly and decided it was the old Wheeler
luck and charm. She lived in Fifty-eighth Street, and we had
to climb about three flights of stairs. She opened her bag and
fished around for her key. She drew a blank.

"Must have forgotten it," she remarked. "I'll ring the bell."

"What for?" I asked nervously.

"I'll have to wake my husband up," she explained.

"I don't think I care for any scrambled eggs and bacon
tonight," I said as I hustled down the stairs, expecting to hear
or feel a shot any second.

I never saw the lady again until years later, and we both
joined in the laugh. By this time it was a funny situation and
probably always was.

One of the colorful and outstanding figures in baseball was
Cap Huston who, with Jake Ruppert, owned the Yankees. Cap
had made his money in Cuba just after the Spanish War and
spent it freely wherever you could buy a drink. He always
wore a black derby and was dubbed by Bill McGeehan "the
man in the iron hat." He was a genial free-wheeling gent.

Now each year the baseball writers have a dinner where
food is of secondary importance. Hype Igoe's wife, having had
some previous experience with these affairs, declined for her
husband by hiding all his clothes except one pair of pajamas.

Hype was equal to the occasion. He sneaked out on the fire escape and dropped from the bottom balcony to the street where he hailed a taxi and directed the driver to the Biltmore Hotel, Cap Huston's temporary headquarters. On arrival, Hype sent word up to get his fare, and then he scurried upstairs in the service elevator.

Cap took charge. First he tried some tailors he knew, but it proved to be a Jewish holiday. Then he began to call up department and men's clothing shops, and these were closed too, since it was Election Day. Ever resourceful, he finally hit on an idea. He telephoned Frank E. Campbell, the big undertaker.

"I would like to rent a burial suit to fit a medium-sized man for this evening," he said.

"For a corpse?" demanded the mortician.

"Not now, but he may be before the night is over, and you will get some business."

The deal was made, and the costume delivered. Hype attended the dinner, but he had to face front all evening. The suit had no back in it.

During the 1919 crooked World Series, Hype Igoe was traveling from Cincinnati to Chicago on a night train. Along about 2 o'clock in the morning he found a tired brakeman asleep in the smoking compartment, with his cap and lantern on the seat beside him. Hype was able to take these without stirring him. He proceeded to go through the train, waking up the sleeping passengers in their berths and compartments, demanding their tickets. He had them fishing in their wallets and complaining loudly. This was a typical Igoe performance. The regular conductor caught up with him after two cars had been covered.

There was a famous restaurant in New York on Sixth

Avenue, between Forty-third and Forty-fourth Streets, named
Jack's. The proprietor was Jack Dunston. It had no key, and
the boast of the boss was the place never closed. In the middle
between two dining rooms was an oyster bar presided over by
a fellow who, on nights when he felt good, would open the
bivalves with his thumbnail. Occasionally after a football
game, some boisterous students would invade Jack's with the
idea of roughing it up. The oyster man was the official bouncer.

There is the story of several Princeton youths, headed by a
famous gridiron star named John Dewitt, who paid a call at
the restaurant to stir things up. The fellow behind the oyster
bar was patient and tried persuasion without avail. Then, according to Irvin Cobb, a reliable reporter who was present, he
wrapped the boys up in a neat bundle and tied one around
the outside. He threw the package out into Sixth Avenue with
a warning not to come back.

Tad, the cartoonist, used to visit Jack's pretty regularly in
the early-morning hours, usually with Hype Igoe. The latter
kept a banjo or a guitar in the icebox, and with the consent of
the proprietor, they would put on an act for the rest of the
patrons. The old Hippodrome was across the street where
Annette Kellerman, the swimming star, was appearing in a
giant tank act.

"Let's see you do the standing, sitting, standing dive, Hype,"
the cartoonist would suggest.

Whereupon Igoe would stand on a chair and attempt it,
winding up sprawling on the floor. Once he broke his wrist.
He was no Annette Kellerman without water.

Tad had a wife he seldom saw and affectionately called "the
Moon" because of the contour of her face. His official residence was in Great Neck, but he frequently forgot his own
address. She specialized in entertaining Chinese students of
both sexes, and the house was usually full of these Orientals.

Once in a while when Tad did get home, he had difficulty in finding a place to sleep unless he wanted to crawl in with a Chink. One day some friend asked him how he was getting along.

"Terrible," he answered. "You have to have a laundry ticket to get into my joint."

Both Tad and Igoe are dead. Too bad. They don't come like them any more.

The first time Billy de Beck, creator of "Barney Google," came into my office, he reminded me of Bud Fisher. He was dapper, cocksure, and talented. He turned down our offer to go to work for the Hearst papers—a mistake, but we remained friends until the day he died.

We both belonged to the Artists and Writers Club. The fashionable Mrs. Stotesbery used to give us a party every year which was pretty stylish and luxurious. An unexpected event in which Billy de Beck starred canceled out this one-night stand.

In a cage in her backyard or patio was a friendly chimpanzee or small gorilla. During the festivities on this particular occasion we missed De Beck, but no one paid much attention until we were getting ready to depart. Then a search was started, since we didn't want our hostess to find one of our members behind the coats the next morning. Finally one of the scouts reported our missing companion had gotten into the cage with the ape.

"Now we've got a problem," remarked Grantland Rice, our president. "How are we going to tell which is Billy and which is the ape?"

One of the snootiest and most exclusive clubs for years was

the National Golf Links at Southampton, Long Island. It was run by Charles MacDonald, president, with an iron hand and always had a long waiting list. He was also one of the early U.S. amateur golf champions.

However, if Mr. MacDonald approved of you, you were in. I had a great friend, who is now dead, a big, cordial, generous, warm guy named George Buckley. He had many quaint sayings, such as "May the skin of a gooseberry cover your enemies." He was also a good golfer. Besides, he could eat glass, an accomplishment he displayed after a few drinks. What he did with the pieces I never found out.

He was at the National as a guest several years ago, and after his round of golf, Charley MacDonald and he were together at the bar drinking, to see how long the supply of liquor would last. Finally, Buckley lifted his glass and took a bite out of it, which impressed the president of the club very much. He immediately made him a member, jumping him over all of the other candidates.

Standing at the bar watching the performance was another quiet fellow. After Buckley had chewed up most of the glasses in the place, this up-till-now silent gent turned to him and said, "Aren't you going to eat the stems? The stems are the best part."

A few years before George Buckley died, he had a bad operation and his kidney taken out. When he was recovering, I went to see him one day.

"Buck, did they find any ground glass in your kidney?" I asked him.

"Yes," he answered, "and also the caps of two White Rock bottles."

Years ago, John Golden organized a club called "The Not Very Club." It was a golf and social organization and got its name in a unique way. When one member would hit a drive, another would say, "Nice shot, old boy."

"Not very," would respond Ring Lardner.

There were only six members—Grantland Rice, Ring Lardner, John Siddall, then editor of the *American Magazine*, James J. Montague, Golden, and myself. It met every Friday noon in Golden's office before starting out for some club. Siddall was a great editor and an inquisitive one.

"John," he said, "how much are you making on *Turn to the Right*? How many people go to see it each performance? What do you pay the actors?"

Golden rang for his secretary. "This is Mr. Siddall," he said. "He's a very nosy fellow. Whenever he comes into this office, I want you to show him my books and all the records so he won't be bothering me."

That's the kind of a congenial club it was. It was also snobbish. Golden kept trying to get Charles Dillingham and Flo Ziegfeld in, but the rest of us blackballed them every time he proposed their names. We also experimented with a women's auxiliary of wives, but that didn't work so well. The founder had stationery printed with the name and a rope with a knot in it as the symbol. The club hung together for about a year. Then one fall day after the schools opened, we were playing golf at Ardsley, and the regular caddies were all at their studies. We got big, tough characters about the size of Johansson as caddies. They were fresh and familiar. They called Siddall "Chewy" because he used tobacco instead of gum, and Montague "Shorty."

"That's the wrong club, String Bean," one of them said to Lardner.

The next time we were to play there, Ring reported absent.

"What was the matter?" I asked him when I saw him. "Why didn't you show up?"

"I'm afraid of the caddies," he said.

John Golden belonged to another organization, which was not so high class as the "Not Very Club." It was organized by Tommy Meighan, the old-time actor, and was called "The Husbands' Protective League." The basic idea seems to have been it was a refuge from wives for harassed members, and they all pulled together.

There was a very strict condition about qualifying. A candidate had to insult his wife in front of two members before he would be considered. Mr. Golden made several attempts to get in, but was blackballed. Then one day when his missus was stepping into his car, instead of helping her, he gave her a kick, not very hard, as a boost.

He said, "Here's where I join."

They took him in right away, and his performance was so good they made him the high tycoon.

Riley Wilson was a character who would turn up wherever there was excitement—at a World Series, a heavyweight fight, or just a cocktail party. His official residence was West Virginia, and he was a nephew of a United States Senator. No one ever found out what his square occupation was, except he made you laugh and was a sort of free court jester. He also drank. He had an affliction, a glass eye, but he made the most of this. He carried three or four spares in his pockets. He would go into a bar in the morning after a hard night, wearing a bloodshot orb.

"Have you anything good for a hangover?" he would ask the bartender. Every one of these specialists always had a prescription.

Riley would swallow the dose, which usually had an alcoholic content. When the professor would turn away to attend to his duties, Wilson would substitute a clear eye, much to the astonishment of the bartender.

"That's fine," Riley would compliment him.

"I didn't know it was that good, myself," the bartender would confess.

One night Bud Fisher and I were with this companion when he ran out of money. We happened to be in a saloon by a coincidence.

"Could you let us have twenty dollars until tomorrow?" Wilson asked the proprietor.

"If you will give me your right eye as security I will," he agreed with a smile.

"Sure," replied Wilson, as he took it out and handed it to him.

This surprised the hell out of him, naturally. He carefully wrapped it up in a piece of tissue paper, put it in the cash register, and handed Riley the $20. Riley redeemed it the next day.

One of the most colorful characters in the early days of flying was Roscoe Turner, who won a lot of speed races and was a handsome daredevil. He designed his own uniform with diamond wings. It was a beaut. Then he had a lion he carried around with him on his flights, harmless enough, but a little scary for nervous passengers. Finally the old beast died, and Roscoe had a coat made out of the hide. Also, out of the lion's tail he fashioned a cane that was a little on the ornate side.

I was working in the office one night about 6 o'clock when Lou Maxon called me.

"How would you like to fly to Miami with us tomorrow?" he asked. "Roscoe Turner will take us in his plane, and Rex Cole and Ted Quinn are going along."

"Sounds good," I answered, "but I can't make it. I've got too much to do."

"Well, come over to the Waldorf and have a drink with us anyway."

"Done and done," I said.

That was the first time I met Roscoe. I invited them all up to my apartment for dinner, and we had a fine time. As the evening wore on, the idea of a trip to Miami in the morning seemed to be a good one. I called in our cook, Lee Estrella.

"I am going to fly to Florida tomorrow," I said. "Please pack a bag for me."

Having heard most of the conversation, she had a definite idea I was kidding, and that is the reason why, when I arrived at my destination, I found only a comb and brush and one necktie in my luggage. It served me right. Anyway, I decided to spend the night at the Waldorf, because we needed to get an early start, arising about 4. By now it was around 1:30. Maxon called up a friend of ours who was notorious for having a bitchy wife. She answered in a sleepy voice.

"You'll have to stop that dog barking in your apartment," Maxon said as if he was next door. She banged up the telephone. That was an early A.M. joke.

We crawled out of bed on a bitter cold morning and rolled in the darkness out to Floyd Bennett field. The vehicle was a single-motor Lockheed with a cabin about as big as a telephone booth and the engine practically in our laps. Roscoe sat in the open out back, dressed in his lionskin coat. It was just about dawn when we took off. After we passed Washington, it began to get rough, and I simultaneously began to get airsick. It was not only painful for me but for my companions as well. We stopped at Raleigh for gas. I went into the terminal and spoke to the lady behind the food counter.

"Have you anything that is good for airsickness?" I asked.

She nodded and fixed up a concoction which I swallowed. It was good for my ailment all right, since I was twice as bad as I had been before. When we reached Jacksonville, I dismounted to make an announcement.

"Boys," I said, "you are looking at a retired aviator. From now on I am going to invest only in Pullman and Lily-Cup stock." They persuaded me to get back aboard, and the rest of the trip was fairly smooth, so I was beginning to feel pretty good. However, we were going to stay at the Miami Biltmore Hotel, and our pilot, to show off, banked the plane around the tower. Immediately, I had another spasm.

When I began to settle a little along in the evening, I got a telegram from my wife, who by now had missed me, to inquire whether I had arrived in one piece. Since flying, especially with Roscoe Turner, was quite an adventure in those days, I scribbled out a reply as follows:

"Arrived safely. Vomited all the way from Floyd Bennett Field to Miami. Love John."

It seemed Western Union had a rule, and may still have, that in case of illness, a telegram must be delivered in person with three stars on it. Four mean death. A "boy" of about 40 showed up with this message at 3 in the morning and woke Lee with the bad news. She called my wife, and when they counted the stars, they could hardly open the envelope, thinking disaster had overtaken me. It seems it was the word "vomited" which caused the crisis. And the next morning Pete Jones had me out in one of Henry L. Dougherty's fishing boats by 8, and I was just as seasick in the Gulf Stream as I had been airsick. It's a great way to reduce. We had an enjoyable stay except I had to buy a new wardrobe.

Turner was admired by one and all. Lou Maxon said one day, "Let's put old Roscoe down in the lobby and set a couple of bear traps around him to see what we catch."

I had made up my mind to ride the train back, but the boys talked me out of it. We took off before daylight one winter morning. The airplane was parked at a military field. The pilot found a truck which was not locked, so he ran it down to the edge and turned the headlights on showing where the field ended and the swamp began. He then raced toward these crossbeams. I thought he was never going to get it up, but just as we were on the brink, he lifted the old crate, and we were in the air, ducking and barely missing an Eastern Airlines plane. Otherwise, the trip back was uneventful and smoother than going down, so I stood it all right.

Roscoe was in New York not long afterwards, and we all had dinner together. Then he put on his lionskin coat and unfurled the cane.

"Where are you going?" I asked him, although it was really none of my business.

"I have a date with Peggy Hopkins Joyce," he said proudly, "but don't say anything about it." He strode out with a swagger and arrived back at the hotel rather late.

"Anybody see you?" I inquired.

"I don't think so. We went to the Stork."

"Well, that inconspicuous costume is great for keeping a secret engagement with a lady," I observed.

As far as I know he is still running a flying school in Indianapolis and is a fine fellow in my book. I hear from him every Christmas.

One more social note about the Miami Biltmore Hotel which was then owned by Mr. Dougherty. A bunch of us were staying there about 1931 as the guests of Pete Jones, and our rooms were in the tower. Mrs. Dougherty had a suite which, fortunately, she was not occupying at the time. Around the walls of the living room were racks decorated with many rare and priceless plates she had collected all over the world.

The idea of our trip was to build up good will for the hotel, since it was during the financial doldrums. We had with us a genial guy except when he got drunk, which was most of the time. He also had only one arm which did not interfere with his drinking and other activities. One evening after dinner we were sitting in the patio with the few paying guests, enjoying our liqueurs and coffee. We heard a shotgun go off over our heads, and the pellets sprayed down into our refreshments. Everybody ducked for cover as the firing was repeated.

The house dick ran up to investigate, and the bombardment ceased promptly as he collared the culprits. It turned out the one-armed magazine editor had a friend, and they got into a discussion about marksmanship. They also had a 12-gauge shotgun. One plucked Mrs. D.'s plates from the racks singly and scaled them out over the patio from the balcony like clay pigeons. The other fired at them. Several guests checked out the next day.

Now while we are on the social aspects of life in newspaper circles, I want to report a dinner, given by Kent Cooper, then general manager of the Associated Press. The guests of honor were Lord and Lady Rothermere, and the invitation announced the clambake would take place at the Waldorf and in white tie. This caused no little consternation, since it was right after the last World War. I know I exhumed my tails from the camphor chest and tried the coat on, and then sent it to the tailor to be let out a little. Actually, on the evening of the occasion, the smell of mothballs was overpowering.

Grantland Rice, a gentleman to his fingertips, never owned a dress coat, so he decided to rent one. He stopped on the way back from the race track on the afternoon of the dinner and took the first he tried on. The tails swept the floor. Frank Tinney, the great, old-time comedian, used to wear one like it for laughs. Old Grant was a little embarrassed, so he took on a few martinis as an antidote. The medicine worked.

The only guest who showed up in a black tie was James Forrestal, then Secretary of Defense. Rice sidled over to him and remarked behind his hand, "Jim, I wish to hell I'd known you were going to wear a dinner coat."

It turned out to be an elegant affair at an oval table with the gents and ladies interspersed. I was sitting next to Mrs. Forrestal and Bruce Barton was on the other side of her. Opposite us was a well-known newspaper publisher who is now dead. He was a good drinker and ordinarily paid little attention to the paper. However, this night he put on a show. Right after the soup, a messenger arrived with the proofs of the next morning's editorial page. He adjusted his glasses and studied these.

Barton nudged me. "Sneak around behind him," he said, "and see if they are rightside up."

Naturally I didn't do it. I am a gentleman, and besides, he was a customer then.

Roy Howard and Bill Hawkins used to run the United Press in its early days. Both lived in Pelham. Roy would give an eggnog party every Christmas afternoon, and Bill would invite a few of his friends back for supper at his house. This party grew in dimensions, as most do, and soon the whole neighborhood was crashing the gate as free-loaders. In fact, one "guest" was found two days later behind the coats in the hall closet. Mr. Hawkins was good-natured, however, and continued it for some years, until one of his sons was riding home from school in an airplane and overheard a conversation between a couple of youths in the seat behind him.

"What are you going to do Christmas night?" asked one.

"Nothing," the other guy replied.

"Well, there is an old fellow who lives in Pelham, named Hawkins, who gives a hell of a party every Christmas night, and he doesn't know who he's invited. Let's go."

The other agreed.

When he got home, young Hawkins reported the conversation to his father.

"That settles it. I'm going to stop it," he decided.

"But how?" asked his son.

"I'll go to Hawaii for Christmas and close the house up," he said.

That is just what he did, but even though the place was dark, a crowd gathered and complained loudly when they found there were no festivities. That is one way to stop a party but the hard way.

Did you ever get your hair cut at Elizabeth Arden's beauty shop? It's like what Montague Glass once said politely about wives: "I wouldn't take a million dollars for my present one, and I wouldn't give a dime for another."

We spent several winters in Miami Beach in our more opulent days. I had had a bad siege of flu before I left New York. For the first time in my life, I was apprehensive about my health and figured each day would be my last. In short, I had become a first-class hypochondriac and spent most of the winter with a stethoscope on my chest and a clinical thermometer in my mouth. In the course of things someone prescribed a haircut, and I happened to mention the matter to Florence Mahoney, who then ran the Miami Beach branch of the Arden establishment.

"Why don't you go to my place and get it done?" she asked. "It will be painless."

This suggestion came as a shock to me.

"What's wrong with a regular barbershop?" I asked her.

"Well, Governor Cox and Dan get their hair cut there," she replied in rebuttal. Dan was her husband, a big, roughneck Irishman and a friend of mine.

"What's good enough for the Governor and Dan is good enough for Wheeler," I answered.

So she fixed up an appointment, and, having nothing better to do, I arrived on schedule. I was ushered into an ornate room where a young gentleman who seemed a little on the effeminate side went to work on my hair. He did all right, and then I suggested a shampoo. It seems that was in a different department, so I was ushered into another parlor where a buxom blonde was in charge. She went to it with skill, and next introduced a device I had never seen before. It was a basin with a slot in it.

She tried to fit this into the back of my neck, but the opening was on the small side, so the water and suds all ran down on my shirt and undershirt which scared the hell out of me, making me think I would surely get pneumonia. The lady was sympathetic and helped me shed my garments which she put on a heater to dry while she continued with me bare to the waist.

"Would you like some blueing in your hair?" she asked.

"So long as I am here, give me the works," I answered. "I'll leave it up to you."

When I walked out of the joint you couldn't tell me from the guy who cut my hair. For any men readers, you ought to try it some time. It's expensive, but then a blonde will give you a shampoo.

No social notes would be complete without mentioning the name "Vanderbilt." Here is a story about two Vanderbilts—

Cornelius, Jr., and Gertrude. Neal, as he is known to his few friends and several wives, had asked me to lunch with him to try to sell me a column. I was pretty busy and not too much interested, but finally agreed to meet him at Dinty Moore's at 1 o'clock. I arrived on time and read the newspaper patiently until 1:15. By now you could fry an egg any place on me, I was so hot. I called the waiter over and ordered my lunch.

About 1:30 my host came rushing in out of breath and apologetic. I gave him the hard-to-get-to. He had the usual explanations for his tardiness—couldn't find a taxi, tied up in traffic, etc. He showed me what he had to offer. I barely glanced at it. Then the Irish waiter, whom I knew, brought around the tab and handed it to Vanderbilt. He looked at it and fished in his pockets, finally coming up with two one-dollar bills which did not cover the total. I decided to let him sweat and made no attempt to grab the check. Here was a young fellow who had inherited a fortune and social position without the cash.

"Will you take an American Express check?" he asked the waiter. Mac agreed, and he produced a book of them. He signed one for $20.

The waiter took it and looked at it suspiciously. "Cornelius Vanderbilt, Jr.," he muttered, reading the signature. You could tell he didn't believe he was Cornelius Vanderbilt—either junior or senior—at all.

"Have you anything to identify yourself?" he asked. Again Neal frisked his pockets and came up with an automobile license with a photo attached. Mac studied it.

"Well, so long as you are with Mr. Wheeler, I'll cash it, anyway," he agreed. He did.

I believe that was the last meal we had together—a good many years ago. He has recently published a book about his wanderings. He has a reference to me in it which is not too flattering, but he does not tell the story of the lunch at Dinty Moore's.

Now Gertrude Vanderbilt came from an entirely different branch of the family. In fact, she didn't come from the family at all, but had adopted the name as high-sounding when she was a showgirl. She was a pleasant, fairly good-looking dame, but hard-boiled as they come. One night before we were married, I took my girl to dinner at Luchow's, a famous German restaurant on Fourteenth Street. Of course, I was arching my neck and trying to make an impression.

"Excuse me a minute," I said, "but I see Gertrude Vanderbilt over there and want to speak to her."

I was greeted cordially with a kiss on the cheek, and we chatted amiably for a few minutes. Naturally, my girl thought there was only one Vanderbilt family and that I was moving in high society.

Gertrude was afterwards mixed up in the case of Bill Fallon, "the great mouthpiece," and her reputation was not helped by this publicity. However, before she died, she was doing pretty well as a press agent and organizing and helping out old Ziegfeld Follies girls of her day who were broke. She was really a goodhearted dame.

That same evening I wanted to send a telegram and rang for a Western Union messenger. Eventually an old "boy" of about 60 with a beard showed up. He looked hungry.

"Have you had your dinner?" I asked him.

He shook his head.

"Sit down with us," I said.

He did, before I could change my mind, and enjoyed a hell of a meal at my expense.

These two events probably changed the course of my life. The lady was so impressed she married me.

XXII. CAUTIONARY TALES

When I was a young boy, I discovered a trick. Yonkers was a small town in those days, and my mother would take me by the hand and lead me down to the village when she went marketing. Frequently she would meet a woman friend, and they had to catch up on a lot of gossip. Sometimes the conversation would go on endlessly, and I would become restless. I would begin to bawl. Of course, my mother would try to shut me up, but I would keep yowling until she left her companion. Occasionally I paid for it when I got home, but it was worth the spanking.

This practice of bawling once reacted against me when I was five or six years old. My father owned some property in Yonkers, and one of the stores on Riverdale Avenue was rented as a saloon with cuspidors, a brass rail, swinging doors, and all the old-fashioned equipment. He used to hitch the horse up to the buggy and make the rounds to collect the rents. Sometimes he would take me with him. On this particular day, he tied the mare and went into the gin mill, leaving me alone. When I thought he had stayed too long, I climbed out of the wagon and stood on the sidewalk in front of the entrance and began to cry. Pretty soon an officious old lady came along and sized up the situation.

"What's the matter, little boy?" she asked me.

"My papa is in there," I sobbed, pointing to the gin mill. Of course, she was indignant when my father came out.

She began to bawl him out good for drinking and leaving

me alone. As soon as she had cooled down, my old man shoved me into the buggy and gave me a good lathering when we got home, which I guess I deserved. He was really a very abstemious man—a glass of beer once in a while. Anyway, he didn't take me with him to collect the rents again for some time.

This is a dog story.

James Gordon Bennett, the owner of the *New York Herald* when I worked there, was an eccentric gent who for personal reasons already mentioned elsewhere, lived in Paris. It was his habit occasionally to send for one of the top executives to report to him. Mr. Bennett also had a collection of Pekinese dogs which he admired very much, and a cow he carried on his yacht to be sure of fresh milk and cream on cruises.

The news editor of the *Herald* was John T. Burke, a two-fisted Irishman who had never met the Commodore, as his boss was called. One day he received a message to come to Paris post haste and not let anyone pass him en route. Burke became a little nervous about the meeting so decided to consult the dog editor as to how he could make a hit with Bennett's pooches. Some experienced traveler had told him if the Pekes like you, you were in solid with the publisher.

"Get some aniseed and put it in the cuffs of your pants when you go to see the old man," advised the expert.

Burke laid in a supply big enough for a kennel. After rushing to Paris, Burke was kept waiting ten days before Bennett sent for him. This was characteristic. Finally the big afternoon came.

Now my mother had the same idea about castor oil as the news editor had about the dog bait. She thought if a little was good, a lot would be much better. Burke loaded the cuffs of his pants until his belt sagged.

Of course, the dogs greeted him cordially, but Bennett was cool. The Pekes kept sniffing at Burke's trousers and making affectionate gestures. The Commodore tried to call them away, since after all they were his dogs, but nothing doing. The conference settled down to a contest to see which gent the dogs liked better. Mr. Burke won and had trouble in shaking them when he departed, which he did rather abruptly.

After he returned to his hotel, he found a message ordering him back to the United States at once. He never did see his boss again. The moral, if any, is, "Don't overdo a good thing."

Admiral Cary Grayson, Woodrow Wilson's personal physician, once told me a story about Clemenceau. He lived in a small apartment in Paris and had a garden in the back. The Admiral went out there to visit him one evening. The Frenchman discussed his habits.

"I am healthy," he told his visitor, "because I go to bed at about 9 o'clock. I take this hot-water bag and fill it with gruel and put it at the foot of my bed to keep my feet warm. I get up about 4 and don't like to disturb the servants, so I pour it into a bowl and eat it for breakfast. Then I work in my garden before it gets too hot."

This would seem to be a great recipe for health and toughness.

One of the bravest men I have ever known and one of my favorite characters is Colonel Bernt Balchen. He saved Admiral Byrd when they flew the Atlantic in 1927 in a trimotored Ford by cracking the regular pilot, who had gone haywire, on the head with a monkey wrench and taking over the controls. He also flew the Admiral across the South Pole during the long winter spent in the Antarctic. However, after their return, he remarked to me, "I wouldn't fly Byrd to Hoboken again."

They had had some kind of a row, which often happens under the circumstances.

My favorite story about Balchen is a personal one. In the early days of aviation, Captain Eddie Rickenbacker loaned me a Fokker plane and Bernt Balchen to fly to East Hampton on Long Island. There was a sort of a converted cow pasture which was called an airport. We landed all right on Friday afternoon and planned to go to Saratoga for the races on Saturday, but the weather was atrocious, fog and rain, so we called it off.

That night Percy Hammond, the well-known dramatic critic, and his wife Florence came to my house for dinner. He had never flown but was much impressed by Balchen, so he decided to take a chance the next day. The morning was clear. Percy showed up with several good-luck charms, including a St. Christopher medal, a horseshoe, and a four-leaf clover. He wasn't taking any chances.

My daughter, about ten then, wanted to fly, so Bernt decided to take her and me up first. We flew around for about 20 minutes or half an hour and headed back for the "airport." There was a road with telephone wires running along the edge, and the first time Balchen touched the wheels down and then gunned the motor to take off again. The next time around he made a pass, but zoomed up.

"Bernt," I said to him somewhat nervously, "I think there is a bigger field in Southampton."

"I put dot ship in dot field," he answered with determination.

So what can you do when you are in the hands of a stubborn Norwegian? We circled again, and this time he just missed the wires and then sideslipped to lose speed. He landed perfectly.

He decided wisely, however, that the field was too small for the plane. Percy Hammond was relieved he didn't have to make the flight. Balchen took off for New York by himself, and Percy for home. He was just learning to drive and was so exhilarated by the experience, he forgot which pedal was the brake and which the gas. He ran his car right into the garage and out through the back, taking the wall along with him. He wasn't hurt, but his Chrysler was banged up.

I once asked Captain Eddie Rickenbacker when he expected to retire and his answer was, "After they screw the top down on the coffin."

When Rickenbacker was the leading U.S. ace in World War I and commanded the Hat-in-the-Ring Squadron, some of the younger pilots were nervous at mess. They knew they were scheduled for a combat mission next morning. Finally, Rick got up, stretched, and said, "I'm on my way to bed. I don't know what the rest of you guys are going to do. I want to say, though, that I expect to live to be ninety years old and then be arrested for rape."

A colorful character I knew in my early days was Norman Selby who fought under the name of Kid McCoy. He was a rough, tough mean battler who would do anything to win— or lose if necessary. There was the famous fight he admitted throwing to Jim Corbett.

"Why did you do it?" I asked him once.

"You see," he answered, "I was feeling very low. My first wife had just divorced me for the second time, and I needed the money."

He was in Paris later and, being a big spender, was broke. He agreed to meet a Frenchman who fought *la savate*, which means he could use both his hands to punch and his feet to kick.

"I didn't know anything about it," admitted the Kid, "but I was busted and ready to take a chance. I let him get in the ring first and watched him. He was a slick, handsome fellow and was shadow-boxing to warm up. Then he would greet some good-looking mademoiselle at the ringside. He had his female supporters there, and I played a trick on him which is known as turning your man. After the bell rang to start the fight, I stepped out and pointed to a flashy dame behind him.

" 'Regardez la femme,' I said.

"He was a sucker and turned his head as I had hoped and expected. Then I hit him on the jaw and knocked him colder than a mackerel. I jumped out of the ring and ran for my dressing room, before the crowd could jump on me. There are a lot of tricks to the trade."

For a time the Kid ran a little gymnasium in Thirty-sixth Street, and I used to go there to box with him. I was younger then, and he showed me several smart moves which served me in good stead later.

There was a hotel called the Normandy at Broadway and Thirty-ninth Street, run by Harry Golden's uncle. Kid McCoy rented the cellar for a kind of a night club where the patrons could eat and drink and dance. The place had one problem—a concrete floor.

Now in his street clothes the proprietor looked thin, almost slight. Frequently one of the bolder and drunker customers would decide he wanted to lick a prizefighter.

"I hated to hit these birds unless they got really rough," the Kid told me. "But once or twice I had to, and the guy fell down on the hard floor and hurt his head bad, so I bought a big mat with 'Welcome' on it and would maneuver the belligerent customer around until I had him on it. Then when he went down, he didn't get damaged much, and we would throw him out."

The poor Kid had a sad ending. He got into a scrape in California and killed a woman. He served a long jail term. When he was released, Henry Ford gave him a job, but he finally committed suicide.

Kent Cooper was one of the great figures in the newspaper business up to 1950 when he retired, after being general manager of the Associated Press for several years. Besides being a pro, he is also very musical and has written several songs. He started as a reporter in Indianapolis, and to piece out his meager salary, he played the fiddle in the theater orchestra at night.

Victor Herbert, the great composer, was scheduled to pass through Indianapolis on his way to Chicago, and Kent Cooper was assigned to interview him. He met him at the station, and they rode together on the train while the young reporter asked questions. Finally Herbert began to hum a tune. He pulled up his sleeve and took off one of those old-fashioned detachable cuffs. He drew a staff on it and wrote out eight bars of music as he hummed.

"May I have that, Mr. Herbert?" asked young Cooper.

"I'll remember the melody," he replied. He gave him the souvenir.

When he got home, Kent played the first eight bars and then finished the tune as he thought it should go. It was catchy, and he began to play it around town. Some of the local orchestras took it up. About six months later, Cooper went to Chicago on business and was walking down Michigan Boulevard when he ran into Herbert.

"Have you seen my show playing here?" he asked.

Kent said he hadn't, so the composer produced one of his cards and scribbled on it.

"Here, take this to the box office, and you will get in."

Cooper went that night. The show was *Mademoiselle Modiste*, and the star was Fritzi Scheff. When she sang that great number, "Kiss Me Again," Kent straightened up in his seat. It was the tune Victor Herbert had started to write on his cuff.

When the musical reached Indianapolis, there was a little confusion, because some in the audience thought Herbert had stolen Kent Cooper's song. However, our honest reporter put them straight. Now he will play the tune, first as Victor Herbert wrote it, and then his version. I favor the composer's.

When I first started to write baseball in 1908, there was a fat, versatile guy named Bill Kirke working for the *New York American*. He could write with either hand, and was ambidextrous when it came to drinking. He boasted he consumed a gallon of whisky a day. He figured 15 shots to a quart, and he swallowed 60 in 24 hours.

He could turn out good verse as well as prose. He wrote one about a girl who had two gents in love with her. One worked in a livery stable and one in a greenhouse. This was a favorite of Grantland Rice's, and he would quote it frequently. It was high praise since Grant was a poet himself. Here's how it went:

My love works in the greenhouse,
There always is a smell
Of violets and geraniums
About his coat lapel.

Mind you, I do not blame you,
I'm making no complaint,
But the greenhouse has a fragrance
That a livery stable h'aint.

This note is a reflection on my sartorial splendor, and I resent it, although I was never known as a dude. In 1933, as I've already mentioned, I went to England with a friend of mine, Lou Maxon, who runs a very successful advertising agency in Detroit. He was a genial and generous companion, and we had a nice trip over on the old *Aquitania*, a gallant ship. There was one fly in the ointment. All the U.S. banks closed while we were at sea, but we managed to tap the branch of a British bank on the boat good before the manager found out about it.

Bill Tichenor, then president of Commercial Solvents, was on the ship, and we got to be very friendly. His wife and he stayed at the Carleton, and Maxon and I had a couple of rooms at the Savoy. Mr. Tichenor called up one night and asked for me. Lou answered the telephone.

"Is this Mr. Wheeler's valet?" asked Bill.

"I don't mind being called a valet," answered my roommate, "but I hate to be called a valet to such a damned sloppy dresser as Wheeler."

The night before we were due in Southampton we had a rather festive evening with two young ladies—one good-looking and the other homely, to put it bluntly. We stayed up until about 3:30 A.M., and for some reason Maxon, in his enthusiasm, invited the plain girl to meet him in the cocktail lounge at 10 the next morning, since the ship was to dock about noon.

He did not feel too well and was struggling to get dressed while I was lying in my bunk watching him. Finally I said, "Lou, why do you bother to keep the date? You will probably never see the girl again."

His reply was typical. "I know, but she is so damn homely I don't want to offend her."

Howard Coffin, then a big automobile man, invited a group of us to Georgia to hunt. It was a gay crowd and more time was spent in shooting craps than deer and birds. It was the first time I met Deac Aylesworth, the first president of the National Broadcasting Company. I was sitting in a drawing room on the train about 11 in the morning with Lee Olwell, a banker.

The door burst open and in came Deac. He pulled a pair of dice out of his pocket, threw them on the table, and said, "They tell me you are a tough sonofabitch. Let's see how good you are."

We became fast friends and always roomed together on many trips afterwards.

Mr. Coffin had built the Cloister Hotel on Sea Island, and we stopped at it for a few days. The first night there, we attended a large dinner, and one of our party, a big executive when at home, couldn't stand the hospitality and drank too many martinis. He decided to go to the men's room which adjoined the hotel barbershop. As he came out, he flopped down in one of the chairs and promptly went to sleep. Aylesworth saw him and pulled a five-dollar bill out of his pocket.

"Keep shaving him and cutting his hair until you run out of money," he told the barber.

Finally, the patient woke up and looked around. Seeing where he was, he decided to prove he was in good shape, so he turned to the barber and directed, "Give me a shave and a haircut."

He had already had about five.

William Randolph Hearst was one of the great editors and publishers of his period. Perhaps he would have been the greatest if he had devoted all his time to the newspaper business, but he got sidetracked onto moving pictures, art collecting, and other avocations. Anyway, he was a hell of a guy in my book.

Mr. Hearst had a funny idea about money. Having been born rich, he thought it was to spend. Brisbane is once supposed to have said, "W.R. needs an income of ten million dollars a year."

The *New York American,* his morning paper, was struggling and not doing very well. There was a new general manager who hustled around to make good. One morning the boss came into the office, as he frequently did in those days to check up on things.

"Mr. Hearst," said his new man proudly, "we made four thousand dollars last month."

"That's fine," replied W.R. "Now you send right over to the bank and get me that four thousand."

The fellow had to do it, too, and W.R. pocketed the money and walked out, although the bank account was badly depleted. He believed if the *American* made the money, he should get it.

Several times I visited him at his ranch—La Cuesta Encantada, at San Simeon in California. The houses were fifteen miles from his front gate, and the driveway was frequented by all sorts of strange beasts he had collected. There is one story that Colonel Frank Knox, when he was Hearst's general manager, got out to open a gate on his way to the mansion on the mountain. As he turned to walk back to his car, he was butted in the behind by a wild goat.

One evening, when I was in Los Angeles, Colonel Joe Willecombe, W.R.'s secretary, called me at my hotel.

"The chief would like to have you come up to see him tomorrow," he said. "Our plane is leaving at 10 in the morning. Can you make it?"

"I have an appointment at 9," I replied. "Could you put it off for an hour?"

It was agreed, and I was flown up to the ranch in style, arriving at the private landing field. The dining room was a toll call from one end to the other, and there was a long refectory table. Mr. Hearst sat in the middle, and his guests were strung out down each side. All had departed except Arthur Brisbane, the flashy but great editor, Mr. Hearst, and myself.

"W.R.," said Brisbane, "you used to have some fine old chartreuse. Is there any left?"

The butler produced it, and the three of us sat there talking about the old days in the newspaper business when Mr. Hearst invaded New York to battle Joseph Pulitzer. The dignified *Evening Post* of that time stuck its nose into the row with a line about Hearst's *Evening Journal* being a yellow dog. The next day the *Journal* editor came back with this crack: "Everyone knows what a yellow dog does to a post."

It was a very entertaining evening. Brisbane was reminiscing about the old *New York Sun* and the great men on it. We got talking about Richard Harding Davis who had been on the staff of the *Sun*. I had just read a book by Fairfax Downey about this correspondent, and I sent W.R. a copy of it later, for which I received a grateful note.

Arthur Brisbane wasn't satisfied with the large salary he drew, and was always talking about getting his own paper. Hearst encouraged him, but told him he reserved the right to declare himself in for half of any publication Brisbane bought. While W.R. was in Mexico, where he had a huge cattle ranch, Brisbane purchased the *Detroit Times*. When the boss returned and heard about it, he declared himself in for half. Then Hearst started to spend money like a drunken sailor. His partner, who was not the most liberal guy in the world anyway, began to lie awake nights and worry about the amount he was losing. Finally, one of his assistants said to Hearst, "If you don't want to ruin a good editor and have him go off his rocker, you had better buy him out."

Hearst paid a liberal price, and the *Detroit Times* was added to the Hearst chain. While he lived, he would never sell one of his papers no matter how heavy the losses.

One night I was standing in Grand Central terminal at the gate on my way to Detroit on business. Arthur Brisbane came along with a lot of papers stuffed under his arm and carrying a brief case.

"Where are you headed?" he asked me.

"Detroit," I replied.

"We are going out to dedicate our new building tomorrow. There is a private car on the end of the train. Why don't you come back after dinner?"

I accepted the invitation eagerly. W.R. had retired when I arrived, but Brisbane and Paul Block, another publisher, were having a heated argument as to which one knew the most about Jews. A.B., as we can call him, insisted a comic strip, produced by a Jewish artist, could poke fun at the Jews if the stuff were funny without offense. He cited "Abie Kabbible," as drawn by Harry Hershfield.

"They laugh up here," said Mr. Block, pointing to his mouth, "but it hurts down there." He put his hand on his heart.

"Listen, P.B.," answered Brisbane, "I know more about Jews than you do."

"No, you don't, A.B.," insisted Block.

The argument was never settled as far as I know. I joined another group.

Bill Curley was one of the top Hearst editors for years. As a matter of fact, he bought the first feature we ever put out— a series by Christy Mathewson, the great Giant pitcher.

Toward the end of his life, Bill had trouble sleeping, so the doctor told him to take a nembutal capsule before going to bed. On one of his visits to the Hearst ranch, he heard W.R. complain that he too had insomnia.

"Why don't you try a nembutal when you go to bed?" asked Mr. Curley. "It makes me sleep for eight hours."

"But they are habit forming, I have heard. Aren't they?" W.R. asked.

"Why do you worry about picking up any bad habits at eighty-eight?" replied Mr. Curley.

His boss laughed and said, "How do I get some?"

"You will need a doctor's prescription."

The moral, if any, is when you are 88 years old, don't fret about forming bad habits.

Irvin Cobb was never a great hand for the country, except to go hunting and fishing, but he didn't admire its residential qualities. However, he bought a house in East Hampton where his family and he spent summers.

Shortly after the purchase I saw him one day and asked, "How do you like living out here?"

"Oh, pretty good," he said, "except I was kept awake all night by a robin stomping across the lawn."

During the First World War, I tried to hire the King of Greece as a correspondent. Carr Van Anda, then managing editor of the *New York Times*, told me he had written a dispatch for that paper free and had even paid the tolls.

"He's my man," I said to myself on the way out. "The terms are good."

I sent the King a cable, making the same offer, but I never heard from him.

When John Siddall was editor of the *American Magazine,*

he built up the circulation by following the success formula. He had many articles about the poor boy who started from nowhere and finished a rich tycoon. He also interlarded his contents with occasional stories by George Ade and other humorists.

He asked Rube Goldberg, the cartoonist, to write one for him, explaining his career.

Rube started as follows: "I wasn't born in the gutter."

As a result, Mr. Siddall, an indignant editor, threw it back at him.

George Ade was not scientifically inclined but he worked out a sound method of getting rid of a mosquito. It was to take one of the old-fashioned nets and put it over the bed without letting it down. Then turn in and when the pest comes buzzing around, drop the net, crawl out under the edges, leave the mosquito to himself, and sleep on the floor.

Bruce Barton told me this story about his father who was a distinguished minister. The preacher and his wife were crossing the Pacific when the ship ran into a typhoon. They became worried as to whether the ship could weather it. The preacher went to the captain and asked him what he thought the chances were. The captain led him into the hold and pointed to the roughnecks in the crew who were cursing. He said, "When those men stop swearing and begin to pray, then you will know we are in danger."

Impressed, the minister reported to his wife the optimistic outlook. Still he was anxious, and after a couple of hours he went back to the hold, and found the same situation persisting.

He came back and said, "Thank God they are still cursing."

Charles Lindbergh was a friend of mine and still is as far as

I know, although I haven't seen him in three or four years. He is what Damon Runyon used to call a "loner." I have always admired the man very much.

Shortly after the last war, he telephoned me in the office one evening about 6 and said he would like to stop to see me for advice. Naturally I was flattered.

When he arrived he showed me a typewritten statement which he wished to give out to the newspapers. It outlined his change of view on United States foreign policy. I read it.

"Why do you want to stick your neck out?" I asked him.

Readers may remember that Lindbergh was criticized for being a member of America First which had opposed the United States' entering World War II.

After talking with the flier for a time, I saw he had made up his mind to publish the statement. He had discussed it with General Wood and others. I might have been selfish and suggested he give it exclusively to the North American Newspaper Alliance, but I advised him to send it to the three press associations for release on Monday morning, frequently a rather dull news day.

"What are you doing tonight?" I asked him, knowing he lived in Darien, Connecticut.

"Nothing," he answered.

He came back to my apartment for dinner. There were just three of us. We got to discussing the troubled world, and I asked him what he thought was the matter.

"I believe," he answered thoughtfully, "too much emphasis has been put on science and the development of bombs and destructive devices and not enough on the spiritual side of life."

"Are you religious?" I asked.

"Yes, when I am up in the air or out in the woods, but I don't go to church very much," he replied.

"Why don't you write a story about that for the North American Newspaper Alliance?" I suggested.

"No," he answered. "I'm not ready yet, but later I may." When he said "no," he meant it too.

Afterwards he wrote a book called *Of Flight and Life* which we syndicated. The first part dealt with his experiences and narrow escapes as a pilot and the second part discussed the spiritual side of life. I am proud of the autographed copy I have on my shelf.

One night we invited Mr. and Mrs. Lindbergh to have dinner with us at our farm in Ridgefield, Connecticut. I gave him what I thought were accurate road directions to reach us from Darien. They were late, which was unusual for them. It turned out that my directions had landed them at the Danbury fair grounds about five miles away.

Later, when we went to the Lindberghs' home for dinner our instructions read like a flight plan. We were told to proceed as far as the Darien railroad station and then to set the speedometer at zero. From there we followed closely the route laid out, so we hit his house right on the nose although it is on Long Island Sound in a remote spot.

Lindbergh is a peculiar combination. One evening he was explaining to me how it was possible to drive from New York City to Connecticut without crossing the Triborough and paying the 25-cent toll.

In World War II he made a great record in the Pacific. Having resigned his Air Force commission because of pressure from Franklin Roosevelt, he went out as an instructor.

Colonel Tom Lanphier, who shot down Admiral Yamamoto, told me that when Lindbergh first arrived, the young fliers didn't know who he was and looked down on him as an old man. However, he went out and did stunts with an airplane that none of them could duplicate, and they soon discovered who he was.

General Sutherland, who was MacArthur's Chief of Staff, told me Lindbergh developed a procedure which extended the range of our combat fighters 200 miles and made our air forces much more effective.

Although serving as a civilian, Lindbergh went out on several combat missions at great risk, for if he had been brought down and captured, he would have been shot forthwith as a spy. He actually shot down two Japanese planes.

A well-known book publisher suggested I write my memoirs. Naturally, I was flattered but gun shy.

"You know," I answered, "there used to be a big, boisterous fellow around Broadway named Wilson Mizner. He got his start during the Gold Rush to Alaska, and he cut plenty of eye teeth in those days. He learned a lot of tricks you don't read about in the law library He developed into quite a writer and wit. His cracks and stories became famous. Well, when I was the editor of *Liberty Magazine*, I went to see him, having known him here and there and round and about for years.

"'What about writing your reminiscences for us?' I asked him. 'We will pay you good money.'

"'Listen, young fellow,' Mizner answered, 'I ain't old enough to write my memoirs yet and what's more I never am going to be old enough—and neither is anybody else. You don't live long enough to tell the truth and so you have to leave out the most interesting parts.'"

Since in this I agree with Mizner, I have not written my memoirs, but I hope I've managed to include in this book some interesting anecdotes from my long experience in the news syndicate business. I'm 74, and I look back with pleasure on my life. Yet I would not advise anyone to start in the business now. But maybe that is only the viewpoint of an old and jaundiced gent.

I would like to add a little boast. I have probably made more out of the syndicate business than any individual who ever started in it. Of course, the big syndicates owned by the Hearst papers and the *Chicago Tribune* have been more profitable, but I have no kick. However, I think the best days are now over with newspaper mergers and shrinking markets.

In conclusion, what has been my philosophy of life? I would like to quote a pertinent remark by old Cy Young, the great pitcher. A young fellow came into the Big League and sought him out.

"How do you pitch to these hitters?" he asked.

"I'll tell you," answered the old pro. "I do the best I can with the ball up to the time it leaves my hand, and after that it is up to the batter."

INDEX